"Bouncy title, thoughtful subtitle, tight writing, and nuanced analysis: *Joy for the World* lays out enjoyably what we need to understand to save freedom of religion. Greg Forster brilliantly shows that we should expect, embrace, and work to preserve a crowded and uncomfortable public square, because if we're scared by it, the naked public square that results will weaken Christianity and America."

Marvin Olasky, Editor-in-Chief, World News Group

"The miracle of Christianity is that it offers a joy that goes beyond emotion and a hope that goes beyond time. In *Joy for the World*, Greg Forster presents a picture of this joy that inspires readers to hope and live in such a way that they transform their communities, their culture, and their world."

Ed Stetzer, President, LifeWay Research; author, *Subversive Kingdom*

"This book is against sequestration—the sequestering of Christian life into 'spiritual' enclaves and churchly ghettos. But it also wants the church to be the church—uncompromised, vibrant, and filled with joy. Both are necessary for the Christian community to be an agent of transformation in the civilization in which God calls it to serve, witness, and bear fruit. Greg Forster argues for a renewed form of holistic obedience, and he does so not only with joy, but also hope. Recommended with enthusiasm!"

Timothy George, Founding Dean, Beeson Divinity School; General Editor, *Reformation Commentary on Scripture*

"When I speak or host my daily radio talk show, I deal with three categories of Christians. Many believe we should be isolated from the culture or conclude that Christians who engage the culture can't make a significant difference in the world. Others believe we should engage the culture, but don't know how. Then there is the remnant trying to engage the culture that could use some instruction and encouragement. This book is for all three. Forster encourages us to be salt and light, explaining how Christians can make a difference and be a significant witness for Christ. This is a book for all Christians."

Kerby Anderson, President, Probe Ministries; Host, *Point of View* radio talk show

"Forster's deft grasp of history, philosophy, and theology enables him to offer up this rigorous yet accessible book. He offers rich, unique insights into the story of how Christians lost their civilizational influence. More importantly, he describes how a vigorous embrace by the church of *whole-life* discipleship—that shapes our personal, family, workplace, and community lives—can create Jesus-followers who are genuinely good citizens and good neighbors."

Amy L. Sherman, Senior Fellow, Sagamore Institute for Policy Research; author, *Kingdom Calling: Vocational Stewardship for the Common Good*

"Greg Forster offers a passionate call for Christians to pursue industrious, thoughtful, and patient labor in all of their life's callings for the humble and biblical goal of blessing their neighbors. Those tempted to dismiss their ordinary occupations as necessary evils will find much to challenge and motivate them in these pages. Especially helpful are Forster's chapters on economics and politics, and their stimulating discussion of work, citizenship, and neighborliness."

David VanDrunen, Robert B. Strimple Professor of Systematic Theology and Christian Ethics, Westminster Seminary, California

"With a refreshing depth of biblical, historical, and cultural insight, Greg Forster presents a compelling way forward for the church to rebuild influence in American society. *Joy for the World* opens up broad vistas of the Spirit-filled life with its transforming power, yet remains wisely tethered to the hopeful realism necessary for living with true joy in a fallen world. This book is tailor-made for every follower of Jesus who desires to embrace an integral and influential gospel-centered faith lived out and embodied in every nook and cranny of life. I highly recommend it."

Tom Nelson, Senior Pastor, Christ Community Church, Leawood, Kansas; author, *Work Matters*

Joy for the World

.

Cultural Renewal

Edited by Timothy J. Keller and Collin Hansen

HOW *Christianity* LOST ITS CULTURAL
INFLUENCE & CAN BEGIN REBUILDING IT

GREG FORSTER

FOREWORD BY TIMOTHY J. KELLER

:: CROSSWAY

WHEATON, ILLINOIS

Cover design: Dual Identity, inc.

Cover image: Getty Images

First printing 2014

Printed in the United States of America

Trade paperback ISBN: 978-1-4335-3800-1
PDF ISBN: 978-1-4335-3801-8
Mobipocket ISBN: 978-1-4335-3802-5
ePub ISBN: 978-1-4335-3803-2

Library of Congress Cataloging-in-Publication Data

Forster, Greg, 1973–
  Joy for the world : how Christianity lost its cultural
influence and can begin rebuilding it / Greg Forster ; edited
by Timothy J. Keller and Collin Hansen ; foreword by Tim
Keller.
      pages cm.—(Cultural renewal)
  Includes bibliographical references and index.
  ISBN 978-1-4335-3800-1 (tp)
  1. Christianity—United States. 2. United States—
Church history. 3. Christianity—Influence. 4. Joy—
Religious aspects—Christianity. I. Title.
BR515.F66   2014
277.3—dc23   2013022764

Crossway is a publishing ministry of Good News Publishers.

VP   24   23   22   21   20   19   18   17   16   15   14
15   14   13   12   11   10   9   8   7   6   5   4   3   2   1

To Mike Smith and Dan Kelly

Orestes: Don't stay here to die. I no longer have a city, but you do.
Bring your body home alive to your father's house,
and the safety of his great wealth.
You'll never marry my sister, as we had hoped;
our bond of kinship is dissolved.
Go and marry another; have children.
You must be happy for us, greatest friend,
Since we who are dead have no happiness.
Pylades: How far apart your thinking is from mine!
If I abandon you now, may the bright air no longer
give me breath,
And the green earth refuse to cover my bones!
I joined with you in all those plans you're paying for now;
you can't deny it. . . .
What would my story be, when I came back to Delphi?
What would I tell the Phocians?
That I was your steadfast friend so long as all was well,
But our friendship ended as soon as you were in danger?
For shame! I could never do that. . . .
Orestes: Nothing in the world is more valuable than a friend.
For one true friend I would not take the wealth
and power of a king
Nor the favor of multitudes of men.

Euripides, *Orestes*

He rules the world with truth and grace
And makes the nations prove
The glories of his righteousness
And wonders of his love!
And wonders of his love!
And wonders . . . wonders . . . of his love!

"Joy to the World," Isaac Watts (1719)

Contents

Acknowledgments

You paid good money for this book, so let me begin by thanking you. It's your willingness to trust me and invest in my work—to put your money where my mouth is—that provides me with the opportunity to write books. And if I didn't have that, I'd be in major trouble. "Writing is like a lust, or like scratching when you itch," said C. S. Lewis in the last interview he ever gave. "Writing comes as a result of a very strong impulse, and when it does come, I for one must get it out."[1] So thank you for giving me the opportunity to scratch my itch in a socially acceptable way. I have done my best to deliver your money's worth.

As always, my deepest appreciation goes to Crossway and my editors Justin Taylor and Collin Hansen for helping make this book the book it is, and for putting it between covers and on shelves.

I am honored beyond expression that Tim Keller has contributed a foreword to something I wrote. It's a particularly gratifying honor since I've learned so much from him, as the following pages will show.

An author is always deeply indebted to those who read his work before publication. A special place goes to Dan Kelly, who talked through every chapter with me. This book is dedicated to Dan and to our friend Mike Smith, who went into the church triumphant with an extraordinary display of faith, hope, and love, but too soon. I also got extensive feedback from David VanDrunen, Amy Sherman, and Karen Wilken; thanks additionally to Kyle Ferguson and Frank Marsh.

I owe a special debt to my colleagues at the Kern Family Foundation and particularly to our benefactors, Robert and Patricia Kern. This book is my own project and represents only my own views, but I have learned so much from my coworkers over the years about how human culture works and how the church fits into that equation that it would be a scandal if I didn't record my debt. To the direct, personal influence of the Kerns especially I owe my awakening from the dogmatic slumbers of fundamentalism. I used to divide human activities into a church sphere (loyal to God's Word and transformed by his Spirit) and a world sphere (morally ordered and licit, but irrelevant to the Bible and the Spirit). I drank in that dualism with some of my earliest theological influences, and this book is the victory feast of my liberation. "The heresies that men do leave / are hated most of those they did deceive."[2]

As always, I could do nothing without the colabor of my wife, Beth, who truly gives her all to make my work possible. And my daughter, Anya, continues to bless my writing with the encouragement she brings to so many good things she encounters.

Above all I attribute all success in any endeavor to God. As a pastor of mine once said, the worldly man is puffed up by success but the spiritual man is humbled by it. The joy of the Lord is my strength.

Foreword

Timothy J. Keller

Greg Forster's important and practical new book helps Christians think out how to engage culture. Many would say this is not a proper goal for believers, but that is a mistake.

Acts 17 records Paul's famous visit to Athens, the academic center of the Roman Empire of the day. One commenter likened the intellectual power of Athens at the time to all the Ivy League schools as well as Oxford and Cambridge universities all rolled into one. Though Paul was repulsed by the idolatry he saw there, he did not turn away from the city in disgust. Instead, he plunged into the marketplace, the *agora*, where we are told he daily "reasoned" with those he found there about the gospel. Now when you or I think of a "marketplace," we think of shopping and retail. Of course the agoras of ancient cities contained that, but they were much more. The agora was the media center—the only place to learn the news at a time before newspapers and other technological media. It was also the financial center where investors connected with businesses. It was the art center as well, the place where so much art was performed. It was the place where new political and philosophical ideas were debated. In short, the agora was the cultural center of any city. And since this was Athens—which along with Rome had the most influence of all cities—it could be said to be part of *the* cultural center of the Greco-Roman world. The ideas forged and accepted here flowed out and shaped the way the rest of society thought and lived.

It is instructive, then, to see that Paul takes the gospel literally into the public square. It means that he did not see the Christian faith as only able to change individual hearts. He believed that the gospel had what it took to engage the thinking public, the cultural elites, and to challenge the dominant cultural ideas of the day. He was after converts of course—he was first and foremost a church planter, not a theologian or Christian philosopher. But he wouldn't have been able to engage the hearts of cultural leaders unless he also engaged the ideas of the culture itself. He did not shrink from that challenge. He did not merely try to find individual philosophers to evangelize in a corner. He addressed them as a culture, a public community.

It is often missed that, although later Paul was invited to give an address, he did not start by *preaching* in the agora. He did not get up on a soapbox and merely declare what the Bible said. It says Paul "reasoned" (Acts 17:17) in the marketplace, using a word—*dialegomai*—that sounds like "dialogue." However, as John Stott says in his commentary on Acts, this term probably denoted something more specific than we would think of today when we hear it. Stott says it was something closer to what we might call the Socratic method. This was not a "debate" as we see debates today, where two parties read off talking points at one another. It required lots of careful listening, and in particular it meant asking questions that showed that your opponents were self-contradictory, that is, they were wrong on the basis of their own premises. And indeed, when we actually hear Paul's address to the philosophers in Acts 17:22–31, we can't help but notice that he does the Socratic method even here. He does not expound or even quote Scripture, but rather quotes their own thinkers (v. 28) and then shows them that, on the basis of their own intuitions and statements about God, idolatry is absolutely wrong (v. 29). Many have pointed out how Paul's address lays the foundation for a doctrine of God, contrasting the contemporary culture's beliefs in multiple, fallible, powerful beings who must be appeased with the idea of one supreme Creator, sovereign God who is worthy of awe-filled adoration and worship.

Every part of what Paul says is deeply biblical, but he never quotes the Bible; instead he shows them the weakness and inadequacies of their own views of the divine and lifts up the true God for their admiration. He appeals as much to their rationality and their imaginations as to their will and hearts.

The term "cultural engagement" is so often used by Christians today without a great deal of definition. This account of Paul and Athens gets us a bit closer to understanding what it is by showing us what it is not. Christians are to enter the various public spheres—working in finance, the media, the arts. But there we are neither to simply preach at people nor are we to hide our faith, keeping it private and safe from contradiction. Rather, we are as believers to both listen to and also challenge dominant cultural ideas, respectfully yet pointedly, in both our speech and our example.

When Paul addresses the Areopagus, a body of the elite philosophers and aristocrats of Athens, he was, quite literally, speaking to the cultural elites. Their response to him was cool to say the least. They "mocked" him (Acts 17:32) and called him a "babbler" (v. 18), and only one member of that august body converted (v. 34). The elites laughed at him, wondering how Paul expected anyone to believe such rubbish. The irony of the situation is evident as we look back at this incident from the vantage point of the present day. We know that a couple of centuries later the older pagan consensus was falling apart and Christianity was growing rapidly. All the ideas that the philosophers thought so incredible were adopted by growing masses of people. Finally those sneering cultural elites were gone, and many Christian truths became dominant cultural ideas.

Why? Historians look back and perceive that the seemingly impregnable ancient pagan consensus had a soft underbelly. For example, the approach to suffering taken by the Stoics—its call to detach your heart from things here and thereby control your emotions—was harsh and did not work for much of the populace. The Epicureans' call to live life for pleasure and happiness left people empty and lonely. The Stoics' insistence that the *Logos*—the order of meaning behind the universe—could be perceived through philosophic contemplation was elitist, only for the highly educated. The revolutionary Christian teaching was, however, that there was indeed a meaning and moral order behind the universe that must be discovered, but this *Logos* was not a set of abstract principles. Rather it was a person, the Creator and Savior Jesus Christ, who could be known personally. This salvation and consolation was available to all, and it was available in a way that did not just engage the reason but also the heart and the whole person. The crazy Christian gospel, so sneered at by the cultural elites that day, eventually showed forth its spiritual power to change lives and its cultural power to shape societies. Christianity met the populace's needs and answered their questions. The dominant culture could not. And so the gospel multiplied.

Do we have Paul's courage, wisdom, skill, balance, and love to do the same thing today in the face of many sneering cultural leaders? It won't be the same journey, because we live in a post-Christian Western society that has smuggled in many values gotten from the Bible but now unacknowledged as such. Late modern culture is not nearly as brutal as pagan culture. So the challenges are different, but we must still, I think, plunge into the agora as Paul did.

Greg Forster's new book does a marvelous job of showing us a way forward that fits in with Paul's basic stance—not just preaching at people, but not hiding or withdrawing either. Within these pages, believers will get lots of ideas about how to "reason" with people in the public square about the faith and how to engage culture in a way that avoids triumphalism, accommodation, or withdrawal. Paul felt real revulsion at the idolatry of Athens—yet that didn't prevent him from responding to the pagan philosophers with love and respect, plus a steely insistence on being heard. This book will help you respond to our cultural moment in the same way.

Introduction

Let Every Heart Prepare Him Room

You have been my help, and in the shadow
of your wings I will sing for joy.

Ps. 63:7

As far back as history shows us, Christians have always been anxious about what role Christianity ought to play in the social order of human civilization. However, I would venture to say that since the founding of this country, we American Christians have been more worried about this question than any others before or since. And at the dawn of the twenty-first century, the question has become especially acute.

In 2010, the Pew Forum on Religion and Public Life gathered survey data on the roughly 4,500 evangelical delegates attending the Lausanne Congress of World Evangelization. Lausanne is by far the largest and most important evangelical gathering in the world; its delegates make up a pretty fair representation of evangelical leadership across the globe. Pew found that 71 percent of delegates from the Global South—mainly Asia, Africa, and South America—are optimistic about the prospects for evangelicalism in their countries, but only 44 percent of delegates from the Global North—mainly North America and Europe—said the same. That makes sense. Evangelical Christianity is spreading like wildfire in the South, but in the North it is plateaued or declining.

The Lausanne findings on cultural impact may be more surprising. Christianity is heavily persecuted in much of the Global South, and is often merely tolerated even where it isn't persecuted. In most places it is (or seems to be) a new and radically alien force compared to longstanding traditional culture. By contrast, North American and European civilizations have historical roots in Christianity stretching back almost two millennia. Yet fully 58 percent of delegates from the South said evangelicals were having an increasing influence on the way of life in their societies, compared to only 31 percent in the North.[1] Peter Berger, perhaps the most important sociologist of religion in the past fifty years, comments: "These opinions strike me as empirically realistic in both regions."[2] And the pessimism in Europe and North America isn't just a pessimism about evangelicalism; those regions aren't exactly exploding with Roman Catholic and Eastern Orthodox revivals. This is a pessimism about whether Christianity itself has a place in civilization.

Christianity's lack of social influence is easy to explain in Europe; there aren't a lot of Christians around anymore. In America, however, it's a puzzle. Depending on how strictly you define it, something like a quarter to a third of the population is evangelical. While the role of Christianity in America's history and civilizational institutions is a complex subject (we'll look at it in chap. 1), at the very least Christianity has always been one of the more important components of the story. And a substantial number of evangelicals are present in the power elite of American institutions—from universities to businesses to entertainment to politics.[3]

So how is it that Christianity has so dramatically lost its impact on American civilization? And how can it begin the process of rebuilding that impact? Should we even try, or is cultural impact more dangerous than it is desirable?

In this book I'm going to propose some answers to those questions. The centerpiece of my answers is the joy of God. If Christianity is going to have a distinct impact, it needs to rely on what truly makes it distinct—the work of the Spirit in our minds, hearts, and lives. That's what makes Christians unique, and it gives us a unique opportunity to bless our unbelieving neighbors through the way we participate in the civilization we share with them.

To show what I mean, let's start with something simple: Christmas.

Explosions of Joy

Christmas was always a very big deal in our family when I was growing up. We kept all the traditions, we went through all the motions. Christmas was sacred in our family.

But Christmas never had anything to do with the birth of Jesus. I was raised outside the church, and in contemporary America that means we didn't even think about Christmas having something to do with Jesus. If we had, the idea would have seemed silly—all that was in the past. You might just as well expect us to cook an authentic seventeenth-century figgy pudding and feed it to carolers as expect us to think about Jesus on Christmas. The advertisements that said "Keep Christ in Christmas" and all the rest of that stuff was invisible to us. We didn't ignore them; we didn't have to. We had so completely tuned them out that we didn't even become aware of them long enough to ignore them.

Officially, Christmas in our family was about all the things the TV specials these days say it's about: love, family, peace, being a good person. In other words, you were supposed to spend the whole time wallowing in feelings of moral goodness. If anyone had a nagging sense that there was something phony about it all, that had to be suppressed. Letting that show would have been a repulsive blasphemy.

For me, though, Christmas was really about getting presents. It was an annual greed factory. I'm sure my parents tried to counteract this, and it's not their fault if they didn't succeed. It was an impossible task. All the rituals of moral affirmation ("peace on earth," "be with family") made everything associated with Christmas seem morally legitimate.

As I got older, I noticed that Christmas was also about something else: excruciating stress, exhaustion, and emotional trauma. First all the wearisome toil of buying, selling, and sending; then on the day itself, bickering, tears, and jealousy. As C. S. Lewis wrote, "You have only to stay over Christmas with a family who seriously try to 'keep' it . . . to see that the thing is a nightmare. . . . They are in no trim for merry-making . . . they look far more as if there had been a long illness in the house."[4] In retrospect, this seems inevitable. What else would happen when you take a spiritually dead holiday and force everyone to treat it like it's the center of their lives?

And yet . . . every year, from time to time, there were the moments of joy. And I mean a really unique joy—a special kind of joy that nothing else in our whole lives ever compared with. It was a transcendent experience. The explosive moment might come at any time, in any place.

This unexplained phenomenon is something I never actually noticed at the time. I didn't notice the difference between this kind of joy and the rest of the whole Christmas package. To me, the greedy pleasure of getting presents, the feeling of uplift from the rituals of moral affirmation, and the moments of explosive joy were all one thing. In retrospect, however, I can clearly see how different they were.

Here's the key: the moments of special joy all had one thing in common. They were always prompted by cultural artifacts associated with Christmas that expressed a truly Christian, Jesus-centered spiritual celebration. Songs, cards, stories, images; strictly formal or loosely casual; old standbys and recent creations—it was always something that some Christian had made by taking the joy of God in Christ that he had personally experienced in the power of the Holy Spirit and then embodying it in a cultural form.

I have an especially vivid memory of one year. I must have been something like ten. I ran around the house, leaping from room to room, belting out "Hark the Herald Angels Sing" and "Joy to the World" at the very top of my lungs. All the stanzas. I was transported; I was soaring.

Nobody ever sang "Frosty the Snowman" that way.

Formed by Joy, Even before Faith

These experiences did not create, or result from, a real faith in Christ on my part. Believe it or not, I wasn't thinking at all about Jesus, even as I was singing carols about Jesus! He remained implausible and irrelevant in my consciousness.

I got little tastes of the joy of God without getting God himself. I was washed for a moment by the spray from the breaking wave, without actually going into the ocean—without even knowing the ocean was there. This is actually a common phenomenon. If you really get to know what life outside the church is like, you can see it happening in all kinds of places. I wonder if people who have grown up inside the church all their lives might not realize how much influence Christianity has on the world outside the church through these indirect tastes of joy.

That special experience of joy did change me as a person, even though it didn't bring me to faith. In fact, I think it was very important to my formation; I am who I am partly because of it.

I don't just mean that I was more receptive to the Christian message later on, so these Christian cultural artifacts were valuable as pre-evangelistic "seed-sowing." That's true, but these tastes of joy made me a better person even apart from the role they played in helping prepare me for faith. If I had never heard the gospel, I would have died in my sins, but they would have been much less terrible sins; I'd have been a much worse sinner if I had never been shaped by the influence of Christian participation in my civilization.

The joy of God changed my mind. I fell in love with philosophy at an early age, but I was never even remotely tempted by atheism. It was just so obviously illogical. I wasn't even much interested in the philosophers who acknowledged God but didn't have much to say about him. Nor did I have much time for philosophies that were purely speculative or morally liberalizing. To me, philosophy was pointless unless it was an all-consuming quest to know and understand God and the moral life. Even if the Lord had never converted me, I would still have been a lot less far away from him like this than I would have been if I'd never known real joy.

Not only did the joy of God lead me to love philosophy, but the love of philosophy led me to more experiences of the joy of God. I read the works of great Christians who had fallen in love with philosophy the same way I had. In one sense, philosophy was the same thing for them that it was for me: the quest to know God and the moral life. That's why I listened to them about philosophy even when I dismissed Christian writers in every other context. And for them, philosophy was explosively joyful on a whole different level from any of the pagan philosophers. To contemplate God was an infinitely deeper joy for Augustine and Locke than it ever was for Plato and Rousseau. For the Christians, philosophy was a chance to glorify the God who had transformed their lives through the Spirit. It took a long time for me to notice the difference and understand why it was there, but just as with those Christmas carols, that doesn't mean it didn't change me in some ways.

The joy of God changed my heart. Because of those moments of joy, I sought God not only in philosophy, but in emotional experience. That didn't lead me to Christ, but on the whole, it still did me a lot more good than harm. For some antinomian types, emotionalism in religion is a cover for sin. But I was no antinomian. Before my conversion, I was a very strict legalist—a real Pharisee's Pharisee. So how much worse, how much more demonic, would I have been if I had never even learned that there was more to God than just the law?

Following the path of these emotional experiences, I found more tastes of the joy of God. The cultural artifacts that gave me the kinds of emotional experiences I was looking for—from music to church architecture—were disproportionately made by Christians. Even the super-cheesy, early 1990s "Christian Contemporary Music" that sophisticated people all laugh at was sometimes the only thing in my life that would make me feel like I was living in a meaningful universe where good things might really be hoped for. Again, I didn't realize at the time what was really happening, but that doesn't mean it didn't change me.

And the joy of God changed my way of living. Like I said, I was a legalist—a hypocrite and a prig. But at least I did know that moral goodness was a true and beautiful thing. I wasn't much tempted by either cynicism or naiveté about moral law. I never found it remotely plausible that all goodness in the world was just a phony pretense, but I also never thought that behavioral standards could be relatively relaxed because people are basically good. I believe the connection between those moments of Christmas joy and the Christmas rituals of moral affirmation laid an important foundation for that love of morality in my character.

Bringing the Joy of God Back to Our Civilization

My personal journey is different from everyone else's, of course. But I don't think it's unusual for people outside the church to be powerfully changed by the way they encounter the joy of God through Christians' participation in their civilization. I found it in places like philosophy, but other people find it in everything from works of art to the way their Christian coworkers do their work.

In this book, when I talk about the joy of God, I'm not talking about an emotion. I mean *the state of flourishing in mind, heart, and life that Christians experience by the Holy Spirit.* The joy of God makes us happier, but also wiser, humbler, more patient, and so forth. The joy of God is all the fruits of the Spirit.

Paul describes the joy of God as something that we live out and grow into, not something we just passively feel: "The kingdom of God is not a matter of eating and drinking but of righteousness and peace and joy in the Holy Spirit" (Rom. 14:17). God's kingdom is active, not passive; it is something embodied and manifested in human life. The gospel answer to pharisaical rules and regulations is not mere emotional experiences; it's a human life that's lived in the right way *for the right reasons*, because we are being transformed in our minds, hearts, and lives by the Spirit.

The joy of God—this Spirit-powered flourishing of human beings—can be experienced in a secondhand way by those who don't have it themselves. It can be tasted. That's what happened to me when I sang those Christmas carols.

I think Christianity is losing its influence in contemporary America because people outside the church just don't encounter the joy of God as much as they used to. Christmas provides a perfect example. Look how Christmas specials on television have changed. You may have seen 1965's *A Charlie Brown Christmas*, with its famous recitation of Luke 2:8–14 ("That's what Christmas is all about, Charlie Brown."). Not every Christmas special had a climactic Jesus moment like that, but it was at least normal for them to do so. By the time I was old enough to be watching Christmas specials in the late 1970s and early 1980s, they still had the Jesus moments, but they had started reassuring their audiences that this doesn't imply anything unpleasant for those who don't believe. For example, 1979's *John Denver and the Muppets: A Christmas Together* concludes with a puppet retelling of the nativity, but it also features two songs (one sung by Kermit, one by Denver) that emphasize it doesn't really make that much difference whether you believe in, or have even heard of, Jesus Christ. And now, of course, on mainstream television it's rare for Jesus even to be mentioned. If there are no unpleasant consequences to not having Jesus in your life, why bother shoehorning Jesus into your Christmas special? Obviously, Christmas specials are just one example, and not necessarily a deeply profound one, but I think it's very telling. How many explosive encounters with the joy of God have unchurched Americans been denied because the media feed them a steady diet of Jesus-free, sentimental mush every December?

This book lays out the reasons why I think this is happening, and how I think we Christians can help our neighbors encounter the joy of God through the way we behave in society. Maybe you're not a person who can write songs that will go on the radio, but whoever you are, there is some sector of American culture—your family, your workplace, your neighborhood—within which you have standing to bring the joy of God to people.

Every day, we participate in the structures of human civilization. Our participation ought to manifest the miraculous work the Spirit has done in our hearts. Impacting our civilization is only one of many reasons it ought to do so. Evangelism depends on it; if we preach the gospel but don't live in a way that reflects it, our neighbors won't believe it. Our own discipleship and spiritual formation also depend on it; our "civilizational lives" take up almost all of our waking hours, and we're not disciples if we glorify God only inside the church walls.

So what do you know? It turns out that evangelism, discipleship, and impacting our civilization all require the same thing. It's almost like it was all designed by someone who knew what he was doing.

Joy for the World

Did you know that "Joy to the World" was not written as a Christmas carol? In its original form, it had nothing to do with Christmas. It wasn't even written to be a song.

Isaac Watts was one of the great hymn writers in church history, and I guess nothing shows that better than the fact that he wrote one of his most famous hymns by accident. In 1719, Watts published a book of poems in which each poem was based on a psalm. But rather than just translate the original Old Testament texts, he adjusted them to refer more explicitly to the work of Jesus as it had been revealed in the New Testament.

One of those poems was an adaptation of Psalm 98. Watts interpreted this psalm as a celebration of Jesus's role as King of both his church and the whole world. More than a century later, the second

25

half of this poem was slightly adapted and set to music to give us
what has become one of the most famous of all Christmas carols:

> Joy to the world, the Lord is come;
> Let earth receive her King!
> Let every heart prepare him room
> And heaven and nature sing!
> *And heaven and nature sing!*
> And heaven . . . and heaven . . . and nature sing.
>
> Joy to the earth, the Savior reigns!
> Let men their songs employ
> While fields and floods, rocks, hills, and plains,
> Repeat the sounding joy!
> *Repeat the sounding joy!*
> Repeat . . . repeat . . . the sounding joy!
>
> No more let sins and sorrows grow,
> Nor thorns infest the ground;
> He comes to make his blessings flow
> Far as the curse is found!
> *Far as the curse is found!*
> Far as . . . far as . . . the curse is found!
>
> He rules the world with truth and grace
> And makes the nations prove
> The glories of his righteousness
> And wonders of his love!
> *And wonders of his love!*
> And wonders . . . wonders . . . of his love!

Borrowing a few lyrics from this wonderful hymn, which I
ran around the house singing as a boy, here's how I think the joy
of God flows out from our hearts into civilization.

Let Every Heart Prepare Him Room: The Holy Spirit miraculously
transforms us through our relationship with Jesus, giving us the
joy of God in mind, heart, and life.

Let Men Their Songs Employ: Because God made human beings as social creatures, this joy of God is not locked up in an isolated heart; it flows among us and transforms how we relate to one another.

Let Earth Receive Her King: The church is the special community of people who are undergoing this transformative work, and the Spirit uses the distinct life of the church to further that work by means of doctrine, devotion, and stewardship.

He Comes to Make His Blessings Flow: We live most of our lives out in the world, among people who are not (yet) being transformed in this special way. How we live in the world should manifest the change the Spirit is working in us, carrying the impact of the joy of God "far as the curse is found."

He Rules the World with Truth and Grace: As we learn to manifest the Spirit's work in our hearts through the ways we live in the world, the portions of the world that are under our stewardship start to flourish more fully—not in a way that directly redeems people, because only personal regeneration can save a human being, but in a way that makes the world more like it should be and delivers intense experiences of God's joy to our neighbors.

My prayer is that you find this book helpful in thinking through the exciting opportunities and perplexing challenges we face as we answer God's call to develop godly ways of life within our civilization.

Part 1

Let Men Their
Songs Employ

What Is the Church? What Is Society?

This book asks the question, how can Christianity begin the process of rebuilding its influence in American society? Many people will answer that question with a question: What do you mean by Christianity?

It's a good question. One of the most difficult issues in theology is how we understand the concept of the church—*ecclesiology*, in theological jargon. And our understanding of the church has special relevance for this book. Differences over ecclesiology are probably the most common stumbling blocks in discussions of the church and society. People can't reach much agreement on how the church relates to human civilization—they can't even have much of a meaningful *disagreement* about it—if they mean different things by "the church." I'm not going to get into technical theology here, but since I'm writing a book about Christianity and the church, I think I owe you at least a brief, simple statement of what I mean by these terms.

When I talk about Christianity and the church in this book, I mean here and now. The "church triumphant," made up of redeemed saints who have gone to their reward, is an important part of ecclesiology. And people who are going to be saved in the future are also, from God's eternal perspective, part of the church. But neither of those is relevant when we talk about the church and society.

When I talk about Christianity and the church, I'm talking about a community. All individuals who come to saving faith are part of the "invisible church." But those who never publicly identify as Christians, live visibly as believers, and join the faith community aren't relevant when we talk about the church and society.

We need to consider two main things when we think about Christianity in relation to human civilization.[1] One is the *organizational* or *institutional* embodiment of Christianity. This is centered on the institutional church: the clergy, the church building, and Sunday worship, which play a unique and indispensable role in the faith community. Jesus made special provision for the ordination of officers to lead and steward the institutional church, and he located his people's corporate worship of God within it. That gives it a unique status. However, the institutional church is not the only organizational manifestation of Christianity. Because our faith is meant to be practiced in community, Christians are constantly forming organizations to carry it out beyond the walls of the church building. This includes weekly small groups, accountability partnerships, and Christian schools, hospitals, and service organizations. These other organizations can never substitute for the institutional church; they do not and cannot play its special role. But they represent other ways in which Christianity manifests itself in organizational form.

The other thing we need to think about is the *organic* or *informal* embodiment of Christianity. This is the whole dynamic social interplay of all the ways in which Christians relate to one another and support one another in building up godly lives together. For example, I am currently employed by two different organizations (my full-time employer and a consulting job on the side) that are not officially committed, as institutions, to Christianity. Yet in both organizations, some of my coworkers are Christians. We don't take off our "Christian hats" and put on our "secular hats" when we're at work; we talk about things like how doing our jobs is part of our faith. That's organic Christianity.

A robust, institutionally strong, well-equipped organizational Christianity is critically needed to support every aspect of Christian life, and our engagement with society is no exception. However, while organizational Christianity is necessary, it's not enough. When we step outside the church building, we don't cease to be Christians, and we don't cease to be social creatures who depend on relationships and community to sustain us. We need to maintain an active, intentional life of discipleship in informal fellowship with organic Christianity.

The structure of this book reflects my conviction that it's essential to discuss both organizational and organic Christianity if we're going to talk about Christianity and society. Organizational Christianity will be the main focus of part 2, although organic Christianity will make some appearances there. Then, organic Christianity will be the main focus of part 3, although organizational Christianity will make some appearances.

These two faces of Christianity are distinct but closely related. On the one hand, it's important not to collapse the distinction and talk about only one of them, as though the institutions of organizational Christianity should barge in where they don't belong and do things that only organic Christianity can really do, or as if organic Christianity were capable of getting along just fine without needing organizational Christianity to teach and support it. On the other hand, it's important not to distinguish the two so much that you effectively separate them. In fact, they're closely intertwined— so much so that the boundaries between the two are often hard to draw in practice. Suppose your small group meets for Bible study, then goes out and does a service project, then goes out for pizza and ice cream. Where does organizational Christianity end and organic Christianity begin? The distinction matters, but trying to draw the line exactly would be impossible.

Now here's another question, one you might not have expected when you picked up this book. When someone asks how Christianity can begin the process of rebuilding its influence in American society, it's very common for another person to reply, "What do you mean by Christianity?" But it's rare for anyone to reply, "What do you mean by 'American society'?" Yet that question is just as interesting.

Here in part 1, we're going to tackle that question in two pieces. First, we're going to ask about the "American" piece. How did America get where it is now, and where is it going? Second we're going to ask about the "society" piece. What is a society, and how are we as human beings related to it? Once we've got a better idea of *what* we're trying to influence, we'll be ready to move on to *how* we influence it.

1

Christianity and the Great American Experiment

Then our mouth was filled with laughter,
and our tongue with shouts of joy;
then they said among the nations,
"The LORD has done great things for them."

Ps. 126:2

If we want to understand the question of this book—how can Christianity begin the process of rebuilding its influence in American society?—first we need to know our history. As Christian philosopher Søren Kierkegaard famously put it, life must be lived forwards, but it can only be understood backwards. And what's true of individuals is also true of societies.

So we should start by asking, how did Christianity lose its influence in American society? Our efforts to rebuild its influence can't succeed unless we understand why it declined. Unfortunately, this history isn't well known, so we often end up fighting the wrong battles with the wrong weapons.

Quick quiz: Who said the following, and when? "The Christian people of America are going to vote as a bloc for the man with the strongest moral and spiritual platform, regardless of his views on other matters. I believe we can hold the balance of power."

Jerry Falwell in 1980? Pat Robertson in 2000? No, it was Billy

Graham—in 1951.[1] That a man as intelligent as Graham could be so naive about how the world works points to a deep problem in American evangelicalism. Many evangelical leaders were saying similar things for most of the twentieth century. When we look into the history of Christianity and American society, we start to realize the problem is not what we may have thought it was.

We want to pull a lever and see the world change. Political involvement is not the issue; the joy of God is the issue. Remember, the joy of God is *the state of flourishing in mind, heart, and life that Christians experience by the Holy Spirit.* We've been so anxious to influence society in the past century that we've ended up going after a lot of shortcuts. For some it's politics, for some it's education, for some it's evangelism. We've been pulling a lot of levers. The common thread is that we're pulling these levers so hard, we leave no space for people to encounter the joy of God.

Christianity and America: Three Stories

American evangelicals tell themselves three different stories about Christianity's influence in America. Each of these stories comes from a particular approach to American history. So getting American history right is going to be the key to sorting out the various stories we tell ourselves about Christianity's place in America.

The first story is the "Christian founding" narrative. This is essentially a tale of stolen glory. According to this telling, the American founding was an essentially Christian act. The people who tell this story today might no longer use the phrase "Christian nation," because it can create misunderstandings. But they do depict the American founding as, at bottom, the enactment of a new model of society more in line with Christian teaching than any before. This Christian social order was the culmination of the Reformation. Thanks to Martin Luther, true Christian teaching had been unleashed from its medieval captivity, and eventually it found social expression (however imperfectly) in the American founding. Responsible people will of course be faithful to the facts; the deism of a few founders, and the shaky theology of many more, will be duly acknowledged. However, after all the caveats and nuances are accounted for, this story depicts Christianity—Christian doctrine and practice—as the foundation of America.

The villains in this story are the major anti-Christian intellectual movements of the nineteenth and twentieth centuries: biological and psychological reductionism in science; narcissistic subjectivism in the arts; materialism and dualism in philosophy; pragmatism in ethics. While these movements found great success in Europe, at first they were contained to a minority in America. But they continued to grow and develop, hatching ever more hideous progeny to torment a vulnerable world: Nihilism, socialism, Fascism, Communism, Nazism. Time and again, in the fight against these evils, the only nation that embodied an essentially Christian form of social organization—America—took its natural place as leader and captain. And America triumphed, because its ideas and institutions were better, having been formed by Christianity.

And then the other side got smart. It organized to infiltrate America's leading institutions from within, especially its schools. In the space of a generation, the secularism that had long been a festering sore on America's cultural life became a cancerous tumor. Christianity's rightful place as the source of America's guiding ideas was usurped. At home, disorder in all forms was on the rise; abroad, we lost our ability to fight our enemies.

In stark contrast to this "Christian founding" narrative, the second story about Christianity and America is the "secular founding" narrative. This is a tale of disillusionment. According to this telling, true Christianity never had much influence on American society. The true church is at enmity with the powers that control the world; it flourishes spiritually only when it refuses the temptation to flourish culturally. The world is ruled by evil, so cultural flourishing means selling out to the world. Again, responsible people will be faithful to the facts; the genuine Christian faith of many of the founders and some influence of ideas borrowed from Christianity are too obvious to be denied. But in this story, the American founding was most importantly a product of "the Enlightenment," which is depicted as an implicitly anti-Christian movement. Some of its ideas were good as far as they went (freedom of religion, civil equality, the rule of law) and may be historically connected with Christianity in some ways, while other ideas were bad (Deism, perfectionism). What they had in common was that they were joined together as components of a larger thought system that was antithetical to Christianity. This mixed bag of essentially non-Christian ideas was dressed up in a cloak of theological language for the sake of maintaining respectability and attracting votes in a country with large numbers of believing Christians.

So in this story, the central organizing dynamic of politics in America has always been a process of cloaking non-Christian ideas (good ones and bad ones) in Christian language. The rise of explicitly anti-Christian ideas in the nineteenth and twentieth centuries was only the natural development of the earlier rise of non-Christian Enlightenment ideas in the seventeenth and eighteenth centuries. These ideas reached their logical conclusions sooner in Europe, where the churches were dying so there was less and less need for the pretense of Christianity. (And the European churches were dying because they had sold out their theological integrity in order to influence society!) The final blossoming of explicitly non-Christian social organization in America in the 1970s was really just the revealing of something that had always been there. Now, the competition is between politicians who appeal explicitly to secularists and those who continue to dress up their agendas as Christian to manipulate churches and voters.

This is a story of disillusionment in both the good and bad sense. In the good sense, it is disillusionment because an illusion has been removed. Since the turn away from "Christianity" in the organization of American life in the 1970s, the true nature of the social order has been revealed. American culture has not necessarily become worse than it always was; it has just become more honest about its non-Christian character. In the bad sense, it is disillusionment because it stems from, and teaches, a cynical attitude about society and Christianity's role in it. Politicians—and for that matter any other socially prominent people—are almost always manipulators who want to get something from the church. The third story is not really much of a story at all. It's more of an attitude of indifference. Let's call it the "it doesn't matter" narrative. The church doesn't need to wrestle with the questions of history and American society. That's not our department. Our job is just to preach a message of repentance, faith, personal regeneration, and justification; make as many converts as we can; and leave it up to individual Christians to fit into society in whatever ways seem best to them. If the church invests a lot of effort taking positions on the questions of history and society, that will distract us from our real job: maximizing the number of people who convert.

This doesn't mean that the great questions of history and society are removed from the life of the church. These questions still matter to people, so the church will still talk about them, even if it has nothing distinctive to say about them. Aid to Africa, recycling, civility—the church will endorse whatever causes, ideas, and positions happen to be prominent in the culture, as far as it can do so without betraying its core message. That way the gospel will be situated within the cultural views that people outside the church already hold, so the decision to believe in Christ will seem more plausible to those people. In effect, it becomes part of the church's job to support and reinforce whatever views are already predominant in the population it wishes to reach.

True Facts, False Stories

History is not just facts, it's a story. The facts are important; fidelity to the facts is essential to good history. But it takes a story to turn facts into history.[2]

You can get all your facts right, and still get the story wrong. Here's how a pastor of mine once illustrated this point. Suppose

I told you that I once saw a group of masked men strap someone down to a table, rip his chest open, and cut out his heart while it was still beating. Now suppose I told you that I once witnessed a life-saving heart transplant operation. Same set of facts, but two totally different stories.

Unfortunately, all three of the stories we've been telling ourselves about American history are inadequate. They can point to true facts, but they don't quite arrange those facts into a true story. And, as will become clear later, these false stories have been undermining our engagement with American society for a century.

The inadequacy of the "it doesn't matter" narrative becomes clear as soon as we identify its real implications. Where this story predominates, churches take the facts about Jesus and insert them into whatever sociocultural story the world is already telling itself. Thus the church becomes, in practice, captive to the world's story. Functionally, the church reinforces everything the world says about human life *except for* the relatively narrow set of facts that the church identifies as the gospel message.

That brings us to the two substantive stories. Both of these stories highlight true and important facts in the historical record. However, both of them are false as stories. They string the facts together into a larger structure of meaning that misleads.

The Christian founding story highlights—accurately—that the ideas of the American founding were importantly influenced by Christianity in numerous ways and were better aligned with biblical principles than the aristocratic and confessional political systems of the old regime. It also pushes back against the tendency to treat anything associated with the Enlightenment as necessarily anti-Christian. The Enlightenment was not a single movement but was manifested very differently in different parts of Europe, and in some places Christian ideas were an important part of it. You cannot prove that an idea is non-Christian merely by connecting it in some way with something called "the Enlightenment."

The secular founding story highlights—accurately—that the

American founding was not a Christian movement as such and was importantly influenced by anti-Christian thinking on several fronts; that the American social order is not a Christian social order as such (not even "unofficially"); and that the founders all called themselves Christians but were very uneven in their doctrinal orthodoxy. In that environment, all sorts of ideas were plausibly labeled as "Christian"—sometimes in manipulative ways.

While both stories highlight facts that are true, neither story is true as a story. The quickest way to see this is to notice that neither story is able to explain the facts that are highlighted by the other. If a story not only contains true facts but is true as a story, it ought to be able to account for the key facts that might be brought to challenge it. Significant unexplained facts are good reasons to doubt a story; too many unexplained facts of too great a significance will undermine our belief in the story.

For example, the Christian founding story can certainly acknowledge, but it cannot really account for, the rationalism of the founders. If this story were true, we would expect that whatever failings the founders had would be a matter of inadequate forward movement—a failure to challenge old, unreformed (literally, pre-Reformation) ways. Yet their failings were much more modern than medieval. In some ways, you will not find three people more diverse in ideas, goals, and personalities than the three men who led the drafting of the Declaration of Independence: Thomas Jefferson, the man of great discoveries and new frontiers, of romantic idealism, perfectionism, and radicalism; John Adams, the man of justice and civilization, of law, conservatism, and discipline; and Benjamin Franklin, the man of practicality and compromise, of trial and error, negotiation, and comity. Yet all three believed that reason—and a pretty narrow concept of what counted as "reason"—was the proper organizing principle of all life. If their project was really the Reformation overthrowing the vestiges of medievalism, where did this all-encompassing rationalism come from?

Meanwhile, the secular founding story can acknowledge, but cannot account for, the critical role played in the founders' thought by the idea that human life is sacred and sinful at the same time. With few exceptions, we find the founders relying consistently on this assumption—that the human person combines irreducible dignity and systematic moral dysfunction. This is the bedrock wisdom upon which their whole system is based. And it was just this integrated understanding of the simultaneous goodness and badness of human nature that made their system superior to the aristocratic and confessional systems that came before it.[3] But where did they get this idea? The Enlightenment provides no sources for it. Indeed, wherever Enlightenment thinkers deviated from earlier Christian approaches to human nature, it led *immediately* to tyrannical political ideas far worse than the old medieval aristocracies and confessionalisms. When Thomas Hobbes introduced into the modern world a reductively materialistic understanding of human nature he had picked up from ancient Greco-Roman writers, there was no gradual unfolding process of realization through which people eventually figured out that materialistic anthropology implies authoritarian and unlimited absolutism in politics. Hobbes himself saw this implication and made it the organizing principle of his political thought. Similarly, when Jean-Jacques Rousseau reintroduced Plato's ethical subjectivism to the modern world, he recognized that it implied a revolutionary social radicalism that would override all civil protection for personal freedoms, and he made this the organizing principle of his political thought. The Enlightenment writers who replaced medieval aristocracy and confessionalism with constitutional democracy and freedom were the ones whose thinking about human nature retained a firm grounding in Christianity—Locke, Montesquieu, Smith, Blackstone. Where, then, did the American founders get the anthropology upon which they built their whole system, if they did not inherit it from Christianity?

Ambiguity: A Glorious American Achievement

This critique of the two substantive stories about Christianity in American history might be summed up in this statement: The American social order was never either clearly pro-Christian or clearly anti-Christian. Ross Douthat has described America as a civilization driven not by Christian orthodoxy nor by heresy, but by a perpetual social tension between the two.[4] The relationship between Christianity and the nation's political and social structure has always been ambiguous. In fact, the relationship between the church and the social order is ambiguous in America in a way and to a degree unlike anything seen in any other country in the world, either before or since the founding of this country.

And by that remarkable fact there hangs . . . a story. This ambiguity was not a historical accident; it was, in fact, the whole point of the American founding. An adequate history of Christianity and America ought to be built around the story of this ambiguity. And quite a story it is. We might call it the "cooperative founding" story, because Christianity and its spiritual enemies created America together.

Every society needs agreed-upon moral rules to govern people's public conduct. It's obvious that society won't survive long unless certain basic moral rules (don't kill, don't steal, keep your promises, help your neighbors) are voluntarily obeyed by at least most people most of the time. Moreover, just agreeing on the abstract rules isn't enough; people need a shared understanding of the concepts behind them. We may agree that murder is wrong, but what is murder? What acts count as murder?

That's why, until recently, all societies in history had an institutional authority whose job was to say what was good and evil. In short, they had a state-sanctioned community religion whose clergy were part of the civil order. There was often toleration for the presence of religious minorities, either out of generosity or to gain some calculated advantage (such as to facilitate the expansion of empire or commerce). But it was understood that the law and the common life of society were based on its official religion.

In the fourth and fifth centuries, as Christianity was legalized and gradually became the predominant religion of the Roman Empire, the church suddenly found that Rome was looking to it to play this role. It had to wrestle with an entirely new set of questions. What does Christianity have to say about the business of running a society? Anything? Everything? Is there only one Christian way of governing? Is there *any* Christian way of governing?

In some ways, the fourth- and fifth-century Christians introduced new ideas about social order that had revolutionary consequences. Christianity's emphasis on the dignity and moral responsibility of all human beings had transformative consequences. We'll highlight some of these in part 3 of this book, looking at a few stark contrasts between social systems before and after the rise of Christianity as a force in civilization.

However, one idea that the Christians of this period did not much question was the basic idea that every society needed to have an official religion. It seemed obvious that somebody had to have authority to say what was just and unjust in public life, or society couldn't function. No society had ever done things any other way. So Christianity stepped into the role of state religion relatively easily. Even as the theologians declared that only the Spirit could give faith and that civil government was based on moral justice rather than the gospel, those same theologians justified civil laws against heresy, blasphemy, apostasy, and other essentially theological "crimes" on grounds that only state patronage of the church could sustain the moral fiber of society.

This entanglement between church and state didn't cause much disruption through the Middle Ages, but during the Reformation, it became the source of a major civilizational disaster. All laws and social institutions were built on the understanding that the church would settle disputes over what was good public conduct, and hence that the state and the church were interdependent.

Then suddenly, as a result of the division over the gospel between Protestants and Catholics, multiple institutions claimed to be the true church and thus to have the right to partner with the state and define the boundaries of public conduct. The system didn't work once there was persistent disagreement over who gets to speak for the church and say what is or is not Christianity.

Because civil authority was deeply intertwined with church authority, the disagreement over the gospel and the church immediately produced a violent conflict. The ensuing wars of religion lasted for two centuries and encompassed some of the cruelest persecution and most massive slaughter in history. And beyond all the torturing and killing, there was a deeper uprooting of the moral order in society. Everything was at stake in these political conflicts—not just all worldly interests, but all goodness and holiness whatsoever—and there was a very real sense that total catastrophe was always just one defeat away. People felt they had to do whatever was necessary to win. Moreover, the people on each side knew that those on the other side were feeling the same desperation, so lies, double crosses, false incriminations, and atrocities on every scale seemed necessary if only for self-protection. All sense of common citizenship or even common humanity across religious divisions became tenuous.

And then, almost as rapidly as they had begun, the wars of religion ceased. People found a solution that would restore moral order to society: freedom of religion.

The basic idea behind freedom of religion is that societies need some level of moral agreement, but don't need—and shouldn't expect—agreement on all moral questions. It was based on the expectation that the basics of public morality (don't kill, don't steal, keep your promises, help your neighbors) don't require a shared theology to be sustained in society. _See pye_ 71

This is not to say that moral rules don't have theological roots. They do. Rather, the point is that we can agree on enough morality to live together without needing to agree on the theology behind it.

Standing behind this basic insight are two principles. One is that religious differences persist in spite of all attempts to enforce orthodoxy; religious enforcement only produces a false appearance of unity. The other is that the basic moral concepts sufficient for social life are implicit in human nature and known to all. This explains why we must remove the enforcement of a community religion, and why we can still expect the moral basics to persist without enforced religious orthodoxy.

Both of these ideas have historic roots in Christian theology. That's why they were plausible to the militantly Christian partisans engaging in the wars of religion. The idea that religious differences aren't removed by enforced orthodoxy grew historically from the doctrines of the fall and the necessity of the Spirit's work for regeneration. In a fallen world where the power of regeneration rests with the Spirit, we must expect that society will always be made up of many who are born again and many who are not—in addition to the diversity of opinions we should expect within both those groups. The idea that basic moral agreement could be sustained anyway on the basis of human nature grew historically from the doctrine that the image of God remains in all human beings. As Paul writes in the second chapter of Romans, those who are without the specially revealed law of God nonetheless reveal through their behavior that the law of God is written on the heart.

But both of these ideas are also philosophically plausible without Christianity. That's why they later came to be championed by critics of Christianity as well as by Christians. The idea that enforced religious orthodoxy only produces hypocrisy fit easily into the narrative that Christianity had been a destructive social force. And the idea that basic moral concepts are knowable by nature fit easily into philosophies that wanted to turn away from revelation, spirituality, and metaphysics, instead seeking fulfillment of all human needs in nature.

In fact, these two ideas, and their synthesis in freedom of religion, came to be prominently championed by Christian and anti-Christian figures alike during the Enlightenment. This kind of intellectual commonality among opposing camps is one of the reasons we speak of "the Enlightenment" as a single phenomenon. It's also a reason why we have such trouble disentangling "Christian" from "non-Christian" influences in the Enlightenment period.

These organizing principles of religious freedom require that the boundary between the church and the social order remain ambiguous. A clear and fixed boundary between the church's turf and the social order's turf could only be drawn if the government defined and enforced the boundary. That would obviously violate the whole idea of freedom of religion, since it would require government to adopt and enforce very specific views about what is and is not the church's turf—in essence, it would require civil enforcement of theology.

Freedom of religion is therefore a totally new approach to social organization, one that is unprecedented in all human history before the wars of religion. It is a comprehensive model for how to run a society, not just a law or policy we adopt alongside all the laws and policies that govern other public questions. Thus, our commitment to freedom of religion reorganizes the way in which we deal with all other policy and social questions.

The American founding was the pinnacle of the historic forces that produced freedom of religion as a social model. Other nations grew slowly and imperfectly toward something approximating freedom of religion. None of them has fully arrived there yet. America, by contrast, was organized from the beginning around freedom of religion.

Thus, history denies us the easy answers we want on the relationship between the church and the social order. America is the one place of all places where such answers are not to be had. It is this, above all else, that makes America exceptional. Frustrating as this ambiguity can be when we are struggling to answer tough questions, it is only through this ambiguity that such freedom of religion as we have enjoyed has been maintained. That is the special achievement of America, and it is worthy of celebration.

The Paradoxes of Religious Freedom

Freedom of religion does have weak points, though. All systems do. The American founders were highly confident that a sufficient shared morality could be sustained without civil enforcement of religious orthodoxy. As I've already indicated, there are irreligious reasons to think so, but there are also sound biblical reasons to think so.[5] However, there's a catch. This kind of robust public morality requires certain social conditions to make it work. But in a society with religious freedom, no one has clear authority to see to it that those conditions are maintained.

This weak point in the model is, again, the price of our freedom—and it's well worth paying. But if we become naive about the social conditions necessary for robust public morality, or (worse) fall into the lazy assumption that public morality is somehow automatically self-sustaining, the freedom of religion model will slowly collapse.

Freedom of religion requires a delicate balancing act: it does not enforce religion, but it requires religion. Only people who have a comprehensive moral and metaphysical view of the universe will actually obey the shared public morality (don't kill, don't steal, keep your promises, help your neighbors) society needs. Mere enlightened self-interest cannot restrain people's destructive behaviors enough. It may be true, as the apostles of enlightened self-interest claim, that we all get more goodies in the long run if everyone refrains from lying and stealing. But I personally will get more goodies in the long run if I encourage *you* to follow the rules against lying and stealing, then turn around and lie and steal like crazy whenever I'm not likely to get caught. Moreover, enlightened self-interest can't sustain a social consensus on what the content of the shared rules should be. What counts as lying? What counts as stealing? What counts as murder?

To sustain moral behavior, people need more than simply a list of rules. They need to be people who have a comprehensive view of the universe—a religion, or an ideology that functions like a religion—that stands behind those rules. Only such a comprehensive view can explain the rules (supplying answers to the crucial "ethical content questions" mentioned above), organize the rules (so we know how to handle difficult ethical judgments), justify the rules (making them seem plausible, and therefore worthy of obedience), and sacralize the rules (making them sacred and truly moral, rather than merely prudent advice). Without a comprehensive view of the universe, no body of ethical rules remains coherent for long.

In short, the basic public morality that we all need to agree upon presupposes exactly the kind of metaphysical grounding that we don't all agree upon, and never will. Thus the freedom of religion model will fail if we reduce our morality to merely the stuff everyone agrees on. If beliefs that go beyond the public moral consensus are stigmatized as crazy or dangerous, or even if they are just relegated to secondary importance for the sake of social peace, the public moral consensus itself will soon collapse.

Society needs to see it as normal and expected, not scary and threatening, when people have different beliefs about the universe—beliefs that are unspeakably precious to them and organize their whole lives. These unshared beliefs will create uncomfortable social tensions. Society must embrace these tensions as healthy and beneficial, rather than shying away from them in fear. Societies where people feel free to have disagreements about the meaning of life are strong and confident in themselves, as they need to be to thrive. Societies where people keep their uncomfortable disagreements hushed up for fear of what might happen if they were aired are weak and hollow. Look back through history and you see the same pattern. The society with lots of open disagreement and social conflict is the one surging with power in art, science, commerce, constructive social reform, and (most of all) religious revival; the hushed-up society where everyone is afraid to say what he thinks is on the brink of violence and collapse.

Another, closely related social condition we must sustain is even more controversial: the institutional embodiment of these comprehensive metaphysical views. It's true that freedom of religion has an individualistic side; it gives civil expression to Martin Luther's dictum that "every man is responsible for his own faith."[6] But this is a responsibility that cannot be carried out by each person in isolation, as Luther himself well knew. Social life requires institutional grounding. Behavior patterns disintegrate if they are not given coherent and enduring expression in institutions. That goes double for moral behavior patterns, which cut against the grain of our disordered desires. Hence, we need institutions specifically dedicated to sustaining our comprehensive views of the universe in their coherent totality, and calling us to account when we fail to live up to them.

The freedom of religion model therefore requires that citizens join and provide support for exactly the kind of institutions that the model itself excludes from civil authority—religious and quasi-religious institutions. Just as the content of our beliefs must not be reduced to only the rules that we all agree on, our institutional life must not be reduced to only the organizations that we all have to join. Society must sustain a strong expectation that its citizens will invest a significant portion of their lives in institutions that embody comprehensive beliefs about the universe to which the social order as such is not dedicated.

These two related expectations upon which religious freedom rests—that people will be religious and support religious institutions—are hard to maintain. And in a society with religious freedom, no one has authority to see to it that these expectations are maintained. That's the essence of religious freedom; nobody can order you to believe or to join a church. So it becomes all the harder to maintain them.

America's Turning Point

In the twentieth century, through this point of vulnerability, the system of religious freedom began to unravel. But the key turning point wasn't in the 1970s; it was in the 1920s. Theological and organizational changes within American Protestantism had profound impacts on the social order far beyond the walls of Protestant churches.

At the time, America was predominantly Protestant. Although Protestantism's predominance was not legally enforced in most cases, it was one of the most important influences in society. Most Americans saw the world through Protestant eyes. So the shape of society was informally and inconsistently—but really and importantly—shaped by Protestant assumptions.

The predominance of Protestantism was a mixed blessing, socially speaking. Obviously those of us who believe in Protestantism will always prefer to see people be Protestant, because we love our neighbors and want them to know the truth. However, looking at the way things played out in the functioning of American civilization, there was both a bright side and a dark side.

On the bright side, the Protestant predominance kept the citizenry moral. Among many other blessings, this was critical to maintaining freedom of religion. The state cannot safely take its hands off religion unless it can trust the citizenry to obey the moral rules necessary to civilization (don't kill, don't steal, keep your promises, help your neighbors) on their own.

The dark side of American Protestant predominance was the unjust treatment of non-Protestants that often resulted. Beyond the bounds of state power, America expected its leading institutions to be predominantly defined by and loyal to the Protestant view of the world. In practice, this meant that Roman Catholics, Jews, and others were excluded from equal participation in the life of American civilization in a variety of ways.

In the first two decades of the twentieth century, as a result of theological developments that had been brewing for centuries,

American Protestantism underwent a drastic schism. On one side were the "modernists" or "liberals," who wanted to make most of Christianity's historic doctrinal commitments (the Trinity, the incarnation, the atonement, the authority and inerrancy of Scripture, the occurrence of the biblical miracles) optional—even for clergy. The overarching aim of the movement was to detach Christianity from claims about supernatural historical events, reinventing it as a collection of timeless ethical/philosophical teachings and edifying cultural rituals. Christianity's historic commitments to supernatural events were increasingly coming into conflict with claims being made in the name of science; the liberal strategy was to ensure Christianity's survival by withdrawing from all questions concerning historical facts (and thus from all questions where Christianity might come into conflict with claims made in the name of science). The major denominational bodies, along with the largest schools and other leading cultural institutions, mostly went this way. On the other side were the evangelicals, who insisted on fidelity to what we might call "historic Christianity" in a double sense: to the doctrinal commitments that had historically defined Christian orthodoxy, and to Christianity's basic character as a religion based on historical events.

This schism undermined both of the key social conditions of public morality described above: that people are religious and support religious institutions. At first, America was still predominantly characterized by "Protestantism." But now, no one could say with any kind of finality what Protestantism stood for. Effectively, it stood for whatever you wanted it to stand for.

Under such conditions, America could not maintain the social expectation that citizens have a comprehensive view of the universe. Most of its churches were no longer even preaching such a comprehensive view, having degenerated into mere ethics and ritual. Predictably, even the ethics and the ritual degenerated over time, since they had no deeper metaphysic to sustain them. Pretty soon, it no longer seemed plausible to most people that everyone needs to have a comprehensive view of the universe sustaining a robust metaphysical basis for morality.

It's important to note that at first, this change did not involve actually denigrating people who believed in a comprehensive view. That would come later. The key change, the one that made all the difference, was that you were no longer *expected* to have a comprehensive view. If you found that kind of thing attractive, that was fine—for you. It just wasn't something that people in general needed to have for society to hold together.

It took longer for the importance of investing in church life to fade. For quite some time, decent people continued to go to church on Sunday simply because that was the decent thing for decent people to do. Eventually, though, as the content of church life became thinner and thinner, it became harder and harder to sustain the expectation that everyone ought to go. Why was it so important? Once again, it wasn't necessary to denigrate institutional religious life; it was only necessary to remove the expectation that everyone ought to participate.

The Evangelical Response

The problem wasn't all on the liberal side. In some ways, the evangelical response to the crisis was inadequate. Evangelicals recognized the problem, but did not fully grasp its causes and effects.

One aspect of their response was right on target. They correctly foresaw that the breakdown of consensus on church teaching would ultimately undermine public morality far beyond the specifically theological subjects of the controversy. Even from the earliest stages of the schism, and with growing alarm in later decades, they sounded the warning that an America where churches are no longer unified in the historic teachings of Christianity would be an America without a moral compass.[7] They were widely dismissed as doomsayers at the time, but subsequent history has largely vindicated them.

Evangelicals did what any good citizens would do in the face of a threat to their country: they mobilized to save it. It speaks well of them that they did. Good citizens don't stand by while their nation is threatened, and evangelical activism has accomplished much good. Although the rising tide of moral disorder has not been reversed, its progress has been halted in many respects, and forces of renewal are gathering. All this was made possible largely by evangelical efforts, though the world will never give evangelicals credit.

But evangelical strategies for dealing with the problem were inadequate. Evangelicals invested in strategies that created short-term positive impacts but depleted their cultural capital— sacrificing their standing in the American social order—over the long term. So the good that has been accomplished through a century of activism has also diminished the social resources we need to sustain that activism. That's how we got to the frustrating position we are now in.

In the past century evangelical strategy followed three different paths. Unsurprisingly, they correspond to the three stories about Christianity and American society outlined above. And since the stories didn't do justice to the full realities of history, the responses they produced were unable to maintain Christianity's standing in American civilization.

Those who adhered to the Christian founding story saw the crisis as a function of power. They believed Christianity was under attack; its rightful place at the top of American society was being dislodged by hostile forces. Thus, it seemed only natural to mobilize for a fight. If Christianity could fend off its foes, it would naturally return to the center of American life, like a gyroscope returning automatically to an upright position after being tipped over.

For most of the twentieth century, the most prominent evangelical leaders spoke and acted as though they were entitled to stand as the moral compass of American society. The Billy Graham comment quoted above is only one example from hundreds. One of the century's most important evangelical broadcasters, William

Ward Ayer, explained in 1942 that the founding of the National Association of Evangelicals was necessary to "save American democracy."[8] At the founding convocation of Fuller Seminary in 1947, cofounder Harold Ockenga declared that because Western civilization was built on Protestant premises, only evangelicals could rescue America from destruction at the hands of secularism and "Romanism"; if they mobilized to meet these threats, they could "rebuild the foundations of society."[9]

Of course, it was true that Christianity was under attack. Christianity is always under attack. That was nothing new, and if attacks on Christianity were going to dislodge its influence in American society, they would have done so long before.

The important new development occurred not outside the church, but inside. The Protestant religious consensus that had once—informally and inconsistently, but really and importantly—predominated in American life had dissolved from within. It was fragmented by centuries of accumulated theological and philosophical divisions. By 1952, the old order was so hollow that Eisenhower could casually remark that "our form of government has no sense unless it is founded in a deeply felt religious faith, and I don't care what it is." To be fair, he quickly added: "It must be a religion with 'all men are created equal.'"[10] But the initial indifference to doctrine was the real indicator of where America's religious consensus was going.

Evangelical leaders who went down this path were trying to prop up a structure that no longer had enough integrity to stand. There was no longer anything to be returned to its "rightful place." The liberal secularists had not dislodged it; they were just rushing in to fill the void after it disintegrated.

Moreover, evangelicalism itself could not play the social role that Protestantism had played before the schism. It was only one among the fragmented voices of many religious factions. Evangelicalism was faithful to the doctrinal commitments of the earlier Protestant unity, but a church is more than a set of doctrinal commitments. People did not view the evangelical fragment as identical to the earlier organic unity, and rightly so. In most respects, other than doctrinal commitments, evangelicalism was different from the earlier religious consensus.

Most importantly, American evangelicalism was never the repository of a social consensus on religion. From its birth in the early twentieth century, the American evangelical movement has been a combatant in a religious conflict. This has shaped almost everything about it. That's a good thing; evangelicalism preserved the gospel through a period of intense attack. But its status as a combatant also excluded evangelicalism from being a genuine continuation of the prior consensus.

So the effort to position evangelicalism in a leadership role in American society was not a restoration of a *status quo ante*. It was an attempt to introduce a radically new situation. And it was correctly perceived as such by the large majority of Americans not affiliated with evangelical churches. Evangelicalism could rightfully claim to be the *doctrinal* heir of the historic Protestant churches, but it had no standing to claim their cultural or historical place.

Many Americans resent evangelicals because they perceive us as thinking we have a right to rule them. That perception is not always unreasonable in light of the way many evangelical leaders spoke and acted throughout the twentieth century. This is one of the most important reasons Christianity has gradually lost influence over the past century.

While the believers in the Christian founding were struggling to conquer America, those who believed in the secular founding story followed a different path. As the leading institutions of American Protestantism went liberal one by one, these believers felt vindicated. They took the liberalism of American Protestant leaders as confirmation of their view that when churches act as cultural leaders, they compromise on sound doctrine in order to maintain respectability. Seeking to play a role in the social order leads churches astray.

Evangelical leaders who took this view sought to create an impact on society from the cultural sidelines. They withdrew (or, in some cases, withdrew further) from the existing social order, which they viewed as anti-Christian in its historical roots. Instead, they sought to influence society by "focusing on evangelism" and making more converts.

However, their cultural withdrawal hindered their evangelism. Culturally separatist Christians obviously encounter unbelievers less often and have more difficulty understanding them. However, a far more serious obstacle is how to communicate the gospel itself from a position of cultural isolation. "Gospel presentations" as an approach to evangelism were originally developed in the context of a culture where people encountered the whole life of Christianity on a regular basis. As a former pastor of mine put it, gospel presentations were designed when most people already knew all or most of the various "puzzle pieces" of the gospel, and just needed to be shown the "picture on the box top" so they could see how the pieces fit together. In a social context where people have never even encountered the pieces, there's too much new information to be meaningfully conveyed in one sitting.

Active participation in the whole fabric of society is an important element of evangelism. Jesus tells the disciples that their evangelism is succeeding because "here the saying holds true, 'One sows and another reaps.' I sent you to reap that for which you did not labor. Others have labored, and you have entered into their labor" (John 4:37–38). American evangelicals today often read this to mean that a person may hear a gospel presentation from multiple people before believing. I think it refers to much more. I think Jesus is talking about how people encounter believers in the whole ecosystem of cultural life.

Cultural withdrawal has also undermined discipleship. As the culture changes and withdrawn churches don't keep up, they are less and less able to guide congregants on how to live godly lives within contemporary American society. Their guidance on how to navigate daily life in a faithful way is obsolete. (We'll come back to this subject in chap. 2.)

These two inadequate approaches have actually reinforced one another. Periodically, evangelical leaders following the "Christian founding" model would mobilize to take the world by storm. Each time, these efforts would enjoy early successes and then peter out in disappointment. They could not overcome the world's inevitable resistance, because they relied too much on short-term power and left insufficient space for the joy of God. Then, those who favored cultural withdrawal would claim vindication and lead churches their way. Isolationist churches would predominate for a time. But then evangelicals would grow frustrated with their withdrawal and suffer "uneasy conscience" (to use Carl Henry's famous phrase) about their failure to do anything about the slow moral disintegration of their country, and the cycle would repeat. Oversimplifying history just a little bit, the story of the last century is one of big mobilizations for cultural impact in the 1920s, 1940s–1950s, and 1970s–1980s, alternating with periods of relative cultural quiescence among evangelicals in the 1930s, 1960s, and 1990s.

Meanwhile, those who are satisfied with the "it doesn't matter" story have stayed on the sidelines of these battles through cultural accommodation. This accommodation can be political, as when churches identify with fashionable public causes in hopes of connecting the gospel to them. Or it can be as simple as striving to reach people based on their "felt needs" without doing enough to confront people with the disturbing fact that their felt needs are not always the same as their actual needs. This approach was less common earlier in the century, largely because the American evangelical movement was first forged by its rejection of liberal cultural accommodation during the great schism. As the century wore on, however, those conflicts became distant. More evangelicals in subsequent generations simply never thought seriously about either the meaning of America or Christianity's role in

American society, and had no strong commitment to any "story" about these issues.

The Joy of God—Whole, Not in Pieces

In spite of their differences, all three approaches have something in common. Intentionally or unintentionally, they all end up channeling Christianity's social engagement through one aspect of Christian life. They pick the one lever that they think is most likely to have a positive impact on the world, then relentlessly focus on pulling that one lever. Of course, the advocates of these approaches don't *intend* to narrow down their engagement with society to one aspect of Christian life. However, that is what they all tend to do in practice.

While this kind of narrow focus does produce short-term benefits, in the long run it isolates Christianity from society. Most people never encounter holistic Christianity and the whole life of the church; people encounter Christianity only through its narrowed-down cultural lever-pulling. So they think these isolated activities are actually the whole purpose of Christianity and that they define the life of the church. They don't know what the church really is. The life of the church in its fullness and wholeness is hidden from them.

I'm not against doing any of the things Christians do to impact culture. In fact, I do them all myself. I'm for politics; my degree is in political science and I've been a political activist continually since I was a teenager. I'm for academic scholarship; I'm a practicing scientist who has published twenty empirical statistical studies. I'm for worldview education; I've published three books (four, if you count this one) and taught many Sunday school classes on the distinctive contributions of Christianity to intellectual life in the English-speaking world. I'm for evangelism, and I'm even for gospel presentations when rightly used; I've been an Evangelism Explosion trainer, and I know what it's like to watch while someone's life is permanently transformed as the result of hearing a gospel presentation. I'm for meeting felt needs; later in this book I'm going to argue at length that Christians should show the world (in the right way) that Christianity makes life work better. And although I'm not necessarily a supporter of whatever cause happens to be fashionable at any given moment, I'm for causes in principle; I've been professionally involved in the school choice movement for over ten years.

These aspects of Christian life (politics, scholarship, worldview, evangelism, emotions, causes) are all good in themselves. Each is doing something that is right. But each is only doing one thing. The problem arises when we take these things, which are meant to be pieces of the Christian life, and leverage them as though they represented the whole life of the church. That doesn't stay effective over the long term.

The pieces all have to stay integrated. That's the only way the world can encounter holistic Christianity. Regular encounters with Christianity in its totality are the only way people will come to understand that this totality, not any of the isolated pieces, is what the life of the church is really all about.

I call this holistic Christian life "the joy of God." When I say *joy*, I don't mean an emotion. I mean the flourishing of the whole person in mind, heart, and life. This flourishing is a transformation that extends to all of life as an integrated totality. It is not a natural phenomenon. It is a miracle. It is a supernatural work of the Holy Spirit; nothing else can produce it.

This joy is what makes the church distinct from the world, precisely because it is a miracle. None of the secondary assets, the pieces of Christian life (politics, scholarship, worldview, evangelism, emotions, causes), makes the church distinct. The world possesses all those things in some measure. Each of the particular things that Christians do in social life can be copied by unchanged, natural humanity. Only the supernatural joy of God in its totality can really make us distinct, because only the Spirit can create it.

This joy can't shine through if we smother it with cultural

lever-pulling. Rushing to have an impact on the culture in the short term, we seize one piece of Christian life and work it for all it's worth. In isolation, each of those pieces expands to fill the whole picture, displacing the broader vision.

Efforts to mobilize power and return Christianity to its rightful place at the top of society produce this problem most obviously. Not everyone is called to be an activist, but participation in political life is good and part of God's plan for human civilization. However, when Christians isolate political participation from the holistic Christian life and use it as the main lever of social impact, the world encounters Christianity as a selfish interest group, mobilizing political power to seize advantages for itself at the expense of others.

Those who follow the "Christian founding" story will often try to broaden their cultural engagement beyond politics by sponsoring intellectual development. They invest in the promotion of Christian scholarship in universities, and in "Christian worldview" education in churches, schools, summer camps, etc. These are all good things in themselves. But when academic scholarship is isolated from holistic Christianity, it doesn't create much of an encounter between the church and the world. The scholarship of Christian academics isn't recognized as scholarship at all unless it conforms to the prevailing rules of scholarship in the academic disciplines. This forces Christian scholars to accommodate and blend in; even when their work is excellent, it isn't identified as Christian. As for worldview education, when this approach is isolated from the Christian life as a whole it has a tendency to reduce Christianity to a combative ideology. Christianity lines up alongside Marxism, pantheism, postmodernism, and so forth—just one more esoteric and culturally implausible philosophy.

Those who withdraw Christianity from the social order to "focus on evangelism" narrow down our engagement in a similar way. I hope it goes without saying that evangelism is a critical aspect of the life of the church! But when evangelism is the only way in which Christians seek social influence, the world encounters the church in two ways: gospel presentations, and activities designed to manipulate people into hearing gospel presentations. In the eyes of the world, the church comes across as a sort of spiritual Amway. I have a friend who sold vacation timeshares before his conversion. He says he learned every trick there is for pressuring and manipulating people, making them feel like they had to agree to something that they didn't really want. And he sees all the same pressure tactics and manipulative tricks being used in evangelism ministries. I have to say, that resonates pretty powerfully with my own experience in Evangelism Explosion. For example, we were taught to get people to "agree" to a gospel presentation by making a cryptic comment ("that was the second best gift I ever got") designed to prompt the person to ask you a question ("what was the best gift?") that invites a presentation. You get to feel like you're not foisting the gospel on people—they asked for it!—but they experience this as underhanded trickery. I wish my experience was an isolated exception, but it's not; you can see a number of these techniques used in the gospel presentation scenes in Christian movies like *Courageous*.

Accommodationism is also a form of narrowed-down engagement. We ought to show people how the gospel meets their felt needs. But where churches focus only on meeting "felt needs," the world encounters the church as a provider of ecstatic emotional experiences. The church is a sort of spiritual entertainment center.

We also ought to support good causes. But where churches seek cultural impact only by signing on to support the latest fashionable cause, Christianity is reduced to a marketing agency for secular do-gooder movements. And we don't have a great track record of distinguishing the do-gooders who really do good from those who just mean well. (As one wit has remarked, we often say "do-gooders" when we ought to say "mean-wellers.")[11] Far from Christianity having an impact on society, the impact seems to run much more the other way. Evangelical churches are quick to adopt the rhetoric and stories formulated by professional activists, often without much critical reflection on whether they're consistent with the biblical narrative. It's not clear whether the churches have any reciprocal impact on the activists.

These isolated pieces of Christian life (politics, scholarship, worldview, evangelism, emotions, causes) might be called the "secondary assets" of the church. God has equipped Christians with these things as components of Christian life. None of them *is itself* Christian life.

Christianity did not initially become influential in society by leveraging these secondary assets. The church rose to social prominence in the fourth and fifth centuries because large numbers of people encountered the whole flourishing totality of Christian life—the joy of God—in its fullness and were blown away by it. They wanted to have it, and to pass it on to their children and neighbors.

The joy of God is more than the sum of its parts; that's part of the miracle. You may ask: if some evangelicals are doing political activism while others are doing evangelism and others are doing worldview education and so on, doesn't that provide all the pieces? Yes, but the pieces don't fit together. Only the whole provides joy. You can go on piling up thousands upon thousands of jigsaw puzzle pieces, pile them up to infinity, but the picture won't be visible until you start putting the pieces in their proper places where they fit together.

Joy Has a History, and We're Part of It

The joy of God can do what cultural lever-pulling can't do. It can restore the social expectations that people should have religious beliefs and support a religious institution. We can't force a religious society upon our neighbors; we must persuade them to *want* a religious society. People who don't share our beliefs and our churches must nonetheless have their own intrinsic reasons to view our beliefs and churches as socially beneficial. That's a battle we can win only by living out the gospel in all of life, so people encounter the joy of God and see how it transforms civilization for the better.

This is a longer, harder, slower road than lever-pulling. It will take a full generation's worth of time to walk it. I'm not promising a quick path or an easy path. All I am promising is a path that actually leads in the right direction.

The good news is that we still possess the flourishing totality of the whole Christian life. It is ours by the work of the Spirit and can't be taken away:

> Who shall separate us from the love of Christ? Shall tribulation, or distress, or persecution, or famine, or nakedness, or danger, or sword? As it is written,
>
> > "For your sake we are being killed all the day long;
> > we are regarded as sheep to be slaughtered."
>
> No, in all these things we are more than conquerors through him who loved us. For I am sure that neither death nor life, nor angels nor rulers, nor things present nor things to come, nor powers, nor height nor depth, nor anything else in all creation, will be able to separate us from the love of God in Christ Jesus our Lord. (Rom. 8:35–39)

In this passage, Paul emphasizes the world attacking the church. Remember that theme; it's going to come up repeatedly in this book, especially in chapter 2. If you were afraid I was going to say we should reduce the level of conflict between the church and the world in order to have more impact on society, you can put your mind to rest. I'm not offering any of that.

For the moment, I want to emphasize something else Paul says here. We always have the joy of God. Nothing can take it away. That means the church can begin the process of rebuilding its influence by finding new ways to bring the total Christian life into contact with the life of the world.

Take a fresh look at the Scripture at the beginning of this chapter:

> Then our mouth was filled with laughter,
>   and our tongue with shouts of joy;
> then they said among the nations,
>   "The LORD has done great things for them." (Ps. 126:2)

Consider the relationship in this passage between the joy of God among God's people and the way the nations respond to God's people. What do the nations notice about God's people? "The LORD has done great things for them." And how do they notice that? "Our mouth was filled with laughter, and our tongue with shouts of joy."

And there's more good news: God creates joy within history. He made human beings as historical creatures. It is of our deepest essence that we exist within an unfolding stream of time, and can take action within it.

Christianity is preeminently the historical religion. Other religions offer escapes from time and history, whether through traditionalism (some collection of rituals and institutions is really—somehow—timeless and eternal) or negation (time itself and all events within it are—somehow—all a gigantic illusion, from which the enlightened can escape). Among the world's religions, only Christianity really gives us history. It even locates its whole message, including redemption itself, within history. The indispensable key that unlocks all the secrets of human existence is not some set of timeless philosophical truths, nor some body of eternally recurring rituals and unchanging institutions. It is a series of events unfolding in history: creation, fall, redemption, glorification. The Christian message is good news. Good news is not just good, it's also news. "News" is just another word for a report of history.

So as we look at the story of how the joy of God has lost influence in American history, we don't have to feel trapped or fatalistic. The story of history is God's story, and he has called us to act within it. Of course, God is in control of history, not us. But when the Spirit creates the joy of God in us, that's God intervening in history. He does it *through* us. We're not passive. We have a job to do.

2

The Church
and the World

Let the nations be glad and sing for joy,
for you judge the peoples with equity and
guide the nations upon earth.

Ps. 67:4

The joy of God influences society through relationships. Human beings are made to be in relationship with each other. Just about everything we do is relational on some level.

Some relationships are obvious because they're direct and personal. However, we have other relationships that are so far in the background of our lives that they're hard to see. For example, as an American, I'm related to every other American as a fellow citizen. It's these larger, less immediate relationships that determine the character of a civilization.

That's what this chapter is about. The joy of God can't influence society unless it's a part of society. These larger relationships that define us as members of the American community provide the connective tissue between our own minds, hearts, and lives (which are being transformed by the Spirit) and the life of American society.

The World Shapes the Church—and That's Good!

When we ask how Christianity can begin the process of rebuilding its influence in American society, the first question that will occur to many people is, can it? Followed by, should it?

I think the quickest way to get the answer to those questions is by turning the tables and seeing what things look like from the other side. Does American society influence the church? Can we prevent that? Should we?

They didn't have to ask such questions in the Old Testament period. God had called his people to be a distinct civilization, and he gave them detailed instructions on how that civilization was to be structured. The laws of the Old Testament defined its overarching social order; they also structured its family, economic, religious, and political systems. The Israelites did not have to worry about whether their society was influencing their religious institutions. All the structures of their civilization were directly ordained by God.

This was a major challenge for those outside Israel who came to faith. They were called to abandon the civilizations in which they had been reared, and move to Israel. They had to integrate and adapt themselves to a new and alien civilization.

This involved far more than a change of address. It was a radical change that went to the very heart of the person. Our social membership—the whole dense web of relationships that connect us to others in family, church, the economy, and the civil community—is an essential component of our identity and personhood.

To get a sense of how much this matters, try to think of everything about you that would be different if you had never had these relationships—if you were never a son, daughter, brother, sister, husband, wife, father, or mother; never an employee, employer, manager, coworker, student, teacher, client, customer, or vendor; never a congregant, pastor, witness, or servant; never a friend, neighbor, member, or participant. With no other people around, you would never know the very idea of affection, or of making someone else's life better, or of being useful to anyone. Beyond bare survival, you would never have tasks to perform. You wouldn't even use language—never speak, read, or write. It's even hard to imagine what your *thoughts* would be like if you never learned language. You would have no concepts of good and evil, or truth and falsehood. You would probably not rise very much above the mental level of a smart animal. There wouldn't be much of you left that could be called "you."

God made human beings so they can't be human except within relationships and social groups. Each person is not *merely* a product of society; you cannot reduce a person to his relationships and nothing else. Every individual is able to think and act for himself, and is irreducibly precious in his own right. However, Tarzan fantasies aside, there is no such thing as an asocial human being. (Even Tarzan had the apes to raise him.)

This shouldn't be surprising to those who believe in the Bible. We're created beings. Our very existence and every aspect of our being is dependent on a relationship—with God. And the only thing ever pronounced "not good" before the fall was that Adam should be alone (Gen. 2:18). The story of Adam and Eve's creation shows us both the intrinsic dignity of every individual and the social nature of humanity. The dignity of the individual is manifested because God started by making one person, alone. Adam had integrity and preciousness in God's sight even when he was the only human being in existence.[1] But Adam was made to be in relationship, and not just with God. He was incomplete until he was in relationship with another human being.

For that matter, personal identity is dependent upon relationships even within the triune godhead.[2] Who are we to think we possess a form of personal identity more independent from others than that of God himself?

So the convert moving to Israel was uprooted from the whole social system that formed him as a person. His identity had to change in a way that people within Israel would never have to face. An unfaithful Israelite who came to faith would undergo a radical change of heart and life, but not of his social identity. The foreign convert, in addition to the change of heart and life, also had to undergo a radical social transplant.

This helps us see why the exile to Babylon was such a catastrophe for God's people. Israel was uprooted from its God-given civilization and forced to conform to another civilization's political, economic, and other social systems. Suddenly they had to worry about losing their identity as God's people under those influences. Psalm 137 is all about this: "How shall we sing the LORD's song in a foreign land?" (v. 4)

Today, in the New Testament era, that exilic challenge—to live as God's people within the forms and structures of natural human civilization—is the permanent state of the church (1 Pet. 1:1, 17; 2:11). God calls us to be good citizens of every civilization. Thus, while God has given us general principles to live by in the Bible, we are not given any specific set of civilizational forms. We are called instead to inhabit the social forms of the civilizations in which we find ourselves.

However, in the New Testament era the exilic challenge has been transformed. The Israelites did not go to Babylon on a mission; they had no mandate to spread the gospel. Exile is our permanent state in the New Testament church because we have now been commissioned—sent on a mission—to the nations (Matt. 28:16–20). Jeremiah sent the Israelites out to a long period of exile in Babylon, but they were always looking forward to the promised return. Jesus sent the church out to permanent exile everywhere.

The church's new mission reorients the exilic challenge. The New Testament church is not a cultural lifeboat for a specific civilization, as the Israelites in exile were. In Babylon, God's people were not keeping alive just God's message and ways, but the remnant of a whole foreign civilization, temporarily sustaining it as best they could until it was time to return and replant it in its native soil. For us, however, there will be no return and no replanting until the world ends. We must keep alive God's message and ways, but we cannot think of ourselves as a separate civilization. Because the church has a mission within every human civilization, we must build godly lives within our home civilization rather than trying to cultivate a separate one. That means working hard to contribute to the well-being and flourishing of our civilization. Otherwise, we're not loving our neighbors.

However, because the church is in exile, we cannot simply identify the church with our host civilization. We cannot reduce the church's work merely to the flourishing of civilization. The church still has to sustain a zone of cultural activity that represents revelation and Holy Spirit transformation. Inevitably, this will mean resisting the dominant culture in some ways. Maintaining balance between mission and exile is one of the central challenges of sustaining the church's identity.

The church is present within every civilization, so it is formed and influenced by those civilizations. As human beings, each one of us is intricately, extensively, unavoidably, and permanently embedded within human civilization. We carry that into everything we are and do. Church is one of the things we are and do. So we carry our formation and identity as members of American civilization into the church. (If you're not American, substitute your particular civilization whenever I say "American.")

This doesn't mean the Holy Spirit isn't working miracles in our minds, hearts, and lives to create the joy of God. It just means that the work of the Spirit takes place within social life. The life of the church is created by the way the Spirit supernaturally transforms human action, but it is still human action that is being transformed. And human action is social action.

The Spirit doesn't make you less American when he transforms you. He converts and sanctifies your Americanness. He transforms your Americanness to make it into the Americanness it ought to be. We don't cease to be Americans when we're converted to Christ. We are dramatically different Americans from the Americans we used to be, because we are Americans who have the joy of God. But we're still Americans. As the Gospel Coalition's vision statement puts it: "Every expression of Christianity is necessarily and rightly contextualized, to some degree, to particular human culture; there is no such thing as a universal ahistorical expression of Christianity."[3]

Consider, for example, how a church worship service can be a different kind of act in three different kinds of societies. In a society where the church is persecuted, attending services is (among other things) an act of defiance against the social order. In a society where the church is sponsored by and closely supportive of the state, attending services is (among other things) an act of affirmation supporting the social order. In a society with religious freedom, such as America, attending a service need not be either of these things.

It's clear that American civilization does influence the church. My possession of the joy of God as a converted American is influenced by my conversion, but also by my Americanness. Not only does becoming a Christian change what kind of American I am; being an American changes what kind of Christian I am.

Would it be better if Christians tried to prevent American civilization from influencing the church? It might seem that way at first. We may think that the more we're shaped by our Americanness, the less we will be shaped by the Bible and the Spirit.

But it's not a choice between being shaped by social forces or by God. Those social forces are part of God's plan for human life. He made them, he blesses them, and he uses them to accomplish his purposes.[4]

God is doing something really amazing in the New Testament era. He doesn't just want to bring people to himself from a single civilization that he directly designed and handed to us. *God wants people of every tribe, tongue, and nation.* Note well: he wants not just people *from* every tongue, tribe, and nation, but people *of* every tongue, tribe, and nation. So the American church is supposed to be constituted by our Americanness. That's the whole plan. That's why Jesus sent the church out to the nations in the first place!

Every nationality, America included, brings unique blessings into the church—blessings the church would never have received if God hadn't sent the church out into the nations. For example, American Christians emphasize the need for personal conversion and authentic belief, probably more than any other Christians have. Freedom of religion, which has always been America's most distinctive characteristic, allows the church to be the church in a more authentic way than anywhere else. And think of how the personal liberties of American society have opened up such a vast and beautiful variety of ways for people to glorify God. We have more freedom than anyone else to follow our callings and nurture our God-given talents to their full flourishing.

When America was founded, what distinguished it most sharply from the old world in Europe were four foundational freedoms: your church, your wedding, your job, and your vote. The first freedom, the one upon which all the others depend, is freedom of religion—you're not required to attend a church or support a religion you don't believe in. There was no clearer break from the old ways of Europe than this! The next is the freedom to select your marriage partner; in Europe women were married off by their parents. Almost all the advances in dignity for women since then can be traced back to that change. You also have the freedom to follow God's calling to the job you are best suited to do, instead of being required to do the job your father did, or at best a job that fits your social station. Since most of human life is taken up by work, the freedom to follow God's calling in your work is radically liberating. And we are governed by rulers of our own choice, which has served as the starting point for uncountable advances in human dignity.

These are all really amazing things, when you compare them to the way most societies have worked in human history. I think we are able to glorify God much more fully when we are stewards of our own lives in these ways. God made us to respond freely to him and to each other. Life works better this way, and that gives us so much more we can offer up to God.

The World Shapes the Church—and That's Bad!

But we can't simply conform to America exactly as it is. Our Americanness presents major challenges. It constitutes us in some ways that draw us away from God and godliness.

Most importantly, as Americans we have a tendency to idolize individual choice and resist institutional claims to authority. That's the flip side of the blessings that come from sending the church out to all nations. The American tendency to elevate the individual and his choices cuts both ways. Like all things in a fallen world, this tendency presents occasions for both good and evil.

We are constantly tempted to abstract ourselves as individuals from the relationships that tie us to others. We want to think we have a sovereign "self" that exists on its own, without being formed by social membership. This self enters into relationships with others, but it does so starting from an Olympian stance of independence. We don't want our relationships to define us.

At best, we are worried that we will be denied our God-given individual dignity as human persons. Naive collectivists have done a lot of damage here. In politics, economics, the church, and everywhere else, we always find people who say that because relationships define us, we have to give one set of individuals dehumanizing and enslaving forms of power over other individuals. (They think they're giving power to the group. In fact, you can never give power to a group as such. Giving power to "the group" always means giving some individuals power over other individuals.) We want to be on guard to protect freedom of conscience, personal liberties, and other aspects of the sacredness of the individual. So we overreact by embracing the idea of the sovereign self.

I think this kind of reaction against collectivism is the main reason many Christians today think in terms of a sovereign self, even though Christianity clearly challenges it. I thought that way myself for a long time. I was a firm believer in the sovereign self because everyone who challenged the sovereign self insisted that the only alternative to it was collectivism, and I knew collectivism was wrong.

I remember listening to a panel of academics arguing that because social membership is core to human identity, Christians need to turn away from the evangelical emphasis on personal conscience and start letting institutions define their beliefs. During the Q&A period, I asked an impertinent question: "I'm just trying to figure out what Martin Luther would say to all this if he were here. I think he would say that if he had followed your advice, he would have denied the gospel, and when he stood before the judgment seat, God would have said, 'I told you to believe and profess the gospel, but you didn't obey me because other people told you not to.' What's he supposed to say to God? 'Well, you see, Lord, the human self is situated in a dense network of social relationships that constitute its personhood . . .'"

I still think that's the right answer to collectivism. However, since then I've realized that I was only seeing one side of the picture. We don't need to deny that our relationships are part of what defines who we are in order to preserve our individual dignity. Luther could acknowledge that relationships were integral to the development of his conscience and still say, "My conscience is captive to the word of God."

However, there is another, less elevated reason why we resist the idea that our relationships help define us. We want to be as free as possible from duties to other people. The social nature of humanity implies that each person is obligated to others. This doesn't mean only that you must refrain from harming them. You have to work actively for their benefit. Hard as it is to fathom, the standard we're held to is that our neighbor's good must be as important to us as our own.

The idea of a sovereign self that's independent of relationships makes us feel like we can ignore or disrupt our relationships without doing much harm to ourselves or others. If a relative, neighbor, or coworker is annoying to deal with, I can just avoid dealing with that person as much as possible. Our relationship may be weakened, but that doesn't do either of us much harm because relationships aren't that important to the sovereign self. If I don't do my best to be productive on the job because it isn't the kind of job I'd like to have, I'm not detracting from the community. If I indulge in a masturbation habit, that doesn't hurt anyone. If some of my fellow citizens are poor or oppressed, that doesn't implicate me.

America has been making law on this basis for years. The Supreme Court declared in a landmark 1992 abortion ruling that "at the heart of liberty is the right to define one's concept of existence, of the universe, and of the mystery of human life."[5] You couldn't find a clearer statement of the view that individuals are sovereign selves, not defined by obligations to one another. If each of us is allowed to make up the meaning of his own life, clearly I can have no obligations to anyone except those that I choose to believe in. Every individual is a little god.

One of the great dangers of our time is the illusion that moral obligations are somehow weaker if they're not chosen. We are blessed with the freedom to make choices that people in most times and places don't get to make. The special temptation of living in a society where we have personal liberties is the seductive idea that obligations are less binding, or not binding at all, if we came under them through birth or other circumstances beyond our control.

The desire to be under obligations only when we choose them isn't realistic. It can't account for the great majority of our actual daily duties. Your duty to care for your parents is an especially clear example. Your duties to your children are clear because you chose to have children (or at least chose to have sex). But you didn't choose to be born. Yet you have a special obligation of care toward your parents that no one else has, whether you like it or not.

Moreover, the whole point about obligations is that you have to do things that aren't intrinsically attractive to you. You have to discipline yourself for actions that cut against your desires. When I'm sitting in my comfortable armchair contemplating my life, it's easy to feel like my obligations to my wife, my employer, my neighbors, and so forth are things that I choose. But in the moment of testing, when a fierce temptation to betray these duties takes hold of me, those obligations will not *feel like* they're chosen. If choice is the only ground of obligation, in that moment of temptation I won't have much motivation to live up to my duties. I need some stronger ground of obligation to strengthen me for those trials.

This is why our society's policymakers and elites are powerless to curb rampant divorce, even though most of them have now realized what a horrible mistake it was to normalize divorce. Of all relationships, the one for which we most value the freedom to choose is marriage—and rightly so. But it's one thing to say that the freedom to choose your marriage partner is unspeakably precious, and another to say that marital obligations are weaker when they're unwanted. At the moment when you want to leave your spouse, your obligation to stay doesn't feel "chosen." Yet our leaders can't quite bring themselves to tell people that they're responsible to their marriages, whether they want to be or not.

This approach fails even on its own terms. The rule that obligations are binding when you choose them is itself a rule that none of us ever chose. Suppose I voluntarily make a promise to do something. If I change my mind later, why am I obligated to keep that promise? Once you teach people that unchosen obligations aren't binding, chosen obligations also go out the window.

You don't get to make up the meaning of your own life. At bottom, that's the message we all need to hear—and it needs to be constantly reinforced on every front. You do get to decide how best to respond to the circumstances and conditions life presents you with, and that kind of personal liberty is a good thing. But you don't get to decide what the circumstances and conditions of your life will be, and those unchosen circumstances and conditions—including relationships and obligations—are a central part of who you are. To a large extent, they determine the scope and significance of choices that you will have the freedom to make.

Sin could almost be defined as the desire to make up the meaning of our own lives for ourselves. This is actually one reason why God designed us so that our relationships with others define us. He wants us to turn away from the desire to make up the meaning of our own lives. Relationships and obligations are a constant reminder that we are not sovereign selves but created beings dependent upon God.

The church cannot just go with the flow of the culture. It cannot be *merely* a part of American civilization. Because the church is created supernaturally by the transformative power of the Holy Spirit, no aspect of the church can ever be reduced simply to a function of human society. Even the civilizational lives of Christians when they are outside the church walls, living out their discipleship in America's homes, workplaces, and communities, are no longer *merely* civilizational lives. The work I do in my daily life, however dependent it is on American civilization for its cultural form, is now a supernatural discipleship with eternal consequences.

How the Church Shapes the World

God is calling us to figure out what it means to live out biblical principles in the context of our society. He has given us the Spirit to empower us for this task, and now we have to answer the call. That's the challenge of this book.

I said earlier that the exilic challenge of the Israelites in Babylon is the permanent state of the New Testament church. If so, we should consider the Lord's instructions to his people during the Babylonian exile: "But seek the welfare of the city where I have sent you into exile, and pray to the LORD on its behalf, for in its welfare you will find your welfare" (Jer. 29:7).[6] This charge provides an excellent starting point for thinking about how we navigate our own exilic challenge.

The flow of influence between the church and society runs both ways. Just as I bring American civilization with me into the church, I bring the joy of God with me into American civilization—because I bring the Holy Spirit with me, who creates the joy of God in me. He does so partly through my civilizational life. Because the transformative power of the Spirit changes me fundamentally, it changes the way I engage in all my relationships. Family, work, and community will be different for me.

Wherever you find an American Christian, you will find the joy of God—that holistic Christian life of transformed mind, heart, and action—intricately, extensively, unavoidably, and permanently embedded within American civilization. Being embedded within civilization is just part of what it means to be human. And the more a Christian intentionally cultivates the joy of God in daily life, the more deeply embedded the joy of God will become in American civilization, through him.

That embedded joy will not consist simply of a changed attitude. Our actions will change. In our families, we will act differently as sons, daughters, brothers, sisters, husbands, wives, fathers, or mothers. In our workplaces and other economic relationships we will act differently as employees, employers, managers, co-workers, students, teachers, clients, customers, or vendors. In our communities, we will act differently as friends, neighbors, members, or participants.

Sometimes we emphasize the need for internal heart transformation so much that we neglect this external aspect of discipleship. But any genuine heart transformation must result in changed action. The Bible is overflowing with testimony that if my works don't change, my heart hasn't changed. (If you doubt it, try reading James or 1 John.)

But we're not done reversing the flow yet. If I act differently in all these roles, the institutions within which I act will also change. The Spirit changes me, therefore he changes how I engage in relationships. So the relationships themselves change. That means the institutions of civilization change, too. A family, workplace, or community with Christians in it will be different from one without them. The more Christians there are, and the more those Christians think and act intentionally to live out their faith in those families, workplaces, and communities, the more different those institutions will be.

So just as American civilization plays a role in constituting the church, the church plays a role in constituting American civilization. When we are doers of the word and not hearers only, the relationships and institutions of American civilization will be different, at least within the scope of our reach.

As an individual, I may not have an extensive range of influence. But that, too, cuts both ways. However small my range of influence is, I do have some range of influence. Within that range I do have the power to create change. I may not be able to impact company policy where I work, but I can change how the coworkers immediately around me experience daily life on the job. I can be the person who goes out of his way to help my coworkers and always prioritizes excellent service to the customer. I may not be able to change the laws of my town, but I can change the social dynamic of my neighborhood. I can organize get-togethers and be intentional about creating a sense of community. That's cultural change.

Moreover, Christians can and should organize to seek change intentionally.[7] The Bible clearly indicates that there should be no Lone Ranger Christians. Every page of the New Testament reinforces the idea that Christians are supposed to be in community, helping each other live more and more into the calling of discipleship. That means we need to get together with other Christians placed near us in the structures of our civilization and ask, how can we work together to do a better job of being good family members, workers, and neighbors? How can we bless those around us more effectively?

This has to be done carefully, because there are a lot of pitfalls to be avoided. We'll talk about some of them in the conclusion of this book. But the only thing worse than Christians working together *badly* to improve their discipleship is Christians not working together to improve their discipleship *at all*.

That's why Jeremiah 29:7 is such an important starting point. We spend 98 percent of our lives doing things in civilization that are supposed to be all about blessing people and making the world a better place: doing dishes, getting our work done at the office, helping the lady next door with her lawn. Since we're supposed to be disciples in 100 percent of life, we need to see blessing our neighbors in civilization as part of our discipleship. Obviously we can't redefine the mission of the church as simply the flourishing of civilization. But if we don't connect our discipleship to seeking the blessedness and flourishing of our neighbors, we aren't practicing discipleship full time and in all areas of life.

Seeking to have an influence in our civilization does not imply captivity to the culture. It just means we're answering the call to be good disciples within our spheres of influence. If the church is being the church by doing the word all week and not just hearing it on Sunday morning, then the church is having such an influence even if we don't realize it. And when Christians intentionally mobilize to do the word better and better in our lives in civilization, the church's impact will be magnified.

We don't need to allow the world to set boundaries for what our lives in civilization must look like. To the contrary, selling out and obeying the world's standards is the quickest way for Christianity to lose its influence in society. When Christians' participation in civilization is the same as everyone else's, the world can simply ignore us. Christianity influences civilization only to the extent that Christians actively participate in it *in ways that obey God's standards, not the world's standards.*

Incarnated within Civilization

All I'm really saying is that, because human beings are social creatures, the transformative power of the Holy Spirit has a social
expression as well as an individual expression, and that social expression is not limited to the inside of the church building. If we
focus on intentionally cultivating social transformation only inside
the church building, we are failing to cultivate discipleship in 98
percent of our lives. God forbid!

The transformation of the human heart by the Spirit has
sometimes been compared—by analogy, meaning it's a limited
comparison—to the joining of human and divine in the incarnation.[8] We obviously don't become joined with the divine nature
in the same way as Christ, but we do become "partakers of the
divine nature" (2 Pet. 1:4). God comes into us to take up permanent residence and live inside us (2 Cor. 13:5). We are his priests
(Rev. 5:10), his temples (1 Cor. 6:19), and his altars (Heb. 13:10). And
wherever there is a priest, a temple, and an altar, there is holy
sacrifice. Just as Christ the Great High Priest offered himself up,
as his priests we are supposed to constantly offer ourselves up as
living sacrifices throughout our daily lives—*that* is our spiritual
worship (Rom. 12:1).

Because human beings are social creatures, the same analogy
can be applied to the civilizational lives of Christians. After all,
when we offer ourselves up as living sacrifices every day, we do
so in our civilizational lives. And the transformation of the Spirit
doesn't just change our participation in civilization. It affects the
institutions where we participate, and thus, civilization itself.

By analogy (and therefore with limitations) we can say that just
as eternal and immaterial divinity joins in mystical union with
temporal and material humanity in the incarnation, so the work
of the Holy Spirit in our minds, hearts, and lives joins in a sort of
mystical union with the life of our civilization. This happens not
through some narrowly defined "cultural agenda" in the church
but through discipleship—through all the various ways in which

our conversion and sanctification transform our participation in the life of that civilization.

Restored for City Building

The need to incarnate the church within civilization is one reason the Spirit empowered Christians to speak every language when he descended upon the church at Pentecost. In that moment, the church was finally released from its long period of training under the Old Testament law. As Paul writes, the Old Testament period was the childhood of the church, and the law was our schoolmaster (Gal. 3:24). At Pentecost, God declared us "all grown up" and empowered us for gospel ministry.

It has been widely noted that Pentecost reversed the scattering of the nations at Babel. The confusion of tongues that began at Babel was reversed, within the church, at Pentecost. However, we don't always grasp the full significance of this reversal. Pentecost is often portrayed in terms of the mission to evangelize the world; Christians were empowered to speak every language so they could bring the good news to all people. Though that is true, by itself it does not capture the full significance of the event.

Babel was not a tower, it was a city. "Come, let us build ourselves *a city and a tower* with its top in the heavens" (Gen. 11:4). Babel was a city that happened to contain a tower. Most retellings of the story concentrate on the tower, but it wasn't physical height people were after when they built Babel: "Let us make a name for ourselves, lest we be dispersed over the face of the whole earth" (v. 4).

It was the city, not the tower, that mattered. Babel was not an attempt to physically invade heaven, besieging the skies. It was the building up of human civilization *on earth* to evil ends. The city manifested humanity's desire to achieve power and greatness without God—to *figuratively* get to heaven without God, not literally. They wanted heaven, but they wanted heaven on earth, through civilizational progress.

Because humanity was fallen and did not yet have the transforming power of the Holy Spirit through gospel ministry, the building up of human civilization could only go wrong. "The LORD said, 'Behold, they are one people, and they have all one language, and this is only the beginning of what they will do. And nothing that they propose to do will now be impossible for them'" (Gen. 11:6). God put a stop to their city building because he knew it would produce evil.

City building is good. God likes cities. (If you doubt it, check out Revelation 21.) God didn't confuse the people and hinder their city building because the building up of civilization is bad. Civilizational life is part of how God made us. To be human is to build the cities and towers of civilization; it's what we do.

The problem at Babel was that people used their city building for evil ends. And they're still doing it, all around us. We're surrounded by people building cities and towers of all kinds, to all kinds of evil ends, still hoping they can get to heaven without God.

And we Christians are building cities and towers alongside them—because we're intricately, extensively, unavoidably, and permanently embedded within a city-building civilization. When we're changed by the Spirit, we're not building to evil ends, as the world is. But we are part of the same city-building civilizational team.

Writing about the Christian life as city building, Timothy Keller draws our attention to Martin Luther's comments on Psalm 147.[9] Verse 13 promises Jerusalem that God "strengthens the bars of your gates." How? By empowering the civil authorities to carry out their callings with excellence. Verse 14 promises that God "fills you with the finest of the wheat." How? By empowering farmers and bakers and merchants in their callings. Verse 19 says God "declares his word to Jacob, his statutes and rules to Israel." How? I would say, by empowering parents, pastors, and other teachers in their callings. The same point could be extended to everyone: through our divine callings we build the city.

Here's where it gets tricky. Psalm 147 wraps up with this: "He has not dealt thus with any other nation; they do not know his rules" (v. 20). But that's not true anymore! In the New Testament era, the gospel has gone forth to the nations of the world. There are now people in cities all over the world who "know his rules." On the other hand, God has not made special promises to today's nations, as he did to Israel in the Old Testament era. How do we make sense of this new situation?

The church is back at Babel. In the New Testament era, to be the church is to be at Babel, because we're in exile. Where did the Israelites go into exile? Babylon. What was in Babylon? Babel. That's where it got the name.

The reversal of the confusion of tongues at Pentecost brought the whole biblical narrative about human civilization full circle. The story of Babel shows us that natural human civilization, before God built a people for himself, could only be built up to evil ends. God confused their language, then extracted a people for himself and cultivated it in Israel. Pentecost shows us that he has sent that people out with a mission to the nations—back to Babel, with the confusion of tongues removed.

Christ's command to the church, the command we were empowered to carry out at Pentecost, was not to go and make converts of every nation. It was to go and make *disciples* of every nation (Matt. 28:19). And what is the difference between a superficial "convert" and a fully formed "disciple"? The transformation of one's daily life. And daily life is lived in human civilization—building up its cities and towers and working within them.

What Christians were empowered to do at Pentecost was transform every aspect of human life through the proclamation of the Word and the doing of the Word. That certainly means personal heart change, building up the church, and extending the gospel to all nations. But it also means discipleship that changes our daily lives.

God confused and divided humanity in order to limit the natural progress of civilization. It was a merciful act, given what sinful man does with his civilizations. Humanity at large is still confused and divided.

But since Pentecost, *the church* is not confused and divided. Among Christians, God has removed the limitations on civilizational progress. Christians now live within every civilization, so city building around the world is changed and empowered by our presence.

We have the Spirit and are therefore able to handle dangerous and deadly things without hurt. Those who had received a special blessing through the laying on of hands by the apostles were able to perform miracles—including handling snakes and drinking poison—to demonstrate the authenticity of their special empowerment from the Spirit. We demonstrate the authenticity of our special empowerment from the Spirit by handling something much deadlier: human civilization.

Are we therefore called to build new Babels that will bring our non-Christian neighbors up to heaven through civilizational progress? God forbid! It's just the reverse. Adam was called to the work of cultivation in a perfect world before the fall, but we are recovering sinners living in a sinful world. We have to limit our expectations and be on guard against temptation. Moreover, we are restored for city building in Christ, not in Adam. Adam was put on probation to fulfill God's covenant with humanity by good works, but Christ has now fulfilled that covenant completely. We must locate redemption in Christ, not in city building.

But we are empowered and commanded to build cities for the purposes God wants them built for, and more like the way God wants them built. God designed human beings to build cities, not to make heaven on earth in defiance of him, but to provide all the good and fruitful things cities are supposed to provide. Blessing your neighbors requires city building.

City Building in Church History

If you're a typical American evangelical, all this talk about extensive two-way influence between the church and the world probably sounds nothing like what you're accustomed to hearing. But this is no new doctrine. This is what the church has always believed.

Even before Christianity was legal, during the second-century Roman persecution the church talked about discipleship in terms of transforming civilizational life. You would have thought that since Rome saw the church only as an enemy of Roman civilization, the church would see Rome only as an enemy of Christianity. In fact, the transformation of Roman civilization through everyday discipleship was precisely the church's argument against its persecutors. The leading teachers of the church argued that Rome should legalize Christianity because Christian discipleship was good for Roman civilization.[10]

So this perspective goes all the way back to the earliest Christians of whom we have any historical records concerning their attitude toward cultural impact. It is not only not new in our time, it was not even new when Christianity first came to cultural prominence in the fourth and fifth centuries. People tend to focus on the church having become allied with the state during that time, and as we saw in chapter 1, that was certainly a mistake. However, it is not true that the idea of Christianity playing a role in civilization originated at that time.

Moving beyond the early church, no one who knows history will need to be convinced that the need to transform life in human civilization was church teaching during the thousand years between Augustine and the Reformation. Augustine, of course, provided the first extended and systematic analysis of the church's relationship with society in his early fifth-century book *City of God*. His thought has provided the dominant framework in the Western church for thinking about the church-and-culture question ever since, right down to the present day.[11]

During the Reformation, the imperative to transform life in civilization was more than just the predominant view. The Reformers emphasized it more than anyone in the history of the church. It was central to the whole message of the Reformation. We have a tendency to boil the Reformation down to two points: the authority of Scripture and justification through faith apart from works. However, the Reformers emphasized three essential components of their message, not two. The third was the doctrine of "vocation" or calling. Discipleship must transform all of life because God has a calling for you in every area of your life. The Reformation's championing of calling took the idea of cultural transformation to a new level.

The Reformation did not begin as a debate about justification or Scripture. It began as a debate about sanctification. Martin Luther's 95 Theses, which began the Reformation movement, are about sanctification. The topics of justification and Scripture came up later, as the Reformation debate made it clear that the controversy about sanctification couldn't be settled without them.

Some leaders in the late medieval church had limited the idea of God's calling on our lives to church life and religious works, arguing that the civilizational aspects of life are spiritually inferior. Life in civilization was permitted—it was morally "licit"—but it was not blessed by God the way church life was. Discipleship was only found in church life and religious works. This idea had been present in the church from its early years, especially in the teachings of Eusebius, but steadily grew in influence over time. By the turn of the sixteenth century this view had become predominant, increasingly displacing the traditional Christian view that discipleship transforms daily life in human civilization.

The Reformers saw this as flatly incompatible with the gospel. It implied that the way to God was through religious works. The Reformers demanded a return to Christianity's historic teaching that discipleship is a change in all of life. They said you can either have discipleship centered on doing religious works, or you can have justification by faith apart from the works of the law, but you can't have both. They found both these views advocated in historic church teaching, but in the Bible they found only the latter view.

Here we see the organic unity of the three pillars of the Reformation—the Bible, justification, and calling. In the sixteenth century, the church had to make a choice between two theologies:

justification through faith apart from works, creating discipleship that responds to God's call in all of life, or justification through faith plus works, creating discipleship focused on religious works and church life. Both alternatives had been advocated in church teaching, but for Protestants, the Bible's authority was dispositive. The Reformers had to balance two concerns. On the one hand, they were fighting against practices that divided human life into two spheres, a church sphere and a world sphere, with different ethical expectations. On the other hand, they didn't want to lose sight of the fact that the church really is different from the world because of the Holy Spirit's transformative work. The Reformers expressed the former concern in terms of calling: God calls Christians to follow him and be transformed in all areas of life. They expressed the latter concern in terms of "two kingdoms": God's providential kingship over the whole universe is different from his special kingship over the church, and that difference needs to be taken into account.

To make sense of how these two concerns fit together, I find it helpful to think about the difference between *institutions* and *types of activity*. The Reformers' concern to distinguish the two kingdoms is primarily focused on institutions; they especially wanted to distinguish the institutional church from other institutions like families, businesses, or governments. However, they did not want this to become an excuse for isolating "religion" as a separate activity that doesn't impact our participation in the life of family, the economy, or civil community.

Affirmation and Transformation

The challenge of building full-time discipleship in American civilization is scary. But God has sent us out into history to navigate its currents. We may find its ever-changing contingencies threatening, but he apparently does not. He has equipped us with reason, conscience, Scripture, and Spirit. It was God who sent us out into the raucous rapids and precipitous waterfalls of the great roaring river of history. He has told the church in each age to find its way down its appointed section of the river. He has promised to be with us and to pull us back up when we threaten to go under. The boat may look small and the oars may look short compared to the tumults of the river, but we may trust that if we are equipped by him, we are equipped sufficiently. Moreover, the difficulties and uncertainties of navigating the river will help us to grow strong in faith—that, too, is part of our discipleship.

Of course, just because God sent us out to navigate the river of history doesn't mean we should just "go with the flow." We are responsible to infuse the joy of God into civilization, not just build comfortable lives within civilization as it already exists. As I've already mentioned, allowing the world to define the terms of our participation in civilizational life is a one-way ticket to captivity and truncated discipleship.

The foundation of all sound cultural engagement is the integration of two things. First, we must begin with *affirmation* of the God-given goodness of civilizational activity. Second, the special *transformation* of our hearts by the Spirit must flow into our civilizational activity, so that we stand against all that is sinful and wrong in the world and pursue a more excellent way. We must integrate these two commissions into a single, unified civilizational life that expresses the joy of God.[12]

Affirmation always comes first and is always most fundamental, for the simple reason that creation comes before fall. Gnostic dualism says evil is just as ultimate as good; Christians say good is primary and evil is parasitic. When we start treating evil as something with independent existence rather than something parasitic on the good, we are lapsing back into dualism. So when we approach civilization, we must always be careful to keep the affirmation of the good in the primary position, and let transformation of the bad follow after.

It seems to me that we don't do very much affirming of civilization in American churches today. We bring missionaries up to the front of the church to commission them to go forth into the world and carry out their callings, but we don't commission the laity to go forth into the world and carry out their (equally spiritual, equally important) callings. We pray for the leaders of our civilization—or at least, we pray for the tiny minority of our leaders who work in politics. But we mostly just pray that they'll stop doing so many evil things. If civilizational activities come up in the sermon, the focus is on abstract ethical injunctions (be good, don't be bad) and the burdens these activities place on us. We're urged to spend more time doing church activities and other religious works, but not to spend more time doing things that serve our neighbors in civilization.

I admit this is only my perception, and your experience may be different. But I think the failure of the American church to affirm the goodness of civilizational life is our greatest failing today.

This doesn't mean we should affirm anything that's bad as if it were good. I'm not even asking us to "tone down" our opposition to things that are sinful. In fact, starting with affirmation will actually help us bear witness more powerfully against sin. Embedding our opposition to the bad within a larger framework of affirming the good is the best way to strengthen and empower our transformative impact, and will be evidenced in at least five ways.

First, within a framework of affirmation for the good, our opposition to the bad will be more accurate. It will correspond to reality. If we pretend that evil is primary when it's not, we will end up saying things that aren't true, and the world will notice. We'll lose credibility.

Second, affirmation of the good will also make our opposition to the bad more meaningful. The only real way to make people feel the badness of evil is by showing how it perverts the good. You have to start with the good to do that.

Third, it will make our opposition more graceful. By keeping our opposition within a framework of affirmation, we can keep it oriented toward building our neighbors up instead of tearing them down. If we start with opposition, we will inevitably seem like we're criticizing because we want to look superior. And that appearance won't always be a false one.

Fourth, it will allow us to criticize aspects of our civilization as members of it, rather than as outsiders. Affirmation confirms that we are members in good standing of our society. If we don't place ourselves within American civilization before we criticize it, we're just busybodies, sticking our noses into other people's societies. We should establish what the lawyers call "standing" to offer our opposition.

Finally, it will make our opposition more effective. This is just a result of the first four things—making it more accurate, meaningful, graceful, and integral is bound to help it accomplish its purposes and successfully roll back evil in the world. And that's what we really care about, isn't it?

Affirmation of the good in civilization takes place at three levels. Most obviously, we should affirm the goodness of the *activities* that make up civilization—family, economic work, civic life, and so forth. God made these civilizational activities. He loves them and ordains them for good. He has explicitly blessed them even after the fall.[13] He loves city building; he made it. And he made us to be city builders—not just once but twice. First he made us human beings, and to be human is to be made to build cities. Then he *remade* us, by the power of the Spirit, to be his special, chosen, and transformed people. So now we're empowered to build cities to his glory. He wants us out there building cities, and doing it well so that we glorify him and bless our neighbors. Step one is to affirm that it's good.

Second, we should affirm the goodness of civilization itself, *as a whole*. God loves the nations of the world. That's why he sent us to them. God loves America, and all the other civilizations. That's not jingoism—not if we're careful to remember that our first loyalty is to God, and to integrate a transformative opposition to evil alongside our affirmation of America's goodness. We can stand against all the evils that take place in America without saying we're against America. We're for America, not against it. In fact, we're against its sins because we're for it—just like we're for our sinful neighbors, not against them, and we're against their sins because we're for them. (In fact, those are really just two ways of saying the same thing, since "America" is just all our American neighbors.)

Finally, we should affirm the goodness of *our own identities as members of civilization.* Just as Paul claimed his Roman citizenship, we should claim our American citizenship. God made us so that our membership in civilization is essential to who we are, and that doesn't change when we're converted. We're Americans, whether we like it or not. We should like it, because God likes it. He wants American Christians. So it's part of our duty to God not just to be Christians but to be Americans, and to be the best Americans we can be.

The imperative of transformation, our opposition to all that's bad, obviously needs to be integrated at all three of these levels. When we see sinful behaviors and institutional structures within the activities of civilization, we need to stand firmly against them—because we love those activities and want them done right. When we see sinful qualities in our civilization as a whole (such as our tendency to idolize individual choice), we need to stand firmly against them—because we love our country and want it to be better. And, perhaps most important, when we see sinful qualities in ourselves that disrupt the lives of those around us in our civilization, we need to confess them—to God, always, and to others, as circumstances guide us—because we want to be better Americans for the sake of our neighbors.

No Such Thing as Neutrality

Here's a good way to summarize what I mean about affirmation. For decades, many Christians have centered their engagement with public issues around the fact that there's no such thing as moral "neutrality" in the social order. From school curricula to the definition of marriage to holiday displays, it is impossible to craft a public policy that is neutral among different moral views of the world. All social activity presupposes a moral basis, because, as we've seen, social systems all arise from relationships, and human relationships are never morally neutral.

This truth is vitally important. The neglect of this truth has been the primary cause of the biggest problems our civilization is facing, from family to the economy. We've been seduced by the deadly illusion that the institutions of social life can be structured so everyone is equally free to practice any morality. But the structures themselves are moral, and by their nature always must be. Awakening our civilization from this deadly illusion is critical to national survival.

However, Christians in public life who have been focusing on this truth have been using it in the wrong way. They've been using it only in opposition instead of beginning with affirmation.

Many use "there's no such thing as moral neutrality" to frame issues in terms of a fundamental opposition between Christians and the civilizational system. The argument is that secularists are using the illusion of moral neutrality as a cloak to exclude Christians who take their faith seriously from public life and to provide official sanction and sponsorship to anti-Christian assumptions. The implicit conclusion is that Christians must mobilize to fight the system, conquer it, and Christianize it. Hence "there's no such thing as moral neutrality" has been the slogan for all efforts to Christianize the state.

In effect, this leads Christians to act as a political pressure group, fighting to get the system to do things our way at the expense of our non-Christian neighbors. It's certainly true that there are secularists who use the illusion of moral neutrality to push Christians out of the public square, and fighting for our inclusion is legitimate. But if that's the only thing we do, if we reduce "there's no moral neutrality" to nothing more than advocacy for

Christianization, then we've been reduced to a self-interested political pressure group. We want the state to give us what we want, and since it's a zero-sum game, every victory for us is a loss for our non-Christian neighbors.

We ought to start instead by affirming the shared moral basis of the system, and affirm it explicitly as a shared moral basis rather than trying to implicitly or explicitly Christianize it. America is built upon a foundation of moral commitments that are genuinely shared across people of different religions: don't kill, don't steal, keep your promises, help your neighbor. The moral fabric of American society is not Christian as such, but it is still good and God loves it, and as Christians we are for it and want to share it in peace with all our neighbors. (We'll come back to this in chap. 8.)

Once we ground our approach in affirmation of the moral consensus we share with all Americans, then we can bring out the message "there's no such thing as moral neutrality" in a way that will work. When we argue that familial, economic, and civic structures need to be morally formed, we can help our neighbors understand that we're not trying to use the law and the state to ram Christianity down their throats. We're trying to help America be America better—and our motive is not our own self-interest but love for our country and our neighbors.

Beating the World at Its Own Game

Christians have the joy of God because we are being transformed by the Holy Spirit in mind, heart, and life. In mind, we have not only been freed from darkness and error, but we have been granted special knowledge through revelation in Scripture. In heart, we have been liberated from slavery to selfishness, guilt, and fear. We have been set free to focus on loving our neighbors instead of wasting our lives on futile efforts to build ourselves up, make ourselves look righteous, and cower behind crumbling walls of false security. And in life we have been granted the strength and perseverance to work diligently, turn away from false pleasures, and endure trials.

We carry all this transformation into our civilizational lives. So if we are really cultivating discipleship and earnestly seeking to bless our neighbors, Christians should be better than others at accomplishing cultural tasks. Joy is not just a fuzzy feeling, it is a transformation under God's power. The joy of God equips us with knowledge, freedom, and strength that others don't have. Certainly not every Christian will be able to do every task better. And it's still a fallen world where things can go wrong no matter how well you do them; God forbid I should ever teach a prosperity gospel! God never owes us success. But on average, most of the time, there should be a noticeable difference in the quality of our lives and our work in civilization.

How could there not be? God has revealed to us inside information about how the universe works. Our identities and motivations are invested in loving others rather than serving ourselves. And we have the power of the Spirit to help us carry that love through in action. Shame on us if we're not experts in making the world a better place!

This—and nothing else—is what can create a real encounter with the holistic joy of God for people outside the church. If they encounter Christianity through our efforts to leverage secondary assets (politics, scholarship, worldview, evangelism, emotions, causes), they will not encounter the joy of God. But when they see that the total Christian life makes a radical difference in homes, workplaces, and communities, they will want to know why.

Then they will know that the joy of God is a real thing. Then they will know that there is a real supernatural power working in the lives of Christians. Then they will know that Christians don't just have politics, scholarship, worldview, evangelism, emotions, and causes. To those outside the church, all those things seem like the same kind of things they already possess—and they like their versions better than ours. Instead, they will know that Christians have something they know they don't have: the joy of God.

Now let me be clear about a critical issue. When I say we should, on average, accomplish civilizational tasks "better," I don't mean better as defined by the world. I mean truly better. When we engage in civilizational activities, we will be more effective at *authentically* improving the lives of others. Our relatives, coworkers, and neighbors will benefit more from our work than from others'. Whether the world defines what we're doing as good or bad is irrelevant.

In fact, we should expect it to do both. Some people in the world will value our contribution, while others will hate it. A Christianity that succeeds in manifesting discipleship within civilization will be more loved by its neighbors and also more hated by the worldly powers. It's true that when people in the world see us perform civilizational tasks better, they will know that we have a real supernatural power—but not all of them will like it. Some of them will. Some will say, "Wow, those Christians have really got something supernatural going for them. I want some of that!" But others will say, "Wow, those Christians have really got something supernatural going for them. They're a threat. We need to stop them immediately!"

How do we measure up by that yardstick? Are we hated? You might think we're hated pretty fiercely today. I actually don't think so. I think the world has contempt for us rather than hatred. The difference between hating something and having contempt for it is whether you take it seriously. Right now, the powers have contempt for us because they don't take us seriously. Why should they? We're not a threat to them in our present condition, after a century of following all the wrong strategies for how to engage with civilization. But if we reconstructed an effective approach and mobilized to actively participate in civilization in ways that were manifestly better for our neighbors than anyone else's ways, we'd suddenly be a major threat. Then we'd see what it looks like when the powers really hate us.

This is why Jesus warned us so clearly to expect the world's hatred. We will be hated not because we drop out of society or treat civilization as evil, but because the Spirit's power can make us better than the worldly powers at serving our neighbors in civilizational activities. That's what makes us a threat. If we serve people better, our neighbors will start to turn to us, not to the powers, to find out how life works best. They'll start to view the church as a spiritual leader. And the powers can't have that.

So, in a sense, we *want* the powers to hate us. Their hatred is an infallible sign we're succeeding in blessing our neighbors. If we see that the worldly powers have contempt for us, we should reexamine our approach to how we live. But if we see that the powers hate us, far from compromising with them in order to minimize conflict, we should ruthlessly double down on whatever it is we're doing that serves our neighbors better.

We see in the Bible how successful ministry is both loved and hated by the world. Consider how Daniel was promoted to the top of the king's household because it was obvious he was superior in wisdom and in managing civilizational work—and the powers of the world tried to kill him for the same reason.

An even more striking example is found in Acts 19:31, a verse I think most people overlook when they read the chapter. In Acts 19, the guardians of the Artemis cult in Ephesus have stirred up a mob against Paul's mission. They make their money from people's spiritual enslavement to idols, and the gospel is destroying their livelihood. The mob has seized two of Paul's colaborers. As Paul is going out to address the mob, some of the disciples attempt to physically restrain him, fearing for his life. Then in verse 31 we are told: "And even some of the Asiarchs, who were friends of his, sent to him and were urging him not to venture into the theater."

That's astonishing. The Asiarchs were very high government officials. The Artemis cult was part and parcel of the religious system that legitimized their rule. Defending it was part of the Asiarchs' job. Sticking their necks out for Paul, even in private, would put them crossways with the cult's guardians—and messing with the Artemis cult was obviously a deadly thing to do. So why did some of the Asiarchs stick their necks out for Paul?

Why was it important to them that Paul and his mission survive? What was Paul doing that they thought was so important, so vital to their community? When gospel ministry is flourishing in the Spirit, its impact on the community is so beneficial that even some unbelievers will risk their lives to preserve it, while others will kill to stop it.[14]

Besieging Strongholds

This idea that the church should be a threat to the worldly powers is pretty radical stuff. When he founded the church, Jesus declared the gates of hell wouldn't prevail against it (Matt. 16:18). That's a telling image. Be careful you don't take it for granted.

The "gates of hell" image implies that the church is on the offensive. It depicts hell as a city that's surrounded by its enemies and under siege. And never mind the dramatic scenes of desperate fighting inside the city walls that you've seen in so many movies; in real life, when the gates of a city broke, that was pretty much the final blow.

Jesus is saying it's not enough for the church to follow Satan's army around and minister to its victims as it rapes and plunders the world. The church should be laying siege to the enemy's strongholds. The final victory comes only with Jesus's return, but we're supposed to be taking the battle to the enemy now.

However, this sense of a mission to besiege the enemy has to be coupled with clear thinking about the right way to do it. Rushing into battle without a sound strategy is exactly what leads people into the approaches that narrowly leverage the church's secondary assets. The first time I heard someone point out that the "gates of hell" image implies the church is on the offensive, that person was advocating some very naive ideas about changing the world through political activism.

Now, as more and more Christians have become disillusioned with those shallower approaches, many are bewildered about what it means to take the battle to the enemy. When we thought we could beat the enemy by getting out the vote, or by signing up for fashionable causes, or by "focusing on evangelism," we knew what to do. Now that we know that's not enough, how do we besiege Satan's strongholds?

When drawing up a battle plan, it helps to know what terrain you're fighting for. I mentioned that serving our neighbors better will lead them to look to the church for spiritual leadership. That's the key feature of our social battleground: leadership. Whom will people look to as spiritual leaders, the worldly powers or the church?

People follow leaders in social life. All civilizations have certain people and institutions that are recognized as leaders. When these leaders describe the world in a certain way, people adopt that understanding of the world. When they say one thing is good and another is bad, people change their behavior.

These leaders include far more than just the most obvious powerful people. It's a dense, complex web. There are many types of leaders, and they exist on many levels. Nationally, the president is a social leader, but so are Oprah Winfrey and Bill Gates. And in the social dynamics of your town, the owner of the local factory and the principal of the high school may be more important leaders than anyone who's nationally famous. And within the factory, the leaders will include not only the owner and the foreman, but also the thirty-year veteran line worker who holds no official position but is known and respected by everyone as "the guy who looks out for people." He's a leader, too, within his sphere of influence; coworkers will change their behavior based on what he says and does.

Institutions are leaders as well as individuals. Consider the vast difference in cultural authority between "a study shows" and "a Harvard study shows." Very few people could actually name the current president of Harvard—or Microsoft, or Disney—and those individuals don't carry a lot of cultural weight apart from the institutions they lead. It's the other way around: the institutions carry the cultural weight, and the individuals matter because they're in them. The publisher of the *Washington Post* has a lot of cultural influence, but only because he's publisher of the *Washington Post*. If he sold the paper, he'd lose most of his power to change culture. And the field is always changing. You can't predict what it's going to do. A generation ago, who would have thought a bunch of obscure entrepreneurs inventing computers in their garages in Silicon Valley would become some of America's most important cultural leaders? And that their inventions would decimate, practically overnight, one of the most important classes of leaders in American civilization—newspaper publishers? Quick: name four nationally important computer companies. Now name four nationally important newspapers. That's how dramatically the field of cultural leadership can change in one short generation.

Culture Change: Co-Opted Entrepreneurship

It's important not to think that attacking the worldly powers means attacking socially leading institutions. On the contrary, institutions of leadership are part of God's good plan for human social life. He calls us to bless these institutions and work for their good. Christians who hold leadership positions in these institutions can steward them for God's glory; other Christians should honor these institutions regardless of whether they're led by Christians.

However, it's equally important not to try to beat the enemy by seizing control of leadership positions and using these institutions' social power to impose Christianity on people. Social life requires the ability to negotiate and compromise among people who disagree, even among those who hold competing visions of the meaning of life. Social leaders above all need to learn the art of compromise if they're to be effective. This means that while Christians can and should steward positions of social leadership for God's glory, the institutions themselves can never be simply Christianized. This was one of the fundamental insights of Augustine's *City of God*, which was written in the early fifth century and is still viewed as one of the most important books ever written on the church and society.[15]

So if our job is not to tear down the leadership positions nor to seize control of them, what is our job? The short, oversimplified answer is that we are to change the way the leaders lead through *co-opted entrepreneurship*. This is how cultural change generally happens. It's a two-step process.

First, people invent new ways of doing things and prove—in practice, on the ground—that these new ways serve people better than the old ways. That's the entrepreneurship part. You have to strike out in a new direction and prove that it makes the world a better place. In Silicon Valley, people invented computers. Pixar invented new approaches to modern cinematic storytelling. The civil rights movement invented new ways of challenging segregation. While the word "entrepreneurship" used to be associated only with for-profit businesses, lately it has become common to talk about "social entrepreneurship" driving change in the nonprofit sector. In fact, all entrepreneurship is social entrepreneurship, because every successful entrepreneur is driving cultural change. Just look at how the entrepreneurs of Silicon Valley have transformed our culture.

Entrepreneurship is for everybody, not just for people who start their own businesses. The heart of entrepreneurship is to do something different, something better than what everybody else is doing. Change the system, not by tearing down the old ways but by devising new ones and showing that they work better. It's a mindset and a lifestyle. (People who practice entrepreneurship within existing institutions rather than starting their own are sometimes called "intrapreneurs.")

Culture-changing entrepreneurs don't start by persuading the established gatekeepers of culture that their ideas are good. The gatekeepers are usually dead set against their new ideas. If entrepreneurs waited for permission from the guardians of the status quo, they'd never get off the ground. Instead, they just go out and do new things and prove that they work.

The need for entrepreneurship is why both individuals and institutions matter. You need entrepreneurially minded individuals to think up and build the new ways of doing things. But the new ways usually can't be proven in practice until they're embodied in an institution, either a new one you create or an old one you change. Without that, your new way of doing things will usually be no more than just a neat idea you have.

If the entrepreneurs are successful, social leaders are forced to respond to their innovations. This is the second step, the "co-opting" part. If the new way is really proven on the ground to serve people better than the old way, leading individuals and institutions have to handle that. Some will try to suppress the new way by force. But usually they will also have to adopt the new way in some modified form. Everyone will see that the new way is better and flock to whoever is offering it. So the leaders will offer some version of it.[16]

Here's an example. Before the modern era, most wealth was managed by aristocratic households. The late Middle Ages saw the introduction of independent commercial firms, which managed wealth outside the control of the great houses. They were a threat to the status quo. But the firms proved by their actions that the whole community benefited from their existence. They were better stewards of the wealth they controlled, and their cities prospered because of it. So the aristocrats were forced to tolerate them. In one of the most striking examples, the tiny city-state of Venice was able to fend off an invasion by the huge Ottoman Empire by mobilizing the wealth and technological superiority of its thriving commercial sector.[17] Eventually, commercial firms became so economically successful that the great households found themselves forced to reform their own management of wealth, just to keep up. They had no choice but to embrace good economic stewardship and promote it as a cultural value. Roughly speaking, that's how the whole modern economy with all of its blessings was born.[18]

All of this may sound like it's something far too big for ordinary people to be part of. But American civilization happens at every level, from the national stage to local towns and cities to particular families, workplaces, and neighborhoods. So does entrepreneurship that changes American civilization. It's true that very few people are positioned for entrepreneurship that will impact America nationally. But everyone is positioned for entrepreneurship somewhere. It may be as simple as finding a better work practice among the five people in your working group at the office or factory floor, or organizing some volunteers on your block. But don't you think God cares about those spheres as much as he cares about the national culture?

In part 3 of this book I offer some concrete observations on the state of American civilization, to help you think through how you may be positioned to change civilization in your own sphere of influence. Taking the lead in those efforts is part of the special role of what I earlier called "organic Christianity"—believers carrying the Christian life with them out into the world.

Before we get there, though, we have to make sure we set up a clear standard for what kind of changes Christians should want to make. How do we know what counts as a "better" work practice? Our efforts for cultural change will go awry unless we measure them by a standard that stands apart from the world. Part of the special role of the institutional church is to steward special knowledge, experience, and practices that maintain such a standard, so in part 2 we'll turn to organizational Christianity.

Part 2

Let Earth
Receive Her King

Three Kinds of Christians

Our impact within civilization ultimately grows from the three-fold office of Christ—Prophet, Priest, and King. Christ exercises these offices supremely. He does so both in his own person, in his being, and through his ongoing ministry to us in the Spirit. As a result of our union with Christ, we exercise (in a subordinate way) the same offices.

The office of a prophet is to tell the world what God says. As Prophet, Christ is, in himself, the supreme revelation of God to man; hence he is called "the Word." He also acts continually to reveal God's word to us through Scripture, by sending his Spirit to make its teaching effective in us. As a result, we know God's word and share it with the world around us. In this way we serve Christ as prophets to the world.

The office of a priest is to make sacrifices that reconcile sinful humanity to God. As Priest, Christ is, in himself, the supreme atoning sacrifice; hence he is called "the Lamb of God." He also acts continually to reconcile us to God as our eternally intercessing Mediator in heaven, and by sending his Spirit to make that reconciliation effective in us. As a result, we continually offer ourselves up as sacrifices (Rom. 12:1) by living for God's sake through Christ rather than living for our own sakes, doing good to our neighbors and inviting them to enter into this new kind of life. In this way we serve Christ as priests to the world.

The office of a king is to exercise stewardship over the creation order. As King, Christ is, in himself, the one whose life gives coherence to the creation order; hence "in him all things hold together" (Col. 1:17). He also acts to steward all creation as its Lord, and sends his Spirit to make his lordship specially effective in us as his people. As a result, we become good stewards over whatever portion of creation God has made us responsible for, managing it and continually cultivating blessing for our neighbors from it. In this way we serve Christ as kings to the world.

Timothy Keller has suggested that each individual Christian has a tendency to gravitate toward one of these roles.[1] I think that's a profound insight. Some Christians gravitate toward doctrine—prophethood—and have a tendency to see everything through that lens. They focus on instructing people in biblical truth, and when they see things going wrong in the church, they tend to blame false teaching. Others gravitate toward devotion—priesthood—and have a tendency to see everything through that lens. They focus on heart transformation, and when they see things going wrong in the church, they tend to blame ritualism or formalism. Still others gravitate toward stewardship of life in civilization—kingship—and have a tendency to see everything through that lens. They focus on whether the church is succeeding in cultivating blessing for our neighbors within the creation order, and when they see things going wrong in the church, they tend to blame irresponsibility.

The church needs all three. Imagine that the church is a car. Doctrine is the road map that helps us find the path to our destination. No road trip could ever be called a success if it ended up in the wrong place! Devotion is the explosive fire that makes the engine run. (You did know, didn't you, that an engine runs by constantly exploding?) That never-quenched consuming fire in our hearts is the engine that makes the church go places. Stewardship is the wheels that actually grab hold of the pavement and take the car to its destination. God's calling in our daily lives to cultivate blessings from the creation order is "where the rubber meets the road"; it gives the church cultural traction.

Unfortunately, a lot of conflict gets started within the church when Christians struggle to push one of these three approaches into a position of dominance over the others. From one point of view, you can say (and rightly so) that doctrine has priority; after all, you have to hear God's Word before you can know him and love him, or carry out his commands. However, from another point of view you can say (and just as rightly) that you will never actually hear God's Word in an effectual way until you are devoted to God because he has removed your heart of stone and given you a heart of flesh. Only heart change allows you to hear truth your pastor is preaching; for that matter, the pastor himself needs heart change! And from a third point of view you can say (still, just as rightly) that it is only by actively striving in practical life to do good and obey the law that we discover both how good the law is and how evil we are. As C. S. Lewis put it, no one can really, honestly know that he is a sinful person until he has really, honestly tried to be good and failed.[2] Thus, a serious effort to live a good life—stewardship—is a necessary prerequisite to both knowledge and heart change.

So all three approaches need to be integrated in the church and Christian life. Each is, really and truly, first in priority from a given perspective. Imagine there's a triangle drawn on the surface of a table. Which corner is the top corner? Each of them is the "top" corner from a given perspective; you can make any corner the top corner just by walking around the table. Similarly, to do justice to the totality of Christ in his threefold offices, we must be equally concerned to know truth, love God, and serve effectively. And we must not keep those things in separate silos as though they were irrelevant to one another, but integrate them into a whole Christian life.

Different Christians focusing on different approaches isn't

necessarily bad. After all, the Bible compares the church to a body, made up of very different members. The foot is not an eye and the ear is not a hand, but that doesn't mean they're not all parts of the same body. God made the body parts different so that the body would benefit from all their diverse functions (1 Cor. 12:14–20).

The problem comes in when the parts reject each other or don't work together—when the eye rejects the hand because it's different and performs a different function. That's exactly why they need each other! It is part of the function of each part to supply what the other parts lack, each according to their various powers and roles (1 Cor. 12:21–26).

Similarly, I think each of us needs to become aware of whatever tendencies we have to focus on one of these three roles. This will allow us to become more aware of our limitations and seek the help of others with different perspectives. It will also help us become more aware of our strengths, so that we can better serve the church and the world by focusing on what we do best. The eye needs to know that it is an eye, not only so it will understand why it needs the hand, but also so it can know the function it's made for—seeing—and get to work doing that.

I'll put my cards on the table and reveal that I'm very much a doctrine person. I've written in chapter 1 about the sinful desire to escape from history; it seems to me that we doctrine people are the most likely to succumb to that temptation. Our besetting sin is to set up once-for-all statements of doctrine (or ethical rules, or cultural forms) and treat those as tests of orthodoxy. We want clarity and certainty, and the contingencies of history and cultural contextualization seem to threaten those values. But God made us as creatures who live within history. Consider 1 Corinthians 11:14–15; apparently even the things we know by "nature" are subject to contextualization and change over time. In fact, we don't have to sacrifice clarity or accuracy to navigate the currents of historical change. In any event, we have to get in the boat and ride the river if we want our doctrinal knowledge to be of any use to our less eggheaded brethren.

Some doctrine people have the opposite problem, and are overly eager to impact history. We sometimes forget that our knowledge of doctrine doesn't give us the right to seize control of the lives of others. We should take care to remember that the Great Commission to make disciples proceeds by persuasion and example, never by force.

Having at least taken note of the beam in my own eye, I will take the liberty of pointing out what may be specks in my neighbors' eyes. I think devotion people are most likely to fall into the trap of "making converts" instead of "making disciples." Heart change must produce life change or it isn't really heart change. We need to set clear and specific moral expectations to guide behavior, or else Christians and churches fall into emotionalism, motivationism, and subjectivism—providing so little specific ethical guidance that the implicit message is "it doesn't matter what you do with your life as long as you mean well." For stewardship people, I would advise against reductive oversimplifications of complex social dynamics. Human cultural systems are not simple, and stewardship people sometimes have a tendency to treat them as though they were. They also seem to me to be especially prone to ethical pragmatism, which says that whatever "works" is the right thing to do. This often manifests itself in hostile rejection of any discussion that sounds like it's just an argument over what words mean. Admittedly, debates about language are often frustrating, and they may seem unimportant. But they're not. It matters what words mean.

Doctrine, Devotion, Stewardship

	Office	Spirit's Work	In Church	Flowing Out
Doctrine	Prophet	Revelation	Authority	Knowledge
Devotion	Priest	Regeneration	Intimacy	Freedom (from guilt and fear)
Stewardship	King	Sanctification	Calling	Responsiblity

A beautiful story in the last section of one of my favorite books, Lewis's *The Pilgrim's Regress*, illustrates how doctrine people, devotion people, and stewardship people need each other. The heroes, John and Virtue, have traveled through the world to reach God's kingdom and become God's people. In the final chapter, they must go back through the world to the land they came from. (This is the "regress" of the book's title.)

They are accompanied by an angel whose sight is so keen that anyone who stands near him can see things as they really are. As they travel back through the world, sticking close to the angel, they see that the entire world is not really what it had appeared to be. The angel's clear sight, imparted to them as long as they stick with him, reveals to them a whole different world. This is the role of the doctrine person; he shares knowledge with other Christians to help them see the world as it really is.

Each of our heroes must fight a dragon. John is a romantic dreamer driven by passionate emotions. His sense of longing for something greater and more completely fulfilling eventually led him to Christ. But along the way it also led him into sexual sin, gullibility, and physical weakness. He must fight the icy dragon who lives in the mountains of the north, ruling over all the greedy and prideful. After he kills the dragon, he inhales deeply to take in its bitterly cold final breath. The chill hardens his mind and muscles, and he gains mastery over all his desires. When he returns to his country, he can work indefinitely without tiring, and the temptress who has been besetting him for the entire novel discovers that she no longer has any power over him. Devotion by itself was not enough. John becomes the complete Christian when his desires integrate knowledge and stewardship.

Virtue is a smart, strong, and moral man—and he knows it. His virtues eventually led him to Christ, because they drove him to seek truth and duty wherever they might lie. But along the way they also made him a cold, self-righteous prig. He must fight the fire-breathing dragon who lives in the southern swamps, ruling the libertines and sorcerers. After he kills the dragon, Virtue eats its flaming heart. All his false dignity and priggishness are melted by the fire. When he returns to his companions, he comes leaping and bounding impossibly high in the air, leaving a flaming crater in the ground every place he lands, and singing a wild paean to the goodness of desire:

> *Behemoth is my serving man!*
> *Before the conquered hosts of Pan*
> *Riding tamed Leviathan,*
> *Loud I sing for well I can*
> *RESURGAM and IO, PAEAN,*
> *IO, IO, IO PAEAN!!*
>
> *Now I know the stake I played for,*
> *Now I know what a worm's made for!*[3]

Good stewardship by itself was not enough. Virtue becomes the complete Christian when his dutiful nature integrates knowledge and devotion.

As we spend our own post-conversion lives traveling back through the world from which we came, how can we carry the truth, love, and responsibility of Christ with us into it? That's what the rest of this book is about. In part 2 we'll look more specifically at how the Holy Spirit works in our lives to create the church through doctrine, devotion, and stewardship, and how that translates into civilizational life. Then in part 3 we'll look more specifically at the major components of American civilization—family, economic work, and the civil community—to see how the work of the Spirit can transform our lives in those areas, and through us, civilization itself.

3

Doctrine: Teaching and Preaching

Light is sown for the righteous,
and joy for the upright in heart.

Ps. 97:11

I'm not a pastor, but I have been a teacher. I know from experience that teaching is a hard job. It's not enough to just tell people the information they need to know. If it were that easy, we wouldn't need teachers; we could just give people books and handouts. Teaching is a social activity. It's not like delivering an oral version of a written report. It's more like telling a story, but with information. Your primary focus is the audience, not the content.

On one occasion, this distinction between teaching and just regurgitating information had a major impact on my life. When I was in high school, I had a really brilliant physics teacher who spent the whole class illuminating the subject matter in his own highly motivated way. He breezed quickly past the basic principles, then spent most of his time bringing in lots of unusual examples and exploring subtle nuances. As a result, his teaching was incredibly engaging to the few students who shared his intense interest in the subject, and completely useless to the majority who did not. They needed him to invest his time and energy in helping them absorb the basic principles.

One girl in my lab group was completely lost and getting a D in the class. She asked me for help. "Just ignore the teacher," was my main advice. "Read the textbook and learn what's in it. Don't pay attention to anything in class; study the book and disregard everything else."

She went from a D to an A, so it worked out well for her. And I ended up married to that girl, so it worked out pretty well for me, too!

It wasn't so great for the teacher, though. He asked her what she was doing differently to turn around her grade so dramatically, and she told him. He wasn't happy to have his deficiencies as a teacher revealed so clearly.

Preaching and teaching take the Word of God, which is eternal and unchanging, and infuse it into our lives, which are historically contingent and constantly in motion. That's an amazing thing, if you think about it. The pastor's job is to continually renew the Word of God for the present age. Preaching is the most important part of the worship service, because the sermon controls how we understand the meaning of everything else (the singing, the sacraments, etc.).

If a pastor or other teacher pays attention to his information but not the needs of his audience, like my high school physics teacher did, the Word of God won't reach God's people. (And unlike a physics class, which has quizzes, tests, and grades, most churches unfortunately don't use systematic measurements to find out whether the pastor is succeeding as a teacher.) But if the pastor knows his audience as well as he knows his Bible, and is skilled in the social art of teaching, he has the high privilege of infusing God's eternal Word into the rushing flow of human history. And as that Word flows out into civilization through the transformed lives of congregants, civilization itself is changed by its presence.

Revelation for Authority, Authority for Joy

The main function of preaching and other church teaching is to nurture the joy of God in us by renewing our minds through instruction. Like all aspects of the church's life, the renewal of our minds doesn't begin with any merely human action. It begins with the work of the Holy Spirit in our lives. It is the Spirit who creates the church, and every aspect of its life grows from our transformation by the Spirit.

The Spirit's work in renewing our minds began with inspiring the Bible. The text of the Bible is God's Word. It is God's Word because the Spirit superintended the writing of its authors to make it so. The Bible is what God says to the church and to the whole world.

Getting the doctrine of inspiration right is critical to the joy of God. A church that believes in an inspired text has a God-given external standard against which to measure itself. It is responsible to something that is outside its own control. It has an authority beyond its own opinions to which it is answerable.

As one theologian put it, the doctrine that the biblical text is inspired means the church is "under orders."[1] Only a church that knows it's under orders will view doctrinal instruction as an opportunity to be transformed by the Spirit. And only a sound understanding of the doctrine of inspiration can keep the church mindful that it is under orders.

A church that believes in looser theories of inspiration, which don't treat the text itself as the inspired Word, has no external standard. One theory is that the message of the biblical text is inspired, or some part of the message, but not the text itself. A church that believes this can seek to be responsible to the inspired message. But who distinguishes the message from the text? Who decides what is the underlying message that needs to be kept, and what is merely verbal and can be disregarded? The church itself does. So the church ends up being responsible to something that is totally under its own control. Another theory holds that inspiration happens within our own minds when we read the Bible. That's even worse. By that standard, we're not even responsible to some elusive "message of the text" that we have to find and disentangle from the text itself. We can essentially invent God's Word for ourselves with relatively little interference.

Inadequate views of inspiration open the door for merely human religion to substitute for Spirit-powered religion. When we, fallen beings that we are, are the final judges of God's message, we start to discover more and more places where—conveniently!—we can jettison the difficult and scandalous teachings of the text and still feel like we're faithful. Over time, the church's understanding of God's message wanders further and further from the Bible.

In other ages, when the doctrine of inspiration was compromised, the first things to go were the more challenging ethical rules. In the early Middle Ages, the church adopted a view that its Latin translation of the Bible was just as inspired as the original texts (because it was the message, not the texts, that was inspired). But the messages people were actually getting out of that Latin text turned out to be different from those we find in the originals. Perhaps most important was the supposed sacrament of penance, which the Latin text can be read to suggest but the original Greek does not support. The sacrament of penance embedded in the daily life of the church the idea that you could work off the effects of your sins. It was this more than anything else that cultivated an environment where indulgences, church offices for sale to the highest bidder, and brothels for priests could flourish. Then at the turn of the sixteenth century, Erasmus electrified the world by publishing his own translation of the Greek New Testament. Along with his new translation, he provided a devastating list of translation errors in the version the church was using—including the errors that had introduced the sacrament of penance. Martin Luther was in business.

In our own time, however, the ethical compromises didn't come until the end of the process. When mainline American

Protestantism compromised its view of inspiration in the early twentieth century, the first things to go were the miracles. The compromisers chose their target well, because belief in the biblical miracles is what most directly anchors Christianity's character as a religion of historic events. Once you've said there was no virgin birth or feeding of the five thousand, what reason is left to believe in the incarnation, the atonement, or the resurrection? This version of "Christianity" detached itself from all connection to history, and therefore ceased to be Christianity in any important sense, with remarkable speed. We may think it's absurd that the head of the Episcopal Church prays to a female "Mother Jesus," but by the historic standards of human religion, that's perfectly normal.[2] Pagan gods are always changing form, because they're not divine as such, they're imaginary manifestations—symbols—of the divine. The divine hasn't entered history, so by its nature it can't be known to us in any way except through ever-changing manmade symbols. Only a fool would believe that the divine *actually* became a man. Once this kind of shocking apostasy had taken hold, ordaining gay bishops was merely an afterthought.

Only an inspired text creates authority in the church, and only a church that is under authority will continue to be Spirit-created and historically grounded. God has given us a delicious paradox: the only thing that keeps the church historical—grounded in God's redemptive works in history and carrying the faith forward in our own historical moment—is our belief that inspiration rests in an unchanging, ahistorical text. When we believe that inspiration rests in something that changes over time, Christianity loses its historical character.

With a sound view of inspiration, we don't have to take things that are really historical and pretend that they're manifestations of the eternal. We don't need an escape from history to reach the divine. The divine has already entered into history, and we still possess within history one of the ways in which that happened— in Scripture. Because we possess the eternal Word in the text of

Scripture, we are free to rest within history as history. We don't have to pretend we can go up to God; he came down.

Preaching and Teaching for Joy

If we really want to receive joy in having our minds renewed by divine revelation, there's no getting around the big issue: the Bible is deep and complex. There's a whole lot going on in there. And the more you learn about it, the deeper you begin to realize it is. As Augustine put it, speaking to God in his *Confessions*: "What wonderful profundity there is in your utterances! The surface meaning lies open before us and charms beginners. Yet the depth is amazing, my God, the depth is amazing."[3]

That means we'd be fools to just read our Bibles alone at home, or even just read them and discuss them in groups. We need help. We need teachers.

The Spirit doesn't just inspire the Bible and regenerate our hearts, and then leave us to figure things out from there on our own. He raises up teachers in the church to help us understand his Word. Pastors aren't raised up by the church, but by the Spirit; the church discerns the Spirit's calling. Creating the teaching ministry of the church—preeminently the preaching ministry in corporate worship, but all sorts of other teaching, too—is yet another way in which the Spirit operates to make God's Word effectively known to his people.

Certainly it's true that the most basic aspects of the Bible's message are relatively easy to grasp. They're sitting right there on the surface, right in front of your face where you can't miss them. It's hard to take an honest look at the Bible and not come away with the message "trust Jesus." Although to convey how obvious it is, we really should print it like this:

Trust Jesus!

So we're not irretrievably lost and without hope in the world if we don't have the teaching ministry of the church.

That said, while we can be saved without the church's teaching ministry, we need to know a lot more than "trust Jesus" if we're going to get what we ought to be getting out of the Bible. We're supposed to be constantly relying on the Bible throughout our daily lives. If all you know from the Bible is "trust Jesus," you're not going to get far. And remember how we saw in chapter 1 that the gospel requires not just getting the facts right, but getting the story right?

When you get beyond the obvious stuff and into the depths of the Bible, interpreting Scripture involves a lot of difficult and complicated issues. There are paradoxes. For example, there's the paradox of systematic theology and biblical scholarship. We have to interpret each passage of text in light of the coherent testimony of all Scripture, yet what is all Scripture but so many passages of text? Which comes first? Even deeper is the paradox of general and special revelation. General revelation is what God makes known to everyone through reason, conscience, and history; special revelation is what God makes known to his people through the special (hence the name) intervening work of the Spirit, such as in prophecy and inspiration. In practice, they're impossible to clearly separate. You can't understand the Bible without drawing extensively on the knowledge and rational capacities that you bring to it. Your very ability to read and understand language, and hence the Bible, is all of general revelation.

Hence the need for pastors. A pastor is entrusted with many tasks, but preaching is the one that above all makes him a pastor. The preaching of the Word defines the institutional church preeminently. The other marks of a church, such as the sacraments, are all grounded in its preaching.

The Bible is the church's authority, so preaching (and other teaching) conveys that authority. Preaching is the primary way the Lord rules his church as its king, because this is how we hear his scriptural commands applied to our lives. The pastor or other teacher is not himself an original source of authority; only God can ever be that. The Bible has authority as God's Word, and because the pastor is preaching the Bible, to the extent that he is really preaching it, his words have authority from it.

How Can Pastors Have Authority?

The pastor's authority is a delicate point. It comes from the inspiration of the biblical text, but the pastor does a lot more than just read the biblical text. He gives the sense of the text, explaining what it means. And he applies the text, showing how it intersects with our lives today. The pastor's exposition and application of the text is how God's authoritative Word is effectively made known to God's people.

There are biblical grounds for this practice. For example, Ezra and the priests read the law to God's people after they returned from exile. Nehemiah 8 says that while Ezra read the law, a group of priests "helped the people to understand the Law" and "gave the sense, so that the people understood the reading" (vv. 7–8).

However, the position of the sermon in worship raises questions about the role of authority in the church. Obviously when the pastor directly quotes the Bible, God is speaking and the authority is clear. But when the pastor is giving the sense of the text and applying it, he is bringing in his own judgment, which is not inspired. How can his words be authoritative?

This is a good reminder of the limits of pastoral authority. Congregants have the right—and equally important, the responsibility—to discern whether what they hear from their pastor lines up with what they find in their Bibles. "Do not despise prophecies, but test everything," Paul writes to the Thessalonians. "Hold fast what is good" (1 Thess. 5:20–21). The theme that preachers are to be judged by the Bible, not the Bible by preachers, runs throughout the New Testament (e.g., Matt. 15:1–9; 2 John 1:10).

This points us toward a deeper solution to the problem of the pastor's authority. Preaching and teaching are not a separate function from congregants' own personal study of their Bibles. The point of preaching and teaching is to assist congregants in learning from their Bibles. A good sermon uses the pastor's thoughts and words, which are not inspired, to help us learn from the Bible, which is. It is the biblical learning, not the pastor's words as such, that is authoritative.

Because his authority comes from the Bible, the pastor has no right to command. That's not the kind of "authority" a pastor has. His authority is declarative. He declares what *God* commands.

The pastor has authority because he is a person with knowledge, just like when we say an expert is "an authority" in his subject area. To say that Professor Jenkins is an authority on physics does not mean he has the right to command the universe and tell objects how to behave. ("I hereby proclaim that the coefficient of gravitation shall henceforth be . . . five! That is all.") Nor does it mean he has the right to command other people in matters pertaining to physics. ("Congress shall double funding for all physics research this year.") It means people who don't have professional training in physics would be wise to listen to him in cases where knowledge of that topic is relevant. And, to a limited extent and within the bounds of their own consciences, they'd be wise to defer to him in making difficult judgments in such cases.

Because a pastor's authority is declarative, one of the most important skills for a good pastor is to develop a keen sensitivity to how his personal judgment is intersecting with the text. A good sermon needs to include applications and illustrations that are not themselves biblically inspired, and these introduce an element of human judgment. The pastor needs to distinguish the parts of his message that are more certain (and therefore more authoritative) and the parts that are less certain (and therefore less authoritative). He needs to tailor his message in a way that incorporates these subtle distinctions. Pastors need to be bold in asserting the things God really does command, but they need to be equally comfortable using phrases like "it seems to me" or "perhaps we should think about" or "use your own judgment" as appropriate. A sermon that actually explicates and applies the text in an effective way, instead of just pedantically paraphrasing it, will usually contain quite a few passages where phrases like these are called for.

In fact, I think authoritative preaching and cautious phrasing are two sides of the same coin. I agree with those who say we need bolder gospel preaching in churches today. However, when pastors shy away from bold preaching, I don't think it's usually out of cowardice. I think in many cases they're just not confident in their ability to clearly distinguish what's really certain and authoritative from what is just their own judgment. They don't want to accidentally substitute their own opinions for God's Word, so they err on the side of caution. Good for them! I'm glad they're sensitive to the weight of their obligations in the pulpit. But the right solution is not to retreat into safe generalities; it's to hone your preaching skills until you can distinguish these things with confidence.

Going Beyond Mindset to Action

My impression is that most sermons and church teaching today focus on equipping people with the right mindset. By "mindset" I mean our sense of our identity and our motivations. The right mindset is imperative to good Christian life, and hence to good teaching. Without it, teaching degenerates quickly into mere scolding, and ultimately into legalistic heresy, because you aren't giving people the right reasons to obey. People need to obey God because it makes sense to them to do so, not because they were hectored into it. And it won't make sense unless we help them see who they are in Christ (identity) and how obedience to God fulfills and satisfies their renewed human nature (motivation).

But mindset isn't sufficient. Translating all this abstract, airy "mindset" stuff into concrete practice is a big challenge. We can't abandon our people to figure it all out on their own. Preaching that only addresses mindset is subjectivist and emotivist—it sends an unspoken message that it doesn't really matter what you do, as long as you have the right mindset. That doesn't lead to changed lives. Just as leaving out mindset ultimately ends in legalism, talking only about mindset ultimately ends in antinomianism (the heresy that says Christians don't need to worry about obedience). And abstract ethical injunctions—telling people, essentially, "be a nice person"—aren't enough. People need to know, tangibly and specifically, what does a Christian life actually *look* like?

Alongside *mindset* we need to teach specifically about *action*. Like mindset, action is made up of two components. At the broadest level it consists of roles: what does it mean to be a good father, mother, son, daughter, employee, employer, coworker, client, citizen, friend, neighbor, and so forth? Pastors need to equip congregants to see how they can live out these roles as manifestations of the Christian life. That leads us to the other component of action: tasks. What's on my daily to-do list? What does God want me to do tomorrow morning? How could that task list change to bring it more into conformity with what God wants for it?

Obviously pastors and teachers can't get down too deep into details. There are too many different roles and tasks in the world for pastors to get specific about all of them. This is why cultivating a shared life in the broader church community matters. Laypeople need relationships with each other to help one another navigate their specific opportunities and challenges. Small groups, accountability partnerships, mentoring, and even vocational associations provide the necessary relational infrastructure for God's Word to get applied to all of life.

But the job of getting down to specifics can't be totally offloaded. Laypeople won't organize in this way unless the teaching they get from their pastors and teachers makes them realize the need for this kind of specific on-the-ground application. If sermons are disconnected from action, that indifference will spread. The teaching at the top has to connect mindset with action to make biblical knowledge effective in changing lives.

There's also another reason action teaching is critical. The mindset part isn't likely to be done right even on its own terms if it's done in isolation from action. God did not make human beings to sit around Eden having the right mindset. He made them to act! "And God said to them, 'Be fruitful and multiply and fill the earth and subdue it'" (Gen. 1:28). Notice God says fill *the earth*, not Eden. Having stewardship over the whole earth is a big task! But God made us for it; he made us to cultivate. "The LORD God took the man and put him in the garden of Eden to work it and keep it" (Gen. 2:15). If human life was designed for action before the fall, getting our actions right after the fall is all the more imperative— not only because we have to equip people to deal with specific sins, but also because on a deeper level their orientation as people has been turned away from the active life of creating blessings for others that God made them for and calls them back to in Christ. The identities and motivations we possess in Christ are action-oriented. Peter tells us to set our hope on Christ's return, but also to be "preparing your minds for action" here and now (1 Pet. 1:13)! Notice that in this command, Peter connects mind and action. If we teach mindset without action, we're not only not teaching action, we're not really teaching mindset, either.

Mindset and action need to be carefully integrated. If one drives out the other, the teaching is undermined. A pastor friend of mine calls this "the great dilemma of preaching." In his words, you need to call people to make their lives better but not create the expectation that they can do so by their own power, merely by trying harder. If you only call people to make their lives better, that's just scolding; in the extreme it becomes legalism. But if you only remind people they can't change by their own power, that's irresponsible; in the extreme it becomes antinomianism.

It might help to think about this in terms of law and gospel. Calling people to make their lives better is law, reminding them that they can't do it by "trying harder" is gospel. We need both law and gospel, and the message needs to be integrated. We need law to convict people that their lives aren't right and they can't fix them by effort, leading them to the gospel that tells them they need Christ to fix their lives. Then we need the gospel to lead them back to obedience—back to the law—but with renewed hearts and the right motivations.

The more pastors go beyond mindset to action, the more we can expect disagreements within the church about specific applications. That will be fine—it will even be enlightening and edifying—*if* pastors remember to distinguish what's really certain and authoritative from what is less so. If we say, "thus saith the Lord" after all our opinions, we will have nasty conflicts. But if one person says, "It really seems to me that the welfare system creates dependency that robs people of their human dignity," and another person says, "It seems to me that a lot of people are in need and we can't just rely on private charity," that conversation might really go somewhere. They might discover that they agree on more than they think. For example, they may agree that the church should take the lead in creating distinctive, more effective and dignified alternatives to the status quo in how we help the poor.

We can also expect preaching to address things people could potentially learn elsewhere—knowledge about what works and what doesn't in daily life. From sex and family to work and economics, people need to know how to live a functional life to glorify God. Some pastors think it's their job to focus on teaching only the kind of knowledge that is most distinctive to the church, or even to their specific denomination or tradition. But teaching people things in church that they might have learned elsewhere is necessary, because in fact most people are not going to learn those things elsewhere. They will only learn them if the pastor teaches them in church—partly because their time is limited, but more importantly because the church has authority. Only the church can tell them that they really need to know these things, that learning these things is not optional. And there is nothing wrong with teaching a truth just because others, including non-

Christians, also teach it; all truth is God's truth, so all truth is at home in God's pulpit.

What a Christian Life Looks Like

I've just dumped a lot of heavy burdens on pastors and teachers! As a sometime Sunday school teacher myself, I'm keenly aware of how intimidating the burden of teaching is. I'm also aware of how far short I often fall in my responsibilities as a teacher!

It shouldn't be surprising that the pastor and teacher's role is intimidating. The Bible warns that teaching is an awesome responsibility: "Not many of you should become teachers, my brothers, for you know that we who teach will be judged with greater strictness" (James 3:1); "Do not be hasty in the laying on of hands" (1 Tim. 5:22).

One thing Christians can do is take a hard look at how we identify and train our clergy. Are we succeeding in getting highly qualified people into the pastorate and equipping them for that role? It is a major scandal that thousands of American pastors have inadequate theological training. One study found 24 percent of senior or lead pastors in US congregations have no graduate degree; 10 percent don't even have an undergraduate degree.[4] Another study asked pastors their level of theological training, and a shocking 9 percent answered that they had *none*. Another 11 percent had only a certificate from a training program; 3 percent had a Bible college degree.[5]

However, more than just good theology is needed. Preaching must infuse God's Word into the lives of congregants. People will not learn from the sermon if it only recites facts. The sermon does not succeed unless biblical knowledge actually changes the congregants' lives.

That means preaching is about our own history and civilization, not just about the Bible. Just as someone translating a book from Greek to English needs to know both Greek and English, a pastor translating biblical knowledge into the lives of early twenty-first-century Americans needs to know both the Bible and early twenty-first-century America.

You can never give the same sermon twice. A sermon given at a different point in time and space will have a different meaning for its audience. As we saw in chapter 2, human beings are deeply social creatures. The congregants whose lives must be transformed by the sermon are extensively formed by their civilization and their place in history (among other things, of course). If the pastor ignores that, or doesn't know how to deal with it, the sermon's message won't be effective in teaching them.

A sermon needs to tell people "what it looks like when you do it." If you want to teach people to be generous, channel their sexual desires, work hard, reconcile with enemies, or anything else, you have to not just tell them to do it, but also draw them a picture of what doing it looks like in practice. But those pictures depend on your civilization and your place in history; they look different today than in any other time, and different in America than in any other place. (And no doubt they will even be different, in more subtle ways, in different parts of America.) Hence pastors need to know about and talk about contemporary civilizational life if they want to be effective teachers of biblical knowledge.

Moreover, the civilizational aspect of the congregants' lives is the one that the pastor is most able to connect with. He can't necessarily tailor his sermon to just the old or just the young, to just the rich or just the poor, to just the people from intact families or broken families, to just the people of one race or another. Even in a demographically homogeneous congregation, a pastor who ignored civilizational life would isolate his church from the larger American population. But pastors can and should tailor their messages for early twenty-first-century Americans, because that describes everyone in the congregation and in the surrounding community.

In fact, theological education already acknowledges the essential importance of knowing about history and civilization—as long as it's from two thousand years ago. The timeless message of God entered into history in Scripture in a series of particular times and places. Knowing the history and civilizations of those times and places is critical to understanding the Bible's message.

The same principle applies to the sermon. Knowing our own history and civilization is critical to applying Scripture's message to the lives of congregants today.

I suspect that the main reason many pastors and teachers don't sufficiently integrate their teaching with contemporary culture, especially when it comes to concrete action, is because they know they don't know enough about it. They know they can't say what discipleship looks like in the context of being an architect, lawyer, or factory worker. They know they aren't sure how to deal with questions concerning good citizenship without making the church captive to someone's political agenda. They don't want to put themselves in a teaching role when they don't have the knowledge to teach.

That's good! If pastors don't want to teach what they don't know, we're already halfway home. That's a lot better than wanting to teach what they think they know, but don't. Now they have to learn the things they need to know, so they can teach with a greater understanding of the world their congregants interact with every day.

I would say the most important way to make preaching more effective at changing lives is for pastors and teachers to see themselves as learners. In the teaching profession in schools and universities, it's an old adage that you can't be a good teacher unless you're a learner. Lifelong learning is an important aspiration every pastor should have as well.

And here's some really good news. Every pastor is armed with an unspeakably valuable resource for learning about the civilizational context of his congregation's lives—his congregation! If you're a pastor, ask your congregants what they're wrestling with. Go into their workplaces and interview them about their spiritual struggles and triumphs at work. Sit in on the moms' group and ask them what aspects of their lives they struggle with most. Organize small groups of laypeople who know certain areas of contemporary life—business, entertainment, civics—and ask them to teach you. Believe me, they'll love you for it. I've talked to pastors who did this, and they tell me it's transformed their relationships with their congregations.

This requires you to make yourself vulnerable in a somewhat scary way. That's okay. It's called humility. It's hard for all of us, but it's only scary until you actually do it. And it works.

I also think churches should develop better systematic measuring tools for evaluating whether preaching is effective in changing lives. I know tools like this are scary. I've designed survey instruments (though not for churches), so I know they can be destructive if they're abused. But the only reason they're destructive when abused is because they're very powerful. Almost every other public institution in American life has embraced systematic assessment in the past few decades, and the benefits have been extraordinary. Churches and government agencies are the last two major holdouts from this trend. Let's try to get on board the train before Caesar does.

Inside Information

When pastors and teachers succeed in making biblical knowledge effective to change the lives of congregants, that doesn't just nurture the joy of God in the congregants. It impacts American civilization. The changes in the lives of those congregants don't happen in a vacuum. Since we're social creatures, the change in our lives affects those around us and the institutions through which we relate to them.

Christians who have the joy of God are armed with inside information about how the universe works. *Inside Information* was the original title of the C. S. Lewis radio broadcasts later published as the first section of *Mere Christianity*.[6] That's how important this idea is to our faith. The work of the Spirit in inspiring Scripture, raising up pastors and others to help us learn from it, and giving us teachable minds and hearts results in Christians knowing more than others do about all phenomena in God's universe.

What do we do with this inside information? We proclaim it to the world, as circumstances permit and call us to do so, certainly. We don't want this inside information to stay inside. We want it to become "outside information"! We want everyone to know, because we love them.

But that's not all we should do with it. We ought to be intentionally, systematically taking advantage of our biblical knowledge to live better lives. And one indispensable element of living better lives is improving the lives of those around us through our daily work in homes, workplaces, and communities. That's the "action" part. Our inside information about the universe means we can find better ways to serve our neighbors than the world can.

Human behavior is one of the phenomena about which we have especially valuable inside information. The Bible is not a science textbook, so we don't have a lot of inside information about, say, the movements of subatomic particles. But on the subject of human behavior, we have unspeakably precious knowledge that is only available through the Spirit's special work in the church.

The two bedrock concepts of Christian anthropology (the study of human nature) are that all human beings are made in the image of God and that all human beings are guilty and corrupt from the fall. These two concepts explain human behavior much better than any of the available alternatives. Historically, all other approaches to human nature have ultimately collapsed back into three inferior alternatives: the naive optimism that says people are basically good, the naive pessimism that says people are basically bad, and the naive bigotry that says some people are basically good while other people are basically bad. The view that all people are both basically good and basically bad at the same time finds systematic support only in biblical revelation. Non-Christians have often embraced this view, but where they have done so, it is obvious that they have borrowed it from Christianity. There is simply nowhere else to get it from, and they have never found a persuasive alternative framework to justify it.

So of all the things Christians are armed to do better because of their inside information, civilizational activities are near the top of the list. We understand how people and their social systems work in a way no one else does. Or at least we should, if we're paying attention in church.

We ought to be able to take advantage of that knowledge. We ought to be better fathers, mothers, sons, daughters, employees, employers, coworkers, clients, citizens, friends, and neighbors. In part 3 of this book, we'll look at specific examples of how we can accomplish civilizational tasks better as a result of our biblical knowledge.

Moreover, we ought to organize among ourselves to do this intentionally. God does not believe in Lone Ranger Christians. If our discipleship calls us to do something, it calls us to work together to do it better. God has designed us as social creatures, and when we work together, we are many times more effective.

Of course, preaching and teaching should be faithful to the truth above all. It should never be judged based on whether congregants' efforts to embody it in civilization succeed or fail. In a fallen world, any effort may fail. The pastor's job is to teach truthfully and let the impact on civilization play out according to the congregants' callings and the Lord's providence. In fact, in one of those cosmic ironies God seems to be fond of, the quickest way of making our teaching irrelevant to civilization is to make it captive to civilizational relevance. As soon as we care more about impacting civilization than we care about teaching the truth, our teaching will become detached from supernatural revelation, and thus it will lose all its power to impact civilization.

Who Has Knowledge?

When our biblical knowledge leads us to accomplish civilizational tasks better than the world does, and especially when we maximize our discipleship by intentionally working together, the world notices. The world can ignore us if our participation in civilization is the same as everyone else's. It can't ignore us if we're doing a better job of improving people's lives than it is—people will come to rely on us rather than the world.

The more we influence civilization for good, the more the world will have to admit that the church possesses knowledge. Simply proclaiming our knowledge won't force the world to admit that we really do know things it doesn't. It can dismiss our proclamations as false, but it can't dismiss results. When Christians are doing a better job of accomplishing civilizational tasks as a result of the truth they learn in church, the world will be forced to concede that the church has knowledge.

This is analogous to the role miracles played in the work of the biblical prophets, Jesus included. Prophets did not just proclaim God's word. They were empowered to perform miracles, to demonstrate the validity of their message. How else could people distinguish true prophets from false ones (Deut. 18:21–22; Matt. 9:4–7; 11:2–6; John 9:1–7)?

Similarly, our ability to perform civilizational tasks better than the world validates our claim to possess knowledge. The world can't explain our success. According to the world's lights, everything Christians do ought to fail, since we believe so much ridiculous nonsense. Yet, inexplicably, Christians can do the world's things better than the world can. In the world's eyes, Christianity's civilizational success is as wondrous as a miracle. That's because it *is* a miracle. It is the result of the Spirit's miraculous transforming work in our minds, hearts, and lives.

Few things impact a civilization more profoundly than the question of who has knowledge. Those who are seen as lacking knowledge can be ignored, because those people depend on others for knowledge and will always end up following them. Those who are seen as having knowledge must be accounted for, one way or another.[7]

We saw before that there are two ways to have authority. One is to have the right to command, but the other is to possess and disseminate knowledge. The institutional church as an organization should never seek the first kind of authority, but it should always be seeking the second kind. If we both proclaim our knowledge to the world and also put it into action in civilization, both of which are necessary to discipleship, we will inevitably become recognized as having knowledge—and thus we will gain authority.

Some in the world will hate us for having knowledge and (therefore) power that they lack, and for attracting followers as we succeed in serving people better. But others in the world will sincerely value our contribution, even if they're not believers. They will want to benefit from our knowledge. And still others will resent us in their hearts, yet find it more useful to tolerate our rising influence rather than try to fight it.

Both the Bible and the history of our own civilization provide many examples of the world recognizing the church as a source of knowledge and valuing it—thus yielding to the church a level of influence over the direction of civilization. We see this during the two great captivities of the Old Testament church: Joseph in Egypt and Daniel in Babylon. Both men rose to the highest levels of civilizational power because they were able to perform the tasks of managing civilization better on account of their biblical knowledge. And although the American founding was not a Christian act as such, the founders did agree that pastors were vital sources of knowledge upon which American civilization depended.

Many are familiar with the famous passage in George Washington's farewell address where he extols the importance of religion to the republic. Unfortunately, the end of the passage is usually overlooked. After identifying "religion and morality" as "indispensable supports" of the nation, and stressing that we should not expect morality to flourish without religion, he concludes: "Promote then, as an object of primary importance, institutions for the general diffusion of knowledge. In proportion as the structure of a government gives force to public opinion, it is essential that public opinion should be enlightened." Do you see what this implies? *Washington thought religion was a source of knowledge.*

Compare Washington's view with that of our own time. Many Christians have achieved great success and reached positions of high power in the life of our civilization. A recent sociological study interviewed 360 Christians in the most elite social positions. The list included United States presidents and cabinet members; Ivy League professors; major league sports team owners; and officers of Fortune 500 companies, major television networks, and movie studios.[8] Yet no one outside the faith thinks Christianity contributed to these Christians' success. Why would they? They don't view religion as a source of knowledge, and we've done nothing to challenge that assumption.

Of the three offices we perform to the world, this one—prophecy—takes the longest time and the most intentional effort to produce an impact on civilization. My to-do list at work tomorrow isn't likely to create major opportunities for applying inside information about the universe. On a small scale, certainly there will be opportunities to put biblical knowledge into action, but it's not likely to be the kind of thing that will get a lot of attention quickly.

However, over the long term, if Christians work together to discern how biblical knowledge influences civilizational tasks, I think it's likely that this office presents the biggest opportunities for impact. In part 3 of this book we'll look at examples of how Christians have used biblical knowledge to transform civilization in major ways. We'll also look at how we can begin that process again in our own time.

If you're still skeptical, remember that there is continuity as well as discontinuity between the inside information we possess in the church and the knowledge God has made available to all through general revelation. The distinction between the two matters, and we should be careful to avoid collapsing it. But all truth is God's truth, so all forms of human knowledge are properly related and can be integrated, because all knowledge manifests aspects of God's mind. If there were no continuity between general and special revelation, we would have no way to recognize special revelation as true or good; one of the functions of general revelation is to equip us to receive special revelation. Failure to respect the continuity between general and special revelation is a form of dualism.

On the other hand, we need to remember that failure to respect the *discontinuity* between general and special revelation also leads to danger. We may deny the validity of sources of knowledge outside the church. This approach implicitly (or sometimes explicitly) denies that there is such a thing as general revelation. That violates the human dignity of non-Christians, and in practice it leads to an oppressive desire to dominate the unbeliever. Another mistake is to deny that there is any serious difference in kind between general and special revelation. This implicitly (or sometimes explicitly) denies the special work of the Spirit in creating the church, and in practice leads to cultural accommodation and captivity.

But when we respect both the continuity and the discontinuity between general and special revelation, we are equipped to carry out our role as prophets to the world. Like the prophets, we will often be hated. We can expect persecution. But, like the prophets, we will also be hearkened unto by many.

And, like the prophets, we will have carried out our commission from God in the only way God permits. Just remember what happened to the prophets who tried to avoid fulfilling their roles!

4

Devotion: Worship and Spiritual Formation

I will go to the altar of God,
to God my exceeding joy.

Ps. 43:4

Shortly after I was converted to Christianity, I told a pastor at my church that I was struggling because a lot of the people in my life thought Christianity was bad and dangerous. "They think religion makes people crazy," I said. "They're right," he replied. "Religion does make people crazy. Jesus makes people sane."

I knew what he meant. At an earlier period in my life, before I was really converted, I went through a pseudo-Christian phase. I thought I was Christian because I accepted as true—in my head—that God existed and that Jesus was Lord. But my heart and life never changed. I didn't even understand the gospel. I was just using the outward forms of Christianity to feed my phony sense of self-righteousness. Thinking about God made me feel like God approved of me, because I was a such a very good person. My "Christianity" was an excuse to wallow in the delusion of my own goodness. I was not a very pleasant person to be around! I lived up to every terrible stereotype of the self-righteous religious prig. Religion made me crazy.

It took the gospel to make me sane. The liberation of the gospel is the single most profound thing a human being can experience. It creates the joy of God in us by changing every aspect of our being—mind, heart, and life. From here, life begins again. The New Testament uses a very apt phrase when it describes the converted person as "a new creation."

We carry that joy, that fundamental transformation, out into civilization with us. It changes everything we do. We are social creatures, so a change of heart means a change in our relationships with others. Our lives in civilization are being re-created along with our hearts. That, in turn, changes civilization itself, insofar as we touch it.

I've been privileged to see firsthand how life in civilization can be the conduit through which one person's heart change can prompt the beginning of heart change in another person. The most dramatic case was a relative of mine who was raised in the church but walked away from the faith at an early age. Fifty years later, close to retirement, she asked my wife and I if we'd be willing to go see the movie *The Passion of the Christ* with her and talk about it afterward. Of course we did, and we talked about the good news. She was struggling to know what to think, and really wanted our help. At one point I asked her if she believed Jesus was alive or dead. She thought about it for a while and then said, slowly and deliberately, "I believe he is alive, because I've seen how he works in people's lives." I asked her where she'd seen that, and she described how her Christian coworkers had a completely different attitude about their jobs. She worked in a doctor's office filing medical records, which is a burdensome, repetitive job. The Christians in her office were the only people who came into work happy to be there. They were focused on how they were blessing people in their work instead of thinking about themselves. The way their devotion to Christ was embodied in their attitudes at work convinced my relative that Christ was alive and at work in the world. That day, she prayed to receive him. That week she started going back to church.

The heart change she saw in her coworkers was literally miraculous. It was the supernatural work of the Holy Spirit in their hearts. And just like the miraculous signs Jesus worked, their joy pointed others toward the supernatural power that caused it. But it only had the chance to do so because it was embodied in the life of American civilization, in that office. And while evangelism was necessary—my relative never would have known Christ if we hadn't been ready and willing to share the good news when the occasion arose—it was also necessary for her to go through that long, slow time of feeling and responding to Christian joy in that workplace year after year.

Human Religion and Slavery to Guilt and Fear

By nature, people are predisposed to use religion as a cloak for sin. They know in their hearts that they're guilty and judged, so they crave things that give them a sense of righteousness. They crave false dignity and false security. Nothing will do that for you like religion.

It's all a sham, of course. "Crazy" is just the right word for it. Nothing's more phony than people who think they're righteous in themselves. For sinful and fallen man, self-righteousness is the most common and most basic of all delusions. And delusions make people crazy—and make them do crazy things. Some of the craziest people of all are the religious crazies.

A lot of Christians associate the word "religion" only with ritualism and formalism. They don't even want to call Christianity a religion. I don't go that far, but I understand their point. The natural human tendency is to use religious forms as a substitute for a heart that loves God and neighbor.

By nature we don't love God—not the real God, the God who insists on being the only God, instead of letting us be God along with him. And by nature we don't love our neighbors—not really, not in the way that matters, not when we're called to sacrifice our advantage for their good.

However, we don't like to face up to these facts about ourselves. You will rarely find anyone, other than a Christian confessing his sinfulness, who will admit that he wants to be God or that he thinks it's just fine to live for nothing but your own advantage. Atheists almost always profess some kind of moral code and try hard to live up to it, even though they can't explain or justify why they do so. (All the serious atheists I've known have been extremely moral people. It's very noble, in a tragic way.) Even those few militant extremists who try to brazen it out and construct ideologies of self-worship, like Ayn Rand and her devotees, never stick to it consistently. You can always catch them contradicting themselves.

Our problem is that we can't change—not fundamentally, not in our heart of hearts. The basic tragedy of fallen humanity is that we are sinners and don't want to be sinners, but we can't stop being sinners. That's the life story of every person who lives apart from the gospel.

We can only change the shape of our sin. We can constrain our behavior in various ways, so that our sin works itself out differently. A pastor of mine once said that it's like the difference between crushing a tin can and crushing a Nerf ball. People think they can change themselves and become better people by constraining their behavior—just like crushing a tin can will change its shape. You crush the can, it stays crushed. But in reality, our sinful hearts are like Nerf balls. The shape does change when you squeeze it, but the new shape only remains while you squeeze. The moment you let go, *sproing!* It springs right back into the same sinful shape it was in before. And no one has the strength to squeeze the ball all the time.

Our slavery to sin makes us miserable in a thousand ways, but two of them stand out as the worst. We suffer from guilt—the dreadful knowledge that we are not good. And we suffer from fear—the dreadful knowledge that our lives and works will not end well, that we and all we care about will ultimately come to ruin. The specific negative consequences that we suffer as a result of our specific sins—the frustrations, dysfunctions, and impotencies we inflict on ourselves—are relatively light compared to the misery of living under a comprehensive bondage to guilt and fear.

Our slavery to guilt condemns us to suffer from a hunger for dignity. That hunger is perpetually frustrating and ultimately futile. While all people retain the dignity of God's image, fallen people can't rest in that dignity as long as they're not reconciled to God. So instead we turn to every variety of false dignity. In the parable of the prodigal son, the priggish older brother and the libertine younger brother proudly look down upon each other. The prig pretends he can derive dignity from his virtue and responsibility; the libertine pretends he can derive dignity from his freedom and authenticity. All of us do the same, in one form or another.

Our slavery to fear condemns us to suffer from a hunger for security. This hunger, too, is perpetually frustrating and ultimately futile. Obviously created beings can find security only in their Creator. In a universe that is under God's control, the only ultimate peace of mind comes from having God's favor. But fallen people don't have God's favor. So we turn to every variety of false security. The workaholic pretends that his work makes him secure; the miser pretends that his hoarded goods make him secure; the snob pretends that his social status makes him secure; the lothario pretends that his ability to seduce makes him secure; the sloth pretends that his detachment from external demands makes him secure.

✱ These two terrible hungers, for dignity and for security, enslave us. Religion is one of the main tools we use to relieve the symptoms of our bondage, to pretend that we aren't miserable. We invent a tame "God" who approves of us (relieving guilt, providing false dignity) and who will look after us (relieving fear, providing false security). We then arbitrarily select certain rituals and behaviors, which we designate as "things that good people do" and/or "things that will deliver blessings." Doing these things makes us feel like we're good people (relieving guilt, providing false dignity) and will receive blessings (relieving fear, providing false security).

Natural religion, religion that isn't made by the Holy Spirit, consists of manmade goods and services that help people alleviate the misery of their slavery to guilt and fear by providing false dignity and security. The actual slavery isn't alleviated, but the misery is—temporarily.

It's no wonder that people and civilizations are willing to sacrifice so much in order to obey and sustain their religions. Who can blame them? Relief from the misery of bondage to guilt and fear, even if it's temporary and imperfect, is worth almost any price.

This use of religion takes an endless variety of forms. Primitive civilizations tend to have relatively few religious professionals and institutions, but they exercise extremely strong social authority. Such civilizations' religions use simple stories and crude rituals, set relatively low ethical standards but enforce them strictly, and claim to offer supernatural intervention on a regular basis. As civilizations advance, the clergy and their institutions tend to grow, but their social authority becomes diluted among other sources of false dignity and security. Their stories tend to get more elaborate and their rituals more refined, ethical standards tend to get higher but enforcement tends to get looser, and supernatural intervention tends to be offered less frequently.

The one constant is that manmade religions adopt symbols that represent the presence of God. They keep these symbols at a distance from their daily lives, and use them to perform rituals that put them in touch with God. They don't even pretend to have a daily relationship with God—not a personal relationship, such as you have with another human being, where you talk to him and he talks to you, and you do things together. They need some sort of special communication system that connects them to God. They need to filter their encounter with God through religious forms. There is always a clear line of demarcation between living ordinary life and getting in touch with God.

The reason manmade religions treat their religious symbols this way is obvious: the tame "God" they've invented needs to be controlled. If he were to start interfering with daily life—if we really knew God and did things with him every day, the way we know our neighbors and do things with them—that must lead to one of two unwanted results. The tame God might demand that we change; in that case, he would no longer relieve our guilt and fear, since we can't change. Or else the tame God might approve of our lives—not our lives as we like to think of them, but as they actually are in daily reality. In that case he would no longer be credible as a dispenser of approval and blessing, since he would be approving daily lives that are sinful.

Free at Last!

The gospel creates the joy of God by liberating people from this self-imposed prison of insanity. It's the only thing that can. The whole world is sunk very deep in a dark and miserable pit of despairing madness, and it is the high and holy privilege of the church to be used of God in curing people and pulling them out of the pit.

The wild ecstasy of emotion Christians feel about their God, which the world laughs at so easily, is perfectly reasonable. How would you feel if you'd been tortured in prison all your life and someone freed you? Don't ever let the world's laughter get to you; they only laugh to keep themselves from crying.

The Holy Spirit creates the church through regeneration—literally, rebirth. Conversion is not a matter of deciding to change religions, it is the beginning of an entirely new life. After all, the beginning of a new life is exactly what "birth" consists of. Jesus famously said to Nicodemus that no one can even *see* the kingdom of God unless he has been born again, and this new birth comes from the Spirit (John 3:3–8).

To understand that passage, you have to remember that Nicodemus was very religious. As a Pharisee, he strictly obeyed religious laws that governed his actions all day, every day. As a member of the Sanhedrin, he was a religious leader at the highest levels of the community's clerical structure. Franklin Graham has wisely remarked that there isn't a church anywhere in America that wouldn't be proud to have Nicodemus as a member.[1]

Yet when Nicodemus came to Jesus with all that religiosity, Jesus's response (to borrow further from Graham) was: it's not enough. It's not enough that you're religious, it's not enough that you tithe, it's not enough that you do all those good works and obey all those rules. All of it, no matter how much of it there is, is just not enough. Nicodemus, your heart has to change!

Only the Holy Spirit can change the heart. He removes our hearts of stone, that are so cold to God and our neighbors, and he gives us new hearts. He gives us hearts that work properly, hearts that love like they should.

At the moment we receive regeneration from the Holy Spirit, we are set free from guilt and fear. We are free from guilt because we are justified in Christ. We have been declared to be righteous, which means we *are* righteous, because when God declares something, it becomes true. (If you doubt it, see Genesis 1.) And we are free from fear because we know we have God's favor. We know it will never be taken away from us because we have it as a free gift. If you think you're getting God's favor by earning it, you always have to fear you'll lose it. Once you have God's favor as a free gift, there's nothing left to fear (Rom. 8:38–39). That's what John meant when he wrote that "perfect love casts out fear" (1 John 4:18).

We still sin in spite of our justification, and we still suffer all sorts of trials even though we have God's favor. That's beside the point. Our sins no longer enslave us to guilt because we know we have been declared righteous, and our trials no longer enslave us to fear because we know that God is using them to purify us from sin. Whatever trials we endure, the final outcome of our existence is assured: "We know that for those who love God all things work together for good" (Rom. 8:28). We can even rejoice in the Lord as we persevere through trials and suffering (Rom. 5:3; 1 Pet. 1:6). Although we still sin, our lives are different, because our hearts are different. Our behavior changes. The whole book of 1 John is about this. John says that his purpose in writing is to explain how we can have assurance that our faith is genuine and saving, how we can know for sure that we're not self-deceived (1 John 5:13). Accordingly, he uses the phrase "we know" thirteen times in the letter. For example:

- By this we know that we have come to know him, if we keep his commandments (2:3).
- We know that we have passed out of death into life, because we love the brothers (3:14).
- By this we know that he abides in us, by the Spirit whom he has given us (3:24).
- Whoever knows God listens to us; whoever is not from God does not listen to us. By this we know the Spirit of truth and the spirit of error (4:6).
- By this we know that we love the children of God, when we love God and obey his commandments (5:2).

John is careful to note that he is not saying the true believer never sins (1 John 1:8–10). He's saying that the true believer is struggling not to sin, does not acquiesce to the power of sin, and is overcoming sin more and more over time.

It's hard to sum up the fundamental difference in heart between regenerate and unregenerate persons, given that they both sin. The regenerate person is not content to be a sinner.[2] The unregenerate person may *regret* that he's a sinner, but he is *resigned* to being one. The best he can do is set up some border or frontier with his sin—he lets it go this far and no further. Within that boundary he's willing to live with it. Only the regenerate person actually strives, actively, toward the eradication of all his sin.

For this reason, one of the most fundamental elements of the Christian life is our continual effort to uncover and remove our sin. As C. S. Lewis said, God will forgive any number of failures in this effort. The only fatal thing is to give up on it.[3]

Putting heart change into practice is a challenge. We're no longer slaves of sin, but we still sin. The heart is deceitful above all things (Jer. 17:9). While God liberates our hearts from slavery to sin, a significant tendency to self-deception remains with us. So the Christian life is a challenging one; we have a lot of sin to uncover and struggle against.

Here's an example from my own life. After my conversion, when I would assess myself, I felt sure that greed wasn't one of my problems. Throughout my career, whenever I had to make a tough choice, I always chose my intellectual conscience and my family's needs over professional advancement. Then one day, my employer adopted a new compensation scheme that I thought was unfair. I blew a gasket. It turned out I was unconsciously enslaved to greed—in the form of "security for my family" and "fairness." I was still hungry for false security. Thankfully, my boss was a fellow Christian, whom I had discussed these things with, and he called me out on this. I realized I had more repenting to do than I had thought. And then I began to realize how many other ways greed was affecting me—and worse, how much false dignity I still had.

New Birth Always Produces New Life

Technically, this discussion of regeneration is starting to get into sanctification, which means cleaning up the continuing sin in our lives. The distinction between the two is very important theologically, for reasons we'll see in a moment. But in practice it's tough to draw a line between "being aware of my regeneration" and "pursuing my sanctification." If you look at how regeneration manifests itself in human life, you're going to end up looking at sanctification. I'll save most of the discussion of sanctification for chapter 5, but to treat regeneration properly we have to say something about it here.

Earlier, I compared the ecstasy of the new birth with the ecstasy of a prisoner liberated after a lifetime of torture. There's another way in which the life of a Christian resembles that of the freed prisoner. This one is more challenging.

That frenzied explosion of joyous emotion the prisoner experiences when he's set free isn't going to last forever. It's not even going to last a week. Pretty soon, that freed prisoner is going to have to develop some kind of functioning life. He can't just go around being ecstatic that he's free and do nothing else. As he develops a new life for himself, his joy will change. Instead of just being happy that he's free, he will be happy that he's free *to live the life he's now living*. This will be a quieter, less exciting kind of happiness, but it will be deeper and more fulfilling—a sustained joy.

If he keeps going back and trying to whip up that original frenzy of emotion from his moment of liberation, he'll make himself miserable. His liberation from prison is still the foundation of his new life, and no doubt his mind will go back to that moment of liberation frequently. But if he doesn't learn to live the new life and find joy in that, then he wasn't set free *for* anything. The liberation was really worthless. He might just as well have stayed in prison.

The life of the church flows out from the heart change of regeneration, and the resulting continual striving to eradicate sin. This is the critical difference between merely making a decision to "convert" in a superficial way (like walking down an aisle to the altar) and really converting to Christ. Those who are not transformed radically (literally, at the roots) have not been converted. The transformation takes time to work itself out in our actions, a process that continues for the rest of our lives and is not completed until we are purified of all sin after death.

However, while the transformation takes time to work itself out, the transformation is the crucial starting point. You can't even begin the process of cleaning up the sin in your life until you've had a radical heart change. The reason is simple: you can't obey the law of God until you love God and know you have his favor.

If you don't love God, your attempts at obedience are really just selfishness. You're greedy for the blessings that only God can bestow, and you want to be a spiritual mercenary, selling your obedience to God in exchange for the goodies he can give you. Likewise, if you don't know for sure whether you have God's favor, you won't be able to escape the fear of punishment, the need to sell your obedience to God in exchange for his favor. That kind of obedience isn't really obedience at all, because "love me and trust me" is the first moral law God wants us to obey. God doesn't hire mercenaries. The new birth from the Holy Spirit is the only thing that can cause you to love God and know you have his favor, and thus put you in a position to begin really obeying.

You cannot slowly improve yourself and work your way up to a transformation of the heart. It is only because of the transformation that you are able to really improve your life at all, as opposed to merely changing the shape of your sin. That's why it's theologically important to distinguish regeneration from sanctification; regeneration has to come first, and sanctification has to follow.

This point is often overlooked. Because we are not yet perfect, we are continually tempted to treat the church as though it were a system for working on ourselves until we have gotten to the point where we can announce, "My heart has changed!" We want the church to give us things we can do to work our way into the new birth. That's just another version of the "religious goods and services" model. It's a way of using religion to make us feel as if we're doing what we ought to do. The church helps us feel like we're doing the things good people do, the things that will bring blessings.

The church is not a system for working people up to the new birth. It is the community of people who have undergone it. The church doesn't create new hearts; the church is created *by* new hearts. The Holy Spirit creates the church by giving us new hearts.

Evangelism is important, but the church is not a convert factory. If we think we can manufacture converts, we're really holding to works righteousness. We're acting as if people can get right with God as a result of human effort. We must remember that only the Spirit can work conversion, and therefore the church is defined not by our production of converts, but by his.

Regeneration for Intimacy, Intimacy for Joy

In the church, regeneration produces the joy of God by creating intimacy with God. We have immediate (literally—without an intermediary, with nothing in between) access to our Lord and Savior. We know him as a person and have a real daily relationship with him.

What does a personal relationship consist of? Above all, it consists of regular direct communication and interaction. Without regular direct communication, there may be a relationship, but it will be impersonal in nature. If there is regular direct communication but it only goes one way, with one party doing all the speaking, then there's no interaction. It's hard to call that a relationship since neither party is really relating to the other.

Regular two-way, direct communication and interaction with God is exactly what we have as a result of our reconciliation in Jesus. God speaks to us in the Bible, and he acts upon us as the Spirit applies his Word to our hearts. We respond by speaking to God in prayer. That's why Bible study and prayer are so essential to the Christian life. The more you read the Bible and really learn from it, the more God will speak into your life through the work of the Spirit in your heart, applying to you what you've learned. Remember, the Bible is God's Word, and God is really speaking to you when you read it. If Jesus himself appeared to you in person, handed you a letter, and asked you to read it, how long would you wait before tearing it open? Learning the Bible brings us into interaction with God. Prayer is equally important, of course, because that's how the communication becomes two-way.

One of the most amazing revelations in the Bible is that God loves us personally. This is really unique to biblical religion; you never find it in manmade religion. Aristotle depicts a God who couldn't possibly love us, because what would an infinite and perfect being find to love in puny, wicked creatures like us?[4] Aristotle made a terrible error, but from a merely natural standpoint, his view had a lot of plausibility to it. Only biblical revelation provides any reliable ground for thinking that God loves us.

Because God loves us personally and we have a real relationship with him, Christian worship doesn't use symbols to keep the presence of God at a distance. It uses symbols to remind us that God is always with us. And it doesn't provide special systems for getting in touch with God. We're always in touch with God. All we have to do is open our Bibles (to read) and open our mouths (to pray).

This is why God gave us the second commandment. Most people don't realize this, but the second commandment was given primarily to regulate worship within the church rather than to condemn the use of idols among foreign religions. Aaron didn't present the golden calf to the Israelites as a new god to replace the Lord, but as a symbol of the Lord himself. He attributed the Lord's acts to the calf and even called it by the Lord's special covenant name (Ex. 32:4–5). Similarly, in every age the church must struggle against the temptation to point to something and say, "This is the thing that connects you to Jesus." The second commandment is necessary because, in our sinfulness, we don't want to be *too* intimate with God! We want to identify God's presence with a symbol so we can isolate God's presence and keep it from being with us always.

When we awaken from our sin, because of our personal relationship with God we worship him in spirit and in truth (John 4:23–24). This means our worship is not a system for getting right with him. It is an expression of the personal love between him and us—an expression of intimacy.

As is proper for a personal relationship, the worship service embodies two-way communication. God speaks to us (from the

Bible) and acts upon us (by the Spirit) during the worship service. We speak to him through things like prayer and song.

God also touches us physically, by giving us the sacraments. Physical touch is indispensable to love relationships. That's why the Lord's Supper is an indispensable element of intimacy with Jesus. Although Jesus's flesh and blood are not physically present in the Lord's Supper, they are really and truly present spiritually—present to our faith. By ordaining the Lord's Supper, Jesus touches us physically. The bread and wine are his instruments for touching us.

In the Old Testament temple, God's people did not actually make the sacrifice; only the priests did that. But when people brought sacrifices, they sometimes had the privilege of participating in the ritual of sacrifice by eating the sacrificed flesh. This holy meal was a sign and seal of God's acceptance of the sacrifice and the extension of its benefits to his people. Similarly, we do not actually make the sacrifice that saves us from our sin; Jesus did that once for all time back in Palestine. But we are privileged to participate in the sacrificial ritual by spiritually (not physically) eating the sacrificed flesh. This holy meal is a sign and seal of God's acceptance of Jesus's once-for-all ultimate sacrifice and the extension of its benefits to us.[5]

I used to attend a church that held the Lord's Supper every week. The pastor would say that your mother doesn't just *say* she loves you, she seals that love to you with a hug and a kiss. God tells us he loves us in the sermon, and in the Lord's Supper God seals his love to us with a physical act. "This is God's hug and kiss," the pastor used to say before distributing the bread and wine. I don't want to get sidetracked by complicated theological debates, but I do want to note that the only time in my life I have ever consistently, reliably felt the presence of God in worship every week was in that church—because in that church, Jesus touched us physically every week.

The life of the church doesn't stop with the worship service.

✳ Spiritual formation, the building up of believers in godliness, isn't something that can be accomplished with an hour a week of treatment. This is why churches have small groups, accountability partnerships, and all the other things they offer to build us up.

Worship and Civilization

Human beings are formed by their civilizations, and this is especially true when it comes to understanding how relationships work. Our sense of what is appropriate in a relationship cannot help but be formed by the civilization in which we are reared. Thus, since the worship service is an expression of our relationship with God, it will necessarily reflect our civilizational formation. God doesn't mind that; it's how he made us.

The same need for civilizational awareness that we looked at in the last chapter in the context of the sermon applies equally to the whole worship service. If the service is to embody our experience of God's presence and our communion with him, pastors must take into account the ways in which our civilization has shaped how we experience relationships of every kind. Certainly our relationship with God is unique, but it is still a relationship, and our social formation in civilization is the apparatus by which each of us enters into relationships, including this one.

We evangelicals are famously contentious about the content of the worship service—everything from liturgy to church architecture, and above all the music. We have partisans of gorgeous buildings, elaborately structured liturgy, and highly refined music (such as from soloists, choirs, and traditional instrumental groups) to convey the majesty and wonder of God. We have partisans of large but functional buildings, zealous and emotional liturgies, and highly accessible music (such as that which requires no reading of musical notes and can be projected on a screen) to facilitate as much ecstatic experience of God for as many people as possible. We have partisans of humble buildings, simple liturgy, and music that is refined enough to produce harmony but is still accessible with moderate effort (such as that in traditional hymnbooks) to convey the intimacy of God's loving presence.

When we fight over these things, we typically presuppose that these cultural forms have a fixed meaning. But of course they don't. What feels beautiful and majestic to one feels cold and snobbish to another. What one finds accessible and intimate, the other finds lazy and complacent. One of my best friends insists that churches should be big and beautiful, like the European cathedrals. Only that kind of worship space, he says, can make you feel the awesome majesty of God. To me, though, those buildings look more like works of art than places of worship. I feel God's presence much more in small, unadorned spaces. I even feel more humble before God in those intimate settings. In a cathedral, I feel so humble in the overwhelming presence of the amazing building that I don't even notice God.

Don't even get me started about music. My Christmas experiences as a child notwithstanding, in general I produce only very shallow emotional responses to music, and am bored by most hymns. Moreover, I have no musical ear, so I am usually unable to sing in churches that don't provide sheet music to show me the notes. Like C. S. Lewis, my preference during worship would be to have fewer hymns, shorter hymns, and better hymns—in that order.[6]

But I recognize that all these preferences about worship spaces, music, and so forth are relative to my own personal makeup. Others have different responses. I try to remember this and stay humble; sometimes I succeed.

Here's another opportunity for pastors to develop civilizational sensitivity. No church is safe, because there are multiple dangers against which pastors must be on guard. On the one hand, the idolization of individual choice in our society may tempt us to reduce the worship service to a consumer product. The highly accessible, emotional service is particularly at risk in this area. On the other hand, our merely aesthetic and tasteful reaction against what we view as cultural vulgarity may tempt us to bring "highbrow" cultural forms into the worship service for the wrong reasons—to show off that we're not like those vulgar, consumerized churches. The highly refined, aesthetically impressive service is at risk here. Yet again, anxiety about both of those dangers leads some to try to avoid cultural forms altogether, which denies the social nature God gave us. The simple, intimate service, which I love so well, is at risk here. All three types of service can be glorious in their distinctive ways, if they avoid these dangers. None is safe if pastors aren't on guard against them.

Spiritual formation beyond the worship service is likewise informed by our civilizational context. This is typically more obvious, and there's not much need to dwell on it here. Listen to any conversation among ministry leaders, or read any book about how small groups work or the difficulty of introducing spiritual disciplines. You won't have to wait long before the discussion turns to the distinctive ways Americans organize their lives and how these create challenges and opportunities for ministry.

Worship and Religious Freedom

Perhaps the most important way in which contemporary American civilization impacts the worship experience is through freedom of religion. In many ways, freedom of religion is an unspeakable blessing that opens up unique aspects of the experience of God's presence in worship. In places where the church is state-sponsored, the entire worship service is haunted by the specter of hypocrisy. Even where the church's faith is genuine and it speaks with prophetic integrity, congregants (and pastors, for that matter) can never have the same confidence in its genuineness and integrity that we enjoy thanks to religious freedom. Meanwhile, in places where the church is persecuted, every aspect of the service becomes an act of social defiance. Sincerity is obviously not a problem here, but social opposition can create its own temptations to cultural captivity. Looking over our shoulders during worship to see if the powerful are watching us is a hindrance to real devotion regardless of whether we are doing it because we're afraid or because we covet their approval. To be able to walk into church and hold a service in which state power plays no role, other than to protect our right to worship according to our consciences—to be able to forget the state entirely when we kneel before God—is a rare and high privilege for which we should be continually grateful.

Nonetheless, for fallen creatures like us, every blessing carries with it a distinct occasion of temptation to abuse it. This is as true of religious freedom as of all other blessings. One temptation is to stay home and create substitutes for church life in our isolated personal and family lives. We see this in believers and unbelievers alike. The cause is not simply that people pay no penalty for not attending, although that is one aspect of the challenge. The deeper problem (as we have already seen in chap. 1) is that the institutional grounding for the duty to attend church is unstable. Civilizations need institutions to create clear signals of what behavior is expected. Where the role of the church in civilization is ambiguous—which, as we saw in chapter 1, is essential to religious freedom—it's not always clear whose responsibility it is to send signals that people ought to be in church.

Another, closely related problem is the reduction of church life to merely a voluntary association. Now, *legally* the church ought to be a voluntary association; people should not be forced by law to attend! But we should not think of the church exclusively in those terms. My primary reason for attending church should be that the Lord has transformed me and brought me into relationship with his people, not that attending church happens to gratify my personal desires. Going to church is certainly very good for you and your family, but church should not be reduced to a product that we market to people because it will benefit them or their families. (Remember the temptation to "religious goods and services.") Another way of putting this is that my identity as a Christian should be voluntary rather than compulsory, grounded in real faith; but if I do in fact believe, I should not regard church life as something I am free to accept or reject. My rebirth has put me into relationship with God's people, and that is an objective fact, whether I choose to acknowledge it or not. Failing to acknowledge that I am part of the family of God and failing to live in relationship with his people is as sinful as failing to acknowledge and engage in the familial, economic, and community relationships in which I am embedded as a social creature.

Another temptation is to think about people outside the church primarily or even exclusively in terms of their choice not to be in the church. Certainly if our neighbors don't go to church, we don't want to ignore that fact about them. It is something we'd like to see change, and we'd like to help that change occur in the right way. And the church does have a legitimate need to distinguish itself from the world (1 John 2:15–17). But the social environment created by freedom of religion creates a temptation to view our unbelieving neighbors exclusively as unbelievers, rather than thinking of them as fellow human beings, as fellow citizens, as coworkers, as relatives—as *neighbors*. If we truly believe that it is not Paul or Apollos but God who gives the growth (1 Cor. 3:6), we should be humble and remember that *we do not stand between these people and God*. Our job is to love them. That includes telling them the good news, but it also includes looking at them and treating them as fellow human beings, not reducing them to nothing more than potential converts and/or spiritual enemies of the church. We will not love our neighbors the way we ought to if we view them only as potential converts, still more if we view them only as spiritual enemies (which they are, alas, as long as they deny Christ). We have to treat people as though we cared about them as people, for their own sake, and not merely because of their decision not to be in the church. (In case you're wondering, the easiest way to treat people as though you cared about them as people for their own sake is to actually care about them as people for their own sake.)

Liberated Life in Civilization

When the church helps its people live out the joy of God through a personal relationship with God in Christ through the Spirit, the result is freedom from guilt and fear. Since slavery to guilt and fear overshadows all aspects of human life, that precious liberation has a transformative effect on everything we do. Through that Spirit-led transformation in our own lives, our relationships change and we influence the civilization around us.

Our devotion gives us freedom from the frustrating and futile quests for false dignity and false security that consume the lives of our neighbors. Our participation in civilization is how we most clearly distinguish ourselves from the world.

The institutions and activities that define civilization are where human beings most often seek false dignity and security. In fact, very often the desire for false dignity and security crowds out everything else. The legitimate functions of the home, the workplace, and civic life are constantly subordinated to the use of these very institutions for alleviating guilt and fear. In classical Greece and Rome people looked primarily to civic institutions; during the Industrial Revolution it was primarily the workplace; during the Victorian era it was primarily family (earlier, too—we see this prefigured in Jane Austen's novels). The names change, but the game stays the same.

Christian participation in these activities and institutions, however, is radically different insofar as it reflects our freedom. In the home we are free to focus on sustaining a flourishing holistic life partnership and the nurturing of children. In the workplace we are free to focus on serving customers and meeting people's needs. In the community we are free to focus on preserving justice and the freedom to flourish for all citizens.

In short, we are free from what might be called the "culturally high" sins. By this I mean the sins we pursue primarily by perverting civilizational activities and institutions. These are the sins whose primary motivation is to provide a false sense of dignity and security. They include greed, envy, covetousness, workaholism, wrathfulness, and grudge-holding, among much else.

The difference this makes on a daily basis is dramatic and immediately noticeable. Watch a family interact for even a few minutes and you can always tell who is putting the family first and who is using family relationships to feed their egos. Hang around a workplace and you can quickly tell who's there to serve customers and who's there to take home a paycheck. Listen in on a meeting of a community group of any kind and you can pick out who's there to benefit the community and who's there to feel important.

Our changed attitudes and behaviors have an impact on the world around us. Families tend to flourish only when their members put the other family members first. Businesses tend to flourish only when they make serving the customer top priority. Communities tend to flourish only when their civic institutions serve the public good instead of private willfulness.

Lewis summarizes the difference this attitude makes in his exceptional graduation address, "The Inner Ring." He describes how large portions of life in the world are taken up by people's efforts to become insiders, to be accepted in one or another "inner ring" of important or prestigious or enlightened people. He warns the new graduates that they will fall into this way of life themselves unless they make efforts to avoid it. But if they do, they will discover the existence of a whole alternate world of delightful activity and friendship, invisible to the people Lewis calls "inner ringers." This alternate world is the real inner ring, the place where people can do their work the way it's supposed to be done, and have real friendships and loves:

> If in your working hours you make the work your end, you will presently find yourself all unawares inside the only circle in your profession that really matters. You will be one of the sound craftsmen, and other sound craftsmen will know it. . . . And if in your spare time you consort simply with the people you like, you will again find that you have come unawares to a real inside. . . .

This is friendship. Aristotle placed it among the virtues. It causes perhaps half of all the happiness in the world, and no Inner Ring can ever have it.[7]

Lewis emphasizes that life in this alternate inner ring is happier and more virtuous, but he also notes that it has a major transformative impact on civilization. The people who don't need to get into the inner ring are the people who really keep a civilization going:

> This group of [sound] craftsmen will by no means coincide with the Inner Ring or the Important People or the People in the Know. It will not shape that professional policy or work up that professional influence which fights for the profession as a whole against the public: nor will it lead to those periodic scandals and crises which the Inner Ring produces. But it will do those things which that profession exists to do and will in the long run be responsible for all the respect which that profession in fact enjoys and which the speeches and advertisements cannot maintain.[8]

That assessment resonates powerfully with my own experience, and with many accounts I've heard from others. The network of people Lewis calls the "sound craftsmen" are the people who prop up every profession in the long run.

You can be a sound craftsman without being a Christian. But God's people ought to be overrepresented among the sound craftsmen. The freedom we get from the Spirit should be making every Christian more and more into a sound craftsman.

Of course, as with doctrine, we don't want our devotion judged by whether it has an impact on civilization. The same principles apply. Devotion isn't devotion if it looks to the world for its standard; captivity to relevance is the quickest path to irrelevance. However, we'd be foolish to shut our eyes to the impact our devotion has on those around us.

In chapter 3 I said that prophesy was the office that took the longest to have an impact. The office we perform through our personal relationship with Jesus—priesthood—is the one that works the most immediate change. Not only does my to-do list for tomorrow provide opportunities to do things in a radically different way because of my personal relationship with Jesus, it in fact contains nothing that doesn't provide such an opportunity.

By itself, however, the societal impact of priesthood is the most local and short-lived. If devotion isn't integrated with sound doctrine and good stewardship, it will give us changed attitudes but not changed lives. Nor will it spread the change beyond the immediate circle of the person who instigated it. A changed attitude simply by itself doesn't change much. Lewis is right that sound craftsmen have influence and importance in civilization not simply because they don't care about being in the inner ring, but because they get things done. So must the church.

5

Stewardship: Calling and Discipleship

Weeping may tarry for the night,
but joy comes with the morning.

Ps. 30:5

Christians often fall back into the natural "religious goods and services" model we saw in chapter 4, and they seem to be doing so more now than at any time in recent memory. Instead of practicing discipleship in all of life, American evangelicals mostly seem to define what it means to live a Christian life in terms of the roughly 2 percent of our time we spend performing religious works: attending corporate worship, Bible study, evangelism, volunteering at church, giving, etc. Who lives the life devoted to God? Religious professionals—pastors and missionaries. I believe this has become the single greatest danger facing the church in America today.

I recently attended a conference on Christians in business, hosted by a prominent evangelical seminary. The first speaker described how he had grown up believing that only pastors—and especially missionaries—were truly serving God. "When I figured out that God wasn't calling me to be a pastor," he said, "I felt gypped." For the rest of the conference, speaker after speaker echoed this experience, which I have found to be typical among lay Christians across America. Others have found the same thing.[1]

God calls most people to live "the life devoted to God" as lay-people rather than clergy. When the church remembers this, everything in church life is different. The church equips Christians to practice discipleship in all of life rather than 2 percent of life. Discipleship is a new way of doing 100 percent of what we do in a different way, rather than a separate set of special activities (i.e., religious goods and services) that we occasionally find time to squeeze into our schedules.

Nothing illustrates this problem more clearly than the way most American churches think about stewardship. With rare exceptions, that word now refers only to religious works, especially tithing. "Stewardship Sunday" is when the church asks for money. As we'll see in more detail below, that's a major deficiency in our theology.

Practicing good stewardship in all of life is as critical to the joy of God as doctrine and devotion. It determines whether our head knowledge and heart experience of God will be an isolated part of our lives or have a transformative impact on the way we carry out our tasks and roles in our homes, workplaces, and communities.

This in turn transforms our relationships and the institutions that embody them. In fact, stewardship in all of life—the office of kingship—is the most important connection point between the church and civilization. While the king needs to integrate his work with the prophet and the priest, for all the reasons we've seen, it is the king whose work is most relevant to the question of how the church influences the direction of society.

A World Made for Joy

The joy of God is meant to take place in the world. That's why the world is here. God made the world so we could live out the joy of God in it.

Joy is not an emotion, it's a life lived for God. He originally designed human beings to live for his purposes, not our own. Life devoted to God's purposes may cut against the grain of our fallen sinfulness, but it completely accords with the nature we were created with. God originally created human beings to worship him and to bless one another. This truth is not only clear in Genesis, it runs all the way from one end of the Bible to the other. The purpose of human life is worship and service, and we are designed such that we flourish best when we carry out our purpose.

In practice, this means we should be *cultivating blessings out of the creation order.* We're here to make the world a better place. God gives us a whole universe that's packed full of potential blessings. From kind words and simple deeds we can all do every day, to the invention of entirely new products, services, ministries, and organizations, there's a whole world of blessings out there waiting to be brought into being. We were created to take potential blessing and turn it into actual blessing.

In the Bible, the story of cultivation begins in Genesis. We were designed specifically to cultivate blessing from the creation order (Gen. 2:15), and sent out on a mission to have stewardship over all of creation and cultivate blessing from it (Gen. 1:28). After the disaster of the fall and the curse of the flood, this same purpose for human life was reaffirmed with Noah (Gen. 9:1–17) and embodied in Old Testament law (e.g., Ex. 20:9) and wisdom (e.g., Ps. 128:2; Prov. 12:11–14). This provided the backdrop for the New Testament, where our purpose was reaffirmed again: "Whatever you do, work heartily, as for the Lord and not for men. . . . You are serving the Lord Christ" (Col. 3:23–24).[2]

I find the juxtaposition of three parables in Matthew 25 particularly striking.[3] The parable of the ten virgins teaches us to take God's calling to new life with utmost seriousness and urgency. The parable of the talents teaches us what it means to take that calling seriously. Merely avoiding sinful behavior is not enough; that's burying your talent. We have been equipped to cultivate blessing in the world, and we are responsible to bear fruit.[4] Then, the parable of the sheep and the goats teaches us what fruitful service means: creating blessings for those who need them.

The calling to make the world a better place is much larger now that the church has been sent out into all the earth with a mission to the nations. Instead of being embodied in one nation, as in the Old Testament, God's people carry this distinctive way of life out into all the nations of the earth.

This is why most people spend most of their lives in civilizational activity. God wants it that way. The home, workplace, and community are the main places we bless other people and improve their lives. That's what God wants us to be doing! He designed us to spend most of our time living and working in those civilizational arenas. A few people are specially called to the clergy, of course, and their role is greatly precious. But for the rest of us, religious works take up only a small portion of our time because that's the way God wants it. He wants us to do those special works, of course, but then he wants us out in the world with the rest of our time, living and working to bless our neighbors.

It's not all exciting and inspiring, of course. The world is still fallen. A lot of our job in the world is to clean up all the various messes sin has made in God's world, and we often experience that as something we *have to* do instead of something we *get to* do.

But as tough as it can be, this is the kind of life that offers the joy of God, and no other life does. We don't have the joy of God merely in spite of the hardships we endure. Knowing that God is seeing us through, miraculously giving us the strength to accomplish good things for our neighbors in spite of toil, is itself a key part of our joy. We rejoice in all that God empowers us to do.

No Heart Change without Life Change

The Spirit's work in creating the joy of God does not stop with inspiration and regeneration. After we're converted, he works to gradually remove the influence of sin from our lives and magnify the power of love in our hearts and actions. He makes us holy, conforming our lives to the righteousness we received in Christ by grace through faith.

Sanctification must follow regeneration. That statement has two meanings, and both are important. The first is that sanctification must *follow* regeneration. You have to possess the righteousness of Christ first, and then your life can become conformed to that righteousness; you need a changed heart that will act from the right motives before your life can please God. During the Reformation, the Reformers stressed this point, and it was the right point to stress at that time.

I believe in our time it is more urgent to stress the other meaning: sanctification *must* follow regeneration. All truly converted people will in fact be undergoing sanctification from the moment they are converted until the moment they die. You may stumble and fall any number of times, and you may not understand what the Lord is doing with you at any given moment. But if you are not gradually making progress in holiness over time, you were never converted and are still spiritually dead.

Obviously, we never want to rest on our good works for our standing with God. He knows we can never do the kind of good works that would earn his favor. That's why he's so displeased with self-righteous moral effort, and at the same time so pleased to see his children making moral progress no matter how far short they still fall.

However, it's equally disastrous to rest on heart change without life change. Good intentions aren't enough. God cares about what we do, not just what we feel. Too often, we *say* we're putting our good intentions into action, when we're still complacently resting on our good intentions.

God isn't satisfied with a changed heart. He starts with a changed heart, because nothing else is going to go right without that. The changed heart is the foundation of the royal temple that he's building you into. But the purpose of a foundation is to have stuff built on top of it. If you construct the world's best-built foundation and then don't put anything on it, you've wasted your time.

Stewardship in Civilization

One of the major ways the Spirit creates the joy of God in us through sanctification is by restoring our lives in civilization to conformity with God's design. Since we live the majority of our lives in civilizational activities, this is one of the most important forms of sanctification. If our participation in our homes, workplaces, and communities is not sanctified, we are not going to make much progress in sanctification. If we want the church to deliver a serious call to holiness, it's critical that we understand sanctification and discipleship as (in part) reorienting our social nature and civilizational life to God.

Thus our lives in the world are no less spiritually significant than our religious works. Church attendance and other religious works are special because they only exist at all due to the work of the Spirit. They are unique to the community of believers, and they play a necessary role that nothing else can play. But they are not special in terms of their spiritual significance. Everything we do is spiritually significant; all of life is comprehended together in our walk with God. The Spirit uses all our works, not just our religious works, to transform us.

You can't even strictly separate religious works from life in the world. Our religious works have to be part of a total integrated life in which all things work together to glorify God. This is an especially important concern in the New Testament era. In ancient Israel, God's people lived in a distinct civilization constituted by its covenant commitment to the Lord. Because we now live in every civilization, we have to be all the more attentive to how our faith should inform everything we do.

When we treat our religious works as more spiritual than our lives in the world, we are falling back into the "religious goods and services" model of the church. We're building up a separate set of special activities to connect us to God. It's nearly impossible to avoid ritualism and formalism once we go down this road, and what lies at the end of the road is legalism.

Yet too many churches today don't cultivate this call to sanctification in all of life. What does a godly life look like in the context of early twenty-first-century America? There are lots of opinions about that—which is another way of saying that Christianity as such has little to say about it at all. Other than "be a nice person and don't look at porn," the church does not offer a coherent witness and teaching to its people on what their relationship with Christ should look like when it's lived out in their lives beyond the church walls. It seems to me that most pastors don't even try to describe discipleship in terms of a whole life—and no wonder, since Christianity seems to have no coherent teaching to offer. Pastors don't want to teach their personal opinions as though they were church teaching, and they don't have a church teaching to offer.

With discipleship increasingly reduced to religious works in American churches, the gospel itself is at stake. Churches have become less and less able to guide us effectively on what a Christian life looks like. In fact, the church really only gives us one way to identify a Christian life: religious works. Other than abstract ethical injunctions ("be a nice person and don't look at porn") the only way the church knows how to describe the Christian life is to emphasize showing up in church, reading your Bible, praying, evangelizing, and—of course—tithing. This tends to whittle down the meaning of discipleship until it gradually comes to be defined exclusively in terms of religious works. Discipleship is 2 percent of your life. But don't worry, it's a *special* 2 percent that will get you right with God. Buy these religious goods and services, and you can rest content with a family, workplace, and community life that's safe, comfortable, and totally irrelevant to God.

Oh, wait, that reminds me. The Council of Trent called. They want an apology.

One of the clearest signs that we're losing our grip on discipleship is our narrow concept of "stewardship." As I've noted, that word now includes only religious works (especially tithing) in most of American evangelicalism today. In fact, stewardship should be the very last thing we define in terms of specifically religious works. Biblically, stewardship means exercising our God-given responsibility as human beings over the creation order. This is especially relevant to activities that cultivate blessing out of creation—meaning our daily work improving the lives of others in the home, workplace, and community. The Greek word that's translated as "stewardship" (*oikonomia*) literally means "household management" and is the same word from which we get the English "economics." And that makes perfect sense. Economics refers to how we manage God's creation order; stewardship means being made responsible for the management of someone else's resources.

In the New Testament, *oikonomos* refers both to Christians' responsibility to live out the gospel (1 Cor. 4:1) and to the economic duties of a household manager (Luke 12:42) or city treasurer (Rom. 16:23). The Bible doesn't recognize a dividing line between "good stewardship" and our responsibilities in human civilization. You can't reduce good stewardship merely to civilizational activities, but neither can you put the two in separate containers as if they had nothing to do with one another.

Admittedly, some people who focus on political causes have succeeded in connecting the concept of stewardship to environmental issues. But even that concept of stewardship is drastically truncated (in addition to being unhelpfully politicized). The whole point of stewardship is that it redefines your personal identity and thus every aspect of your life. A church where discipleship is so disconnected from daily life that it sees good stewardship as tithing and recycling has gone very badly wrong.

Our Social Nature—Made for Stewardship

The eclipse of an effective call to stewardship in all of life is not happening because we've wandered away from the Bible, at least not in principle. Thousands of churches that are obviously sincere and zealous in their desire to live "by the book" have nonetheless lost the biblical concept of stewardship.

The real problem is that too many churches no longer understand the social nature of human beings. I think this is a major challenge for American Christianity. In fact, I think the gospel itself is in peril in our churches because of our inadequate understanding of how humans are defined by relationships.

God tells us a lot about what he wants from our civilizational lives in the Bible. However, what the Bible gives us are general principles. Don't kill, don't steal, keep your promises, help your neighbor, and so on.

General principles are where we need to start—that's why the Bible, which was given to us as our starting point for life, provides them! But how do we apply those principles? How do we embody them within our own unique time in history and our own unique place in American civilization? How do we figure out what holiness looks like in practice for us?

Figuring out what holiness looks like in our civilizational time and place requires thinking about ourselves as social creatures. A church that is naive about our social nature will come to view its job almost exclusively in terms of creating isolated personal religious experiences. As we saw in chapter 2, Americans like us are constantly tempted to abstract the individual—the sovereign self—from social relationships. We assume that the individuals, considered in isolation, are all that really matter. The church's job is changing individuals "one heart at a time," as the widespread saying goes.

If we think only about the isolated individual, we won't be able to construct godly lives. We'll focus solely on creating personal religious experiences. That's what you're left with when you strip the relationships away. The end result is a church that does almost nothing but create religious experiences—plus evangelizing, in order to get more individuals to have those religious experiences.

We tend to assume that once the individuals are changed, their relationships will change automatically. But in fact, they won't. Relationships are not just "downstream" from individual hearts. They are that to some extent, but they also have their own integrity. We have to think about relationships on their own terms.

Sanctification for Calling, Calling for Joy

Sanctification can be summed up as the power to know and follow God's calling with your whole life and in every area of your life. The concept of God's calling, and in particular the concept that God has a calling for your whole life and for every area within your life that you have the power to know and follow, is one of the most important in the history of theology. It's so essential that during the Reformation, the Reformers considered this doctrine just as critical to their movement as the doctrine of justification by faith apart from works and the doctrine of the Bible's final authority.

The Reformers said if you don't understand that all your daily activities are a calling from God, you don't understand the gospel. That's strong medicine! I think it's exactly the medicine we need.

The doctrine of God's calling is important because it provides an organizing principle for understanding everything we do. Without that kind of integrating framework, our lives become dis-integrated, spinning in many directions. A life without integration doesn't have a center, and a life without a center can't be centered on Christ. Without integration, each separate area within our lives becomes something that stands on its own, rather than something that grows from our commitment to Christ.

Following the calling of God is hard enough, but you have to know it before you can follow it. Our top priority in rebuilding a serious and effective call to sanctification should be to teach people how to know what God is calling them to do.

The wisest church teachers have historically agreed on three factors we need to consider to know the calling of God: gifts, blessing, and deep satisfaction. All three are necessary to a sound approach to calling. Imagine a Venn diagram with three interlocking circles representing these three factors; following God's call means living as much as possible in the center of the diagram, inside all three circles at once. Or imagine a scorecard with three lines. On each line you enter a score (say, 1 to 100) based on these questions: How well am I gifted for this? How much does this bless people? How deeply satisfied does this make me? Following God's call means doing the things that get the highest total score.

Gifts are an important factor because God does not equip everyone to do everything (1 Corinthians 12). Don't think too narrowly; anything that enables you to do something effectively counts as a gift. This means much more than just your "skills" and "talents" narrowly understood. Personal characteristics, ranging from physical endurance to empathy, are gifts that empower you to do things others can't do. Knowledge, whether academic information or practical skills and "know-how," is a gift. Experience is a gift. Relationships and other forms of social position are gifts. No matter who you are, you are connected to a unique combination of people and have a unique set of institutional positions in your family, workplace, and community. For example, what school you went to or what companies you've worked for may open doors for you that are closed to others. Amy Sherman has suggested a list of seven major "dimensions of vocational power." These are various ways in which God equips us with opportunities to accomplish his purposes. Her list is knowledge/experience, platform, networks, influence, position, skills, and reputation/fame.[5]

Even your personal history is a gift, no matter what it is. I once met a relatively new Christian who had come out of a life of drug addiction and crime. He said he wondered how much God could really use a man like him. An older, wiser Christian than I, who was (thank God!) present for this conversation, said to him: "There are a lot of people out there who are still living exactly the same way you were. They need Jesus. But they're not going to listen to us. They will listen to you." I wish I could describe for you the way that man's face changed when he heard this. His personal history, which had been weighing so oppressively upon him, suddenly became a special gift that empowered him to serve God.

Blessing is another factor because we're called to do things that make the world a better place. Blessing others is the reason God put people in the world; Adam and Eve's job in the garden was not to grow plants but to grow blessing. That remains our job today. Thankfully, we're not on probation to earn God's favor the way they were. Christ has taken care of that. But my to-do list for tomorrow morning still looks a lot like Adam and Eve's: make the world better.

Cultivating blessing means doing anything that makes life better. God's calling is to make the world a better place, and that covers a lot of ground! Just as with gifts, don't think too narrowly. Many people have a tendency to put their routine daily activities in one silo and then "things I do to serve others" in a separate silo. Because God made human beings to love and bless each other, we're supposed to be spending the large majority of our time blessing our neighbors. That doesn't mean expanding the "serve others" silo while shrinking the "routine daily life" silo. It means we break down the dividing wall and transform our routine daily lives by making it our goal in all our daily activities to bless others and make the world a better place.

Keeping this aspect of calling front and center is critical for two reasons. Most importantly, it's the only thing that keeps us from becoming self-centered in what we do. The call of God is always a call to serve everyone's good, not to do what we feel like doing. And a focus on blessing others is often the key factor that makes the difference between success or failure in accomplishing God's tasks, because it forces us to pay close attention to how our actions are impacting the world around us and the people in it. Timothy Keller says that asking "how can I be of greatest service to other people?" is what will "lead us to a more sustainable motivation for discipline and excellence at work. If the point of work is to serve and exalt ourselves, then our work inevitably becomes less about the work and more about us. . . . But if the purpose of work is to serve and exalt something *beyond* ourselves, then we actually have a better reason to deploy our talent, ambition, and entrepreneurial vigor—and we are more likely to be successful in the long run, even by the world's definition."[6]

Deep satisfaction is a factor because God has built human beings to enjoy the life he designed for them. He made us so that we experience a profound sense of fulfillment when our lives are structured over time toward meaningful accomplishment of good purposes. I'm not talking about mere short-term gratification, but a deep sense that you have built a life that is making a difference in the world. I call it "satisfaction" because it satisfies our spiritual hunger to answer God's calling.

Among the three factors, this is the one that most often gets overlooked or glossed over. People are reluctant to think of natural human feelings of happiness as something central to the Christian life. But the joy of God does not merely replace or substitute for natural happiness. It draws natural happiness up into itself, by integrating deep satisfaction with God's calling in our lives.

If your search for God's calling doesn't include some reference to your own happiness, you'll be obeying God out of the wrong motivation. The first moral law is to love and trust God. Obedience isn't obedience unless it's motivated by love.

Grounding our callings in deep satisfaction is also necessary for the sake of the doctrine called "Christian liberty." The human conscience is subject only to God. If a person's calling is only where his gifts and opportunities overlap, why not just assign people to jobs instead of letting them choose? In fact, we're in danger of doing this when we rely too much on assessment instruments to measure gifts and talents.[7]

Keller actually advises people to think about their deep desires first when discerning their callings, and only then move on to gifts and opportunities. This way, your desires can reveal to you gifts and opportunities you never knew you had. "Before I came to New

York City I would never have said that I had the gift of evange-lism," he writes. "I had a burden for New York, and that led me to a deeper understanding of my own heart. I did not say, 'I have a gift of evangelism. Where should I use it? I know—New York City!'"[8]

It's important to make sure we're following our deep satisfac-tion to find our calling, not short-term gratification. Gratifying our human desires can connect us to God, when we're gratifying godly desires. But it is not very social; it involves other people only incidentally. If we relied on gratification to know God's call, it wouldn't lead us to serve our neighbors enough. Deep satisfac-tion is the part of our human nature that provides us with a con-tinuing sign of God's design for civilizational life. The home, the workplace, and the community provide deep satisfaction when, and only when, we make blessing others our goal.

Paul's admonition to slaves in Colossae is really God's calling for us all: "Whatever you do, work heartily, as for the Lord and not for men. . . . You are serving the Lord Christ" (Col. 3:23–24). Why is this a calling for us all? Paul tells us earlier in the same letter that Christ "is before all things, and in him all things hold together" (Col. 1:17). If all things hold together in Christ, our lives should be Christ-centered in everything we do.

Gene Edward Veith puts the matter clearly when he says that the doctrine of calling, or "vocation," is "nothing less than the doctrine of the Christian life."[9] It comprehends within it all that the life of a Christian should be, enlightened by Scripture and flowing from our transformed hearts. "The doctrine of vocation shows Christians how to live out their faith in the world. It has to do with God's presence in the world and with how he works through human beings for his purposes. For Christians, vocation discloses the spirituality of everyday life."[10]

Rejoicing in Responsibility

Where the church equips Christians to be full-time stewards and follow God's calling, the Spirit's work creating the joy of God in sanctification flows out into the world through responsibility. Responsibility is fundamental to the image of God in humanity. God made us moral agents—we are responsible for what we do and don't do. And God made us to have dominion over the creation order. Some find the word "dominion" troublesome; it really just means we need to be responsible stewards of everything that comes within our influence. In fact, Bible scholars are increasingly stressing the dominion mandate as central to the meaning of "the image of God" in the Genesis text, rather than the traditional focus on humanity reflecting God's attributes.[11]

Living as stewards of God's world is an exciting adventure, at least much of the time. But the word "responsibility" may suggest burdens and drudgery. There's a reason for that. In those moments when we're really Spirit-powered and excited to be getting great things done, we don't think about concepts like stewardship and responsibility. We think about God and the things we're doing for him! The only time we have to actually think about the concept of responsibility is when we're feeling discouraged, we're tempted by sloth, or there's some especially toilsome task waiting to be done. "Well, I've got to do it," we think. "I'm *responsible* for it." We must remember to keep the good side of responsibility in mind.

Responsibility is one of the most important aspects of our original design as human beings that remains even after the fall. Even when the Bible stresses the impact of the fall most strongly, it always insists that fallen humanity remains responsible for its actions.

This means that responsibility is something we, as believers, have in common with our unbelieving neighbors. Responsibility is one of the most important connecting points between the church and the world; demonstrating responsibility is one of the most important ways in which the church and human civilization influence one another. Our unbelieving neighbors are still responsible creatures, but they are unable to live up to their responsibilities because of the fall, so they abuse the social systems of civilization as false sources of dignity and security. By joining us to Christ, the

Spirit empowers Christians to live up to their responsibilities as human beings. That means living out our responsibilities in the context of the social systems we share with our neighbors. We use these systems the way they're supposed to be used. Because their original design in God's image still shapes their behavior, our unbelieving neighbors feel that and respond to it. Some respond with hatred because we're exposing and refuting the lies they rely on in drawing false dignity and security from social systems, but others come to realize and embrace the deep satisfaction that the responsible social life provides.

Responsibility transforms our participation in civilizational life. It empowers us to resist the culturally "low" sins, like sloth, lust, and gluttony. As long as serving others in the home, workplace, and community is a burden that we bear because we have to, we will continue to struggle with these sins. Abstract ethical commands to serve others don't satisfy the soul, and that spiritual hunger will seek satisfaction elsewhere—leading us to neglect our duties and respond to our impulses for entertainment, sex, food, and so forth. But when we understand that we achieve high fulfillment and deep satisfaction by serving others in civilizational activities, and that doing so is a critical component of our walk with God, our whole lives are transformed. When we stop seeking our satisfaction in entertainment and sensuality, our desires for those things become more orderly and controllable.

Moreover, because the Spirit makes us responsible, we're better at accomplishing civilizational tasks. We're being sanctified and can resist lust and gluttony, so we're not constantly squandering time and energy on ourselves. By seeing ourselves as stewards of God's creation, and by resisting sloth, we put that time and energy into our proper tasks in the home, workplace, and community. We love our neighbors, so we care about tangible results and intentionally shape our patterns of life to produce them.

Think about my relative who filed medical records, the one I mentioned at the start of chapter 4. Her Christian coworkers showed up to their jobs every morning eager to work and make the world better. This had an impact on my relative, but it also had an impact on those workers' job performance. In chapter 7 I'll tell you about a Christian who helped invent the modern factory by seeing how early industrial working conditions could be brought more into line with what's proper for human nature as God designed it.

Here's another example. In the second half of the nineteenth century, Christian ministries to the poor began migrating toward a free handout model. They actually just took stuff out into fields and let anyone who wanted it take it. This ended up destroying jobs, creating dependency, and undermining relationships of interdependence in families and communities. The urban missions movement grew up in response to these problems, creating an alternative way to serve the poor that worked much better. It's a lesson we could stand to learn again, given the state of our international aid ministries. Even at home in the United States, most of the important lessons of the urban missions movement are widely neglected today.[12]

God demands that we care about results. "Little children, let us not love in word or talk but in deed and in truth" (1 John 3:18). "What good is it, my brothers, if someone says he has faith but does not have works? Can that faith save him?" (James 2:14). We're not really serving God if we don't care whether we're succeeding in accomplishing his purposes. We're not really serving our neighbors if we act like it doesn't matter whether our service is effective as long as it's rightly intentioned. As C. S. Lewis said, donating to a ministry isn't commendable if you don't care whether the ministry is fraudulent.[13]

The reason God demands that we care about results is because he wants us to love. Real love demands results. No matter how much you "help" the poor, you don't love the poor if you don't care whether they stay poor or not.

God's demand that we care about results ought to convict us. I think it's a major problem when we set our standard for serving our neighbors mostly in terms of good intentions. We mean well, and we measure our success mostly by how much well-meant stuff we do. If we handed out a lot of turkeys, we had a successful Thanksgiving hunger drive. If we had a lot of teenagers show up for youth group, it was a successful youth group. I've heard people say that we define a successful church in terms of ABC—attendance, building, cash.

It's good to mean well. But how often do we hold ourselves accountable for achieving the tangible goals that really matter? Instead of aiming to give away as many handouts as possible, some churches have had success helping entrepreneurs start small businesses that provide jobs and remove poverty.[14] Others have selected a struggling school and aimed to raise its test scores through tutoring and other forms of help.[15] Some have selected a small neighborhood, or a specific national issue, and come in to provide many types of help at once.[16]

At this point, with kingship in place, we have all three offices ready for integration. I said in the previous two chapters that prophethood only has an impact on civilization over very long periods of time. Priesthood can have a large impact within a small sphere and a short time frame, but (by itself) doesn't sustain and spread those changes. Kingship provides the framework for sustained cultural change. You can't set up kingship by itself. But it is the king who knows how to steer a middle course between an irresponsible short-termism that doesn't ask how change can be sustained and spread, and an irresponsible long-termism that says cultural change is so hard and takes so long that we don't need to have any sense of urgency about getting anything done. And it is the king who knows how to steer a middle course between the tight localism of the priest inside his temple and the boundless universalism of the prophet who may at any moment be spirited away to preach in some far-off corner of the world. When Christians act as kings, they are acting in the office most naturally suited to acting within civilization.

Part 3

He Comes to Make His Blessings Flow

Looking through a New Lens

The social nature of human beings has far-reaching consequences. It can be difficult to grasp how much our social nature matters to our lives in society. To see and understand this aspect of humanity, we have to look through a new lens.[1]

Animals live by instinct. From birth, they mostly know what to do to survive and thrive. They never question or debate these behaviors. The wolves may fight to see who is alpha male, but they don't fight over whether there ought to be an alpha male, or whether they ought to fight. The lions and bears may fight over territory, but they don't fight over whether they ought to be territorial, or change their ways and live like the sparrows or the sloths.

Because the behaviors are never questioned, they never change. The beavers and the eagles and the ants may build, but no animal builds itself *up* over time. Beaver dams, eagle nests, and anthills are the same yesterday, today, and tomorrow. The beavers have built no Hoover Dams, nor the eagles a tree house, nor have the ants produced a miniscule Frank Lloyd Wright who shocks the insect world by daring to make a square anthill.

Human beings are different. We don't live by instinct. We have to be carefully taught how to live. That means we have to think about how we live. We build structures for social life, just like animals, but we are aware of them as social structures. As we make homes and institutions, as we fight for dominance or defend our territory, we think about what we are doing.

Moreover, by the mysterious metaphysical power of the divine image in humanity, we are empowered to perform two great miracles that cause us to tower above the animals like gods. We think rationally about how things are. And we think morally about how things ought to be.

As a result, we become aware at an early age that the structures of human life are created by human action. They are not eternally fixed. They could be different. We know that we are rational creatures, so we know we have some power to make them different. And we know that we are moral creatures, so we know we are obligated to ask whether they ought to be different.

We must avoid two errors when thinking about social structures. The first error is thinking of them as arbitrary constructs of individual human decisions. This implies that there are no limits on how social structures can be changed. We raise children in families now, but if we all decided to live differently, we could just as easily create massive nurseries and drop off all our babies there at birth. We have an economy based on ownership and exchange now, but if we all decided to live differently, we could just as easily redistribute all property to the people we think should have it, or abolish property and live communally. This is the error I described earlier as naiveté about the social nature of human beings.

It's true that families and the economy and all our social structures are created by human action. Children are raised in families because that's how people raise them. There's no magical force outside human will that makes people live this way. But it does not follow that we can arbitrarily change these arrangements.

Take property as an example. What is it that makes a pencil or a car or anything else "mine"? Writing my name on it doesn't make it mine. Possessing it doesn't make it mine. Using it doesn't make it mine. We can't put our finger on *anything* that makes it mine. Everyone just treats it that way. Yet that doesn't mean its status as "mine" can be changed arbitrarily. You can swipe my things, write your name on them, possess them, and use them, but none of that makes them yours. That's exactly what it means to call something mine! My ownership of an object also cannot be traced to some kind of larger social convention, such as the civil law. If that were the case, no one would ask whether one policy or another toward property ownership was fair or just, because fairness and justice in property ownership would themselves be products of the law. But we constantly argue over whether a given law or policy regarding property is fair—again, that's part of what it means to say that my things are mine! This shows that property ownership isn't subject to arbitrary rearrangement. The reality of property ownership is "just there," taken for granted in the human situation regardless of whatever we may think, say, or do.

Admittedly, there is something mysterious about this. It certainly *seems* like social structures ought to be infinitely changeable if they are only the result of human action. But in fact, they make no sense to us if they're arbitrary. If we can rearrange parenthood or ownership at will just by deciding to do so, then really there is no such thing as parenthood or ownership.

The reason is simple: social relationships are embedded permanently in our nature as human beings. They're like reason and morality, which are also embedded in our nature. You can't think logically unless you first assume, without argument, that logic is valid. You can't think morally unless you first assume, without argument, that there is such a thing as right and wrong. Similarly, you can't think socially unless you first assume, without argument, that social systems are real and not arbitrary.

The other error to avoid is treating social structures as though they were not a result of human action at all. This implies they can't be changed, that they're mechanical forces that stand outside our world. They control us, but we have no power to control them. I've already hinted at this error, when I commented that there's no magical force outside human will that makes people live this way. This is the opposite error to naiveté about our social nature. It denies the dignity of the individual person. It denies free will, reducing us to mere puppets who have to do what the social systems tell us to do.

You can refute this error with philosophy and theology, showing that we can't think meaningfully about human action without the assumption that people are responsible for what they do and have the freedom to act differently. Or you can refute it with history. Entrepreneurs and great leaders have changed the direction of social systems in ways that can't be reduced to the mere outworking of the system's existing direction. We'll look at one of those at the start of chapter 7.

This means we do have some power to change civilization. Within limits, and provided we are smart about it, we can have influence. The changes we're observing now didn't come from nowhere, and if they can come from somewhere, then other changes can also come from somewhere—from us.

In the next three chapters, I'm going to do something called "exegeting culture." That is, I'm going to make observations about the state and direction of American civilization today. Exegeting culture is not an exact science. I will rely on some hard data, but for the most part I'm going to be using my judgment and interpreting things that other reasonable people could interpret differently. I offer these thoughts not (God forbid) as authoritative pronouncements but as a lens for seeing the culture that makes sense to me. If it makes sense to you, too, then I hope I've helped you think more clearly about the world we live in. If not, then I hope I've expanded your perspective by showing you what things look like to someone who sees things differently.

6

Sex and Family

Rejoice in the wife of your youth. . . .
Be intoxicated always in her love.

Prov. 5:18–19

Sex is one of the most powerful forces in human life, and not just in the obvious ways. The influence of our sexual desires goes far beyond just our instinctive impulse for a certain act or physical pleasure. In fact, that is just a fraction of how sex shapes us. The most basic building blocks of society—above all, family, but much else as well—arise from our sexual desires.

Because our sexual desires affect us so profoundly, their disorderliness is all the more destructive. When I tried to get started writing this chapter, I relearned that lesson (for the millionth time). I was going to start it during a plane ride, and I was thankful the seat next to mine was empty, given what I was going to be writing about. But just as the doors were closing, a last-minute passenger came on board: a stunning young woman, about half my age and dressed in a manner I can only describe as casually provocative. Down the aisle she came, sat right next to me and greeted me as if she knew me. I decided to work on the economic chapter during that flight instead! I couldn't have concentrated any more intently on the economy if the solvency of my employer had depended on it.

Our sexual desires are insanely disordered. Struggling with unwanted desires, Augustine cried out: "What is the cause of this monstrous situation? . . . The mind commands the body and is instantly obeyed. The mind commands itself and meets resistance."[1] G. K. Chesterton wrote that when it comes to sex, people "scarcely reach sanity till they reach sanctity."[2] The Bible concurs with that observation. Paul indicates that while everything goes wrong for sinful human beings, sex goes wrong first and worst (Rom. 1:18–32).

Sex is different. It makes us crazy. Just look around you, anywhere in America.

Over the past fifty years or so, Christian efforts to influence American civilization have increasingly focused on the issues of sex and family. Yet even as we ramp up more and more aggressive efforts, even as we try one strategy after another, and even as we achieve some significant successes, America's relentless downward march into sexual depravity has continued. Here's a historical lens to look through: in 1969, at a time when evangelical leaders had spent more than a decade talking about a rising tide of immorality that was reaching the ultimate breaking point, the Super Bowl halftime show was Bob Hope and the Florida A&M University Marching Band.[3] We had no idea how much further we had to fall.

Sex is centrally important not only to the lives of individuals but to the core social structures of civilization. So it makes sense that sex is a key issue for public witness. If Christianity doesn't have something to say about sex and family in contemporary America, Christianity really doesn't have much to say about contemporary America, period.

But while the focus on this topic is justified, it seems pretty clear that some strategic rethinking is needed on how we approach it. I know some people who think the last fifty years of Christian effort to influence civilization about sex and family have accomplished important things. I know other people who think we don't have much to show for our trouble. But I don't know anyone who's satisfied with the *status quo*. It seems to me there's a pretty strong consensus that the time is ripe for reassessment. How can we rethink Christian approaches to sex for twenty-first-century America?

Sex Is Not What You Think—Neither Is Marriage

Everyone knows sex is critical to joy. The problem is, most people (even Christians) don't know what sex really is. We are accustomed to thinking of sex as a physical act that produces physical results—most importantly, pleasurable sensations and babies. However, the physical level is not the best place to start.

Sex is two people joining together in a comprehensive, transcendent, and permanent union. Every time we have sex, we form a total and unending union with the other person. This happens regardless of whether we intend to form such a bond, or are even aware of it. Every sex act always involves the whole person, body and soul, and always bonds the whole person of one individual with the whole person of the other individual to create a permanent transcendental unity between them. This is mentioned in the creation account (Gen. 2:24) and reaffirmed by Christ (Matt. 19:6). C. S. Lewis comments that in asserting the reality of this total bond, Jesus "was not expressing a sentiment but stating a fact—just as one is stating a fact when one says that a lock and a key are one mechanism, or that a violin and a bow are one musical instrument."[4] For good measure, Paul makes it clear this does not apply only to sex within marriage but to all sex, even prostitution (1 Cor. 6:16). Whether they acknowledge it or not, two people who have sex will be metaphysically joined for the rest of their lives, and that union will change them in mind, heart, and action.

God made us with a deep-seated longing for this union. That's why sex is critical to our joy or misery as human beings. Our sex-obsessed culture is wrong about many things, but it is right about one thing: getting sex right is one of the very few central keys to whether we end up happy or miserable.

This fact explains the perplexing mysteries of sexuality. We are consumed by a seemingly endless bundle of desires and appetites that clearly have nothing to do with physical intercourse. We want our sexual partners to dress in certain ways, behave in certain ways, move in certain ways, say certain words, and look at us with certain facial expressions. None of this—the high heels, the suggestive stares, the provocative lines, the movements of the body—has anything at all to do with inserting the male organ into the female one. Why does over 90 percent of our sexual behavior have nothing to do with the act of intercourse? Because inserting the male organ into the female one is not the main thing we really want from sex. We want another person to think, feel, and act a certain way toward us. We long desperately for the unity of two *whole* people, body and soul.

Yet these appetites feel so permanent, immutable, and irresistible that we almost can't help but think of them as bodily needs. We interpret all our sexual desires as bodily desires. This is really bizarre when you think about it. A woman moves her body in a certain way while wearing a certain kind of clothing and (most powerfully) wearing a certain kind of facial expression. A man responds in ways that signal his desire for her. These activities cause both of them to become sexually aroused. If you asked them what they were thinking about, they would say they were thinking about the physical sex act: intercourse. Yet what they were really thinking about was each other's appearance and behavior. It's highly unlikely that either of them was actually entertaining a mental image of sexual intercourse.

This is why sex makes us crazy. We misunderstand what we really want. We treat our sexual desires as if they were bodily needs. Today I think even most Christians, including married Christians, think about sexual desires only in terms of bodily needs. In fact, sexual desires are much more spiritual needs than physical ones. I think for most men most of the time, underneath all the layers of materialism and selfishness that we pile up because we're so sinful, what a man really wants deep in his heart might be roughly summed up this way: "My wife admires me." And I think what most women really want most of the time might be summed up: "My husband loves me."[5] Millions of people lack joy because they don't realize that the main thing they want from sex is something spiritual.

The raw biological impulse to insert the male organ into the female one is certainly powerful and important. But the raw biological impulse to insert food into the mouth is also powerful and important, and yet somehow, most people realize that overeating is not driven by an excessive biological urge. Overeating is a spiritual problem; the excessive eater is suffering from a spiritual hole, and is trying to fill up that hole with the wrong things. In exactly the same way, the biological sexual impulse is not the primary reason people masturbate, look at porn, or have one-night stands. In fact, in my experience, the more immoral the sexual behavior, the less it has anything to do with biological urges. Immoral sexuality is trying to fill up an agonizing spiritual hole where spiritual needs are unmet. It is filling up the hole with the wrong things, which is why the behavior is wrong. But it is a spiritual hole, not a physical need, that mostly drives the behavior.

Just as most people don't know what sex really is, most people don't know what marriage really is. Marriage is not a union of two people, strictly speaking. It is sex, not marriage, that creates the union. A married couple who never had sex would never enter this higher union. Marriage is a social structure designed to recognize that sex creates this union, and to manage its consequences.

This is why all sexual activity outside of marriage, even masturbation, is evil. It is indulging, destructively, in a false version of reality. We are denying to ourselves that sex creates a permanent metaphysical union. We want sex to be nothing but a physical act, so we talk ourselves into believing it and try to live as though it were true. But the union is still there, and it changes us. "The truth is," Lewis writes, "that wherever a man lies with a woman, there, whether they like it or not, a transcendental relation is set up between them which must be eternally enjoyed or eternally endured."[6] Elsewhere he writes: "The monstrosity of sexual intercourse outside marriage is that those who indulge in it are trying to isolate one kind of union (the sexual) from all the other kinds of union which were intended to go along with it and make up the total union" of two people in a shared life.[7]

Living out the sexual union through marriage changes you in profound ways. In a marriage, two human beings learn over time how to live as one organism. Most of married life does not consist of having sex, yet the permanent metaphysical bond between you changes all of your life. It even changes the parts of your life that take place outside the home. You are not your own any longer. All your plans and commitments now take into account your primary rootedness in your household. You become a very different person, in a way that nothing else produces. All this is difficult to describe for those who haven't lived through it, but I hope with a little imagination, unmarried readers can get at least an idea of how big a deal this is.

The only thing that changes you as much as marriage does is conversion to Christ. That's no coincidence. The Bible says marriage is a picture of the gospel, conversion, and the love between Christ and the church (Eph. 5:25–33). In our sexuality, God has painted upon the canvas of our deepest nature a portrait of how we relate to him. No wonder it's such a treasure trove of pleasure and joy!

And no wonder it comes under such fierce attack from the Evil One. I've already mentioned that Paul says sex is what goes wrong first and worst for fallen man. It's not hard to guess why. If sex is a portrait of the gospel, it's a living embodiment of what Satan hates most of all. It would only make sense if he invested more effort in disfiguring that portrait than in any of the other ways he attacks us.[8]

Having sex outside marriage also changes us in very profound ways. We usually don't realize how it changes us, because we don't think about it. The whole point of sex outside marriage is to live in a pretend reality where the metaphysical union of sex doesn't exist. But the very act of indulging sexuality *without* thinking about that union changes the kind of person you are.

When we have sex outside marriage, we distort our natural emotions and suppress our consciences. We go out of our way to inflame our sensual lusts, because that makes us feel like nothing but sensuality is involved in sex. And we perform these degrading acts every time we indulge ourselves, so over time we make ourselves more and more into a different kind of person: the kind of person who finds it natural and easy to suppress the conscience and inflame selfish desires.

We become people who have extreme difficulty experiencing joy. Eventually we become dead to it.

Marriage Is Metaphysical

Because sex creates this metaphysical bond, marriage is the keystone in the sexual arch of human nature. Marriage is what makes it possible for human sexuality to achieve all it was made for. Without marriage, sexuality falls to pieces.

Marriage is the most basic social building block in all societies. Familial institutions have varied to a great extent from one civilization to the next. But throughout history and around the world we always find marriage at the center.[9]

Even quasi-legitimate familial structures like concubinage or catamitage, which are fairly common in human history, testify to the superior value of legitimate marriage. These quasi-legitimate institutions undermine the purity and stability of marriage where they are present. However, they prove that even societies that are incapable of channeling sexual desire only into legitimate marriage still have to channel it into institutions that accommodate and restrain its effects. These alternative institutions are clearly just pseudomarriages—pale imitations of the real thing. Moreover, the alternative institutions are never fully legitimized. Marriage is always the fully legitimate arrangement; other arrangements are at best quasi-legitimate.

Marriage is central to society because it is the only known social arrangement that channels all the various consequences of sex in ways that are constructive both for the individuals involved and for society at large. For the same reason, as civilizations develop over time, their long-term historical trajectory has generally been toward monogamous marriage rather than polygamy.[10]

Sexual desires are uniquely intense and uniquely disruptive. Marriage provides structure to these desires, channeling them in the right direction. Marriage can do this more effectively than anything else because only marriage guides our desires constructively—changing the content of our desires "from the inside," so to speak—rather than merely promising external rewards for good behavior and punishments for bad behavior. If our sexual desires are not constructively molded in this way, how we act on them will come down to a contest of willpower. And sexual desires are so strong they almost always win that contest in the end. External incentives to behave are not enough. If we want people to behave themselves, we need to raise them from childhood with an intrinsic motivation for humane sexuality. Marriage provides this motivation. No one has ever discovered anything else that does.

One way marriage channels our desires constructively is by cultivating romantic love in a way that yearns for permanence. Interestingly, marriage did so long before young people were allowed to select their marriage partners based on their romantic interest in one another. The sexual union itself invites a romantic love that longs for permanence when it is lived out in life partnership through marriage. Most civilizations have given parents the power to choose their children's marriage partners, yet every civilization demonstrates its awareness of romantic love (even if not all civilizations have celebrated it). But, of course, the right to select your spouse based on love interest has greatly magnified the ability of marriage to cultivate this form of love. That is one reason the freedom to choose your marriage partner stands as one of the most important advances in the history of human civilization.

Another way marriage constructs sexuality in a humane way is by changing the significance of childrearing. The need to provide for childrearing is one of the most important ways in which civilization is impacted by sexuality, so it is one of the most important determinants of familial structure. In subcultures where marriage is not expected, men are alienated from childrearing. They experience it as an unnecessary burden. Meanwhile, mothers in these subcultures are not only overburdened and facing truncated life opportunities because they are sole caregivers to their children. They are also subject to a greatly increased temptation to think of the child selfishly, as a sort of personal possession. On the other hand, in healthy cultures where people grow up expecting to get married, men view childrearing as intrinsically desirable, while women are safeguarded from both the burdens and the temptations of sole caregiving.

And, of course, at the highest level, marriage cultivates a life partnership that embodies and manifests the metaphysical bond of sex. This is something very different from romantic love. In fact, I have known couples who didn't seem to be in love with each other but who had clearly advanced very deeply into life partnership. I have known other couples who were obviously very much in love but couldn't seem to live as partners. (Guess which of those marriages tend to last, and which end in divorce.) For those who don't cling to themselves, for those who are willing to admit that they are no longer their own, marriage provides a profound transformation. Romantic love, powerful as it is, pales to insignificance beside this.

The deepest heart of marriage, then, is neither sexual exclusivity nor romantic love nor childrearing. It does involve all these things. But the heart of marriage is living in a state of total life partnership.

In fact, marriage breaks down when we treat it as merely a vehicle for romantic love, or even childrearing. The greatest triumph of the radical critics of marriage in the 1950s was persuading Americans to think of marriage primarily in these terms. This was what lay behind, for example, their complaint that a wife who doesn't produce a cash income is in a state of economic slavery, dependent upon her husband's paycheck. The unspoken assumption was that marriage is not an economic union—that his paycheck is really only his, not both of theirs.[11] This makes sense only if we think that sex is not a permanent total bond of two entire people. Once marriage was redefined as a *merely* sexual union, the path was clear for liberalized divorce, illegitimacy, and, ultimately, gay marriage.

This attitude about marriage—treating it only as a vehicle for romance and childrearing rather than the embodiment of a total metaphysical union—seems to be present in most sexual relationships today. I include in that observation not only most married couples, but even most Christian married couples. It is normal in contemporary America to think of your "relationship" with your spouse or partner as something purely emotional and spiritual, and "sex" as a purely physical act that you do with that person because you both enjoy doing it. Sex is treated on roughly the same level as everything else that you both do together because you enjoy it. Its role in your marriage is more important than that of, say, a shared hobby, but it's still the same sort of thing as a shared hobby. The difference is one of degree, not kind. People recognize that sex is important, but they rarely think of it as the thing that most basically creates and sustains the marital (or unmarried "partner") relationship. This has far-reaching consequences.

Perhaps the most important sign of our failure to understand sex is the way married couples today—even most Christian married couples—think about "good sex" in terms predominantly defined by unmarried sexuality. As Gene Veith and Mary Moerbe write, drawing on research by Lauren Winner: "Qualities associated with single sex—being secretive, transgressive, and out of the ordinary—are reflected in the expectations of married couples. Egged on by sex manuals, including Christian sex manuals, they too look for sex to be seductive, forbidden and exotic." Married couples have "date nights," implying that they need to recapture the sexual feelings they had before marriage. "Married people pretend to be single so as to recover a sense of romantic attraction."[12]

Worldly Sexuality Makes Us Frustrated and Miserable

When people who have sunk into sexual indulgence first hear the claim that sex creates a metaphysical union, they don't believe it. After all, they can't see it. Sex does not install in you a sixth sense that "beeps" when you're in the presence of a person you've had sex with, like Spider-Man's spider sense tingling when he's in danger. By its very nature, the sexual bond is something that can't be seen—just like God.

So people think the purpose of sex is pleasure. This seems plausible; we do get pleasure from sex. But this theory can't explain most of our actual sexual behavior. If we are really the kind of creatures for whom the purpose of sexual intercourse is pleasure, why do we have all these extremely intense sexual desires for things that have nothing to do with sexual intercourse—looks, clothes, movements, and so forth? Indeed, why would we have so many intense sexual desires for behaviors that are wasteful and destructive? And why are we so obsessed with sexual pleasures when there are thousands of other things that also give us pleasure—and do so more reliably and with less exertion and general disruption of our lives? If human beings were pleasure maximizers, we wouldn't spend half or even a quarter of the effort we do on sex.

When you treat sex as a utilitarian source of pleasure, it becomes just about the most inefficient source of pleasure there is. Sexuality is deeply pleasurable when our desires are channeled and controlled. But sensual indulgence as it is usually practiced in the world actually makes people miserable.

Worldly sexuality dulls your receptivity to physical pleasure, even as it inflames your craving for the very pleasure that it makes you less capable of experiencing. Think about how heavy drinking destroys people's ability to enjoy alcoholic drinks while also driving them to drink more; or how serious drug users get more and more dependent on their high even as they "build up a tolerance" and get less and less of a high from each dose. In the same way, sexually promiscuous people feel more and more miserable if they don't experience thrills, even as they get less of a thrill from each sex act. Some get bored with "vanilla" sexuality and gravitate toward perversion, in the futile quest to recapture the early pleasure. After an initial thrill, the perversion becomes stale and the misery returns, so even worse perversions must be sought out. Others simply attribute their misery to something else besides sex.

Either way, they are eventually reduced to slaves of their desires. They are hagridden by stronger and stronger appetites that deliver smaller and smaller payoffs. People who are enslaved by sex have miserably warped personalities. (Most normal people can tell a pervert almost on sight, though perverts themselves are unaware of this.)

And, in one of the Lord's supreme ironies, even the ability to perform sexually withers under these conditions. The more sexually immoral people are, the more frequently they will have difficulty performing the sex act. This is a major factor in the misery that sexual immorality always creates. But it isn't much talked about. Those who experience it keep it hushed up, because for those who live in the world of serious sexual immorality, the inability to perform is the ultimate shame.

All of this is why religions and philosophies that teach that pleasure is the only good thing in life, and that have seriously thought through the implications, such as the Epicureans in ancient Rome, have historically de-emphasized sex. Today the word *epicurean* implies debauchery. But the real Epicureans, for the sake of greater pleasure, practiced a severe ascetic withdrawal from sensuality—above all, from sex. Asceticism delivers more pleasure. They were not alone in thinking so. The serious worship of pleasure, when it's carefully thought out and organized as a way of life, always tends to lead toward the hermit's hut rather than the strip club.

Our sexual desires are absurd if we see them as utilitarian sources of pleasure, because in fact they make us miserable when we indulge them. But if we consider them as expressions of a deepseated longing for a total metaphysical union with another person, our desires suddenly make sense. We engage in all this elaborate behavior that has nothing to do with intercourse because we want so much more than just intercourse. We want a total person, not just a body. And sexually immoral people invest so much time and effort on sex even when it makes them miserable because whatever they may tell themselves, pleasure is not really the most important thing they want.

Sex involves the soul, not just the body. Our souls contain evil as well as good. If the parts of a complex machine get bent and twisted, the joints that hold them together will get bent and twisted in exactly the same way. Similarly, if two people's souls are twisted by evil, the sexuality that bonds them together will be twisted by evil as well.

Worldly Sexuality Makes Sex Degrading

Materialistic attitudes about sex change the content of our sexual desires. They make us want things that are bad for us. If sex is about pleasure, it's not enough just to do what comes naturally in the bedroom. We have to feel like we're getting the most pleasure we can. So we become more and more focused on *using* sex rather than simply experiencing it. Sex is instrumentalized—we see it as a tool we can manipulate. We have to invent things we can do in bed so we can reassure ourselves we're having great sex.

Ironically, all this tiresome innovation for the sake of novelty makes sex less pleasurable—not only emotionally, but even physically. Sexual performance becomes a skill, and we inevitably feel like we're being judged by our partners based on how talented we are. We have anxiety about whether we're getting what we should be getting out of sex. And, of course, we also become enslaved, physically impotent, and miserable in all the ways I've described above.

That's not even the worst of it. Whenever we see sex as something we can use as a tool, to some extent we end up seeing the other person as something we can use as a tool. There is a built-in force, often subtle but always present, pulling us toward degrading and dehumanizing the other person. We want to reduce that person, a human being, to the status of a thing—an object we can control and manipulate.

Once again, I'm talking about most people, not just the highly promiscuous people. It's true that this degrading tendency is most obvious when people are sexually promiscuous. We see it in the horrible ways people treat each other when they're prowling for one-night stands, and in the even more extreme cruelty we see in the typical attitudes and behaviors associated with strip clubs and prostitution. Pornography provides the phenomenon in its purest form. In your fantasy, this person you're looking at will say and do whatever you want. The real attraction of pornography lies in ruling over the objects of your desire as their hideous but omnipotent god.

Yet this same tendency toward dehumanizing your partner exists, in a more limited form, in most ordinary sexual relationships. It's limited because both partners have a stake. You can't just take what you want; you have to do some of what the other person wants, too. Sex becomes, in effect, a negotiated bargain where each party gets something from the other. It is a contract for mutual use. He gets certain things, she gets certain things. He uses her as a tool, but she uses him, too, so it all feels equal and fair.

This whole arrangement is made to feel plausible and legitimate by a matched pair of lies. The man fuels his desire with a lie: "This girl will do whatever I want." The woman fuels her desire with a lie: "Men want me more than anyone else." These lies allow us to conceal from ourselves the ways in which we've denied or suppressed our real desires. The hunger to feel that "my wife admires me" or "my husband loves me" must be kept out of our minds, so we don't feel just how distant we are from satisfying that hunger.

The two lies are mutually reinforcing in a way I can only describe as diabolical. The man wants the woman to present herself as an object—a tool of his pleasure. The woman wants to inflame his desire for her and prompt him to demonstrate it, in order to reduce him to an object—a tool of her pleasure. So she does what he wants, presenting herself to him as his object, in order to reduce him to her object. Then, to reward her for this behavior and encourage more of it, he responds in the way she wants, reducing himself to her object in order to continue reducing her to his object.

I wish I could stop there, but it gets worse. These lies create a downward spiral. Over time, the things women do to objectify themselves for male amusement come to feel ordinary. Eventually, they become simply things that women normally do. When these behaviors become normal, they no longer feel objectifying. They no longer excite the same level of desire because they no longer involve degradation; men no longer get the message that you're offering yourself as an object. So women have to seek out something even more objectifying to do. The boundaries always have to be pushed further, because it's only the pushing of the boundaries that creates excitement and arousal.

This is why, in a society with no effective counterweight to sexual immorality, song lyrics and clothing styles and everything else all get more and more degrading over time. Every time we think we've hit the bottom of the abyss, we discover there are further depths we hadn't yet discovered, and nothing we do seems to stop the descent. Lewis saw how this whole dynamic was already forming fifty years ago, and he saw exactly where it was leading: "A society in which conjugal infidelity is tolerated must always be in the long run a society adverse to women. . . . I have no sympathy with moralists who frown at the increasing crudity of female provocativeness. These signs of desperate competition fill me with pity."[13]

Worldly Sexuality Makes Us Slaves to Sex

In addition to changing the content of our sexual desires, materialism also changes how we manage them. We misunderstand where our sexual desires come from and what they are oriented toward, so we adopt the wrong ideas about how sex fits into our lives. We follow the wrong rules and find ourselves unable to reconcile our sexual desires with our other desires in an integrated life.

There certainly is a physical appetite for sex. There is no denying that it's a strong biological need, and responsible people ought to make provision for it. While a few are specially gifted by the Spirit for celibacy, and temporary abstinence from sex can be a spiritual discipline even among those who don't have that gift, for the most part we are called to make provision for satisfying our natural sexual appetites (1 Cor. 7:1–9).

The key mistake is the perception that our sexual desires are unalterable, and even to a large extent uncontrollable and irresistible. People really convince themselves that the sexual arrangements they've made in their lives, whatever they are, are necessary. They feel like human nature requires them to live that way. It's not true, and this fact is obvious to anyone who will see it—if only because people have made a very wide variety of sexual arrangements in their lives, yet each thinks his or her particular arrangements are rigidly required by human nature itself.

Augustine described this as "the overwhelming force of habit." Habit creates the illusion of necessity. When we live by habit, we no longer consciously make choices, so the behaviors feel to us like they're not habits at all but permanent natural necessities. In the end, when all of Augustine's intellectual arguments against Christianity had been refuted, this was the real obstacle to his conversion. He wanted to become Christian but he believed it was impossible to live without the sexual habits he had developed. He writes that as he wrestled with the call to conversion, "the overwhelming force of habit" held up to his attention the sexual indulgences he would have to renounce and said to him, "Do you think you can live without them?"[14]

The illusion that sexual immorality is necessary follows from the materialistic idea that sex is merely physical. If sex is physical, our sexual desires must be a physical appetite, like hunger. Our appetites for food are not habits. They are mostly outside our control, and they're not optional. You can change them somewhat on the margin—a gluttonous person can reduce the strength of his appetites through long and difficult training, or a person who strongly dislikes a certain food can keep eating it until he gets used to it. However, for the most part our appetites for food are pretty much given. And when you get hungry, you have to eat.

In fact, you arrange your whole day, every day—and therefore you arrange your whole life—to ensure your appetites for food are satisfied. And people who think about sex materialistically do the same thing for sex. They rearrange their whole lives in order to make sure they get what they want, because they think they have no choice.

This is why so many people are enslaved by sex. The teachers of sexual "freedom" are really slaves. Peter writes of such teachers: "They entice by sensual passions of the flesh. . . . They promise them freedom, but they themselves are slaves of corruption. For whatever overcomes a person, to that he is enslaved" (2 Pet. 2:18–19). Does that sound relevant to sexuality today?

Being enslaved to sex is miserable and incredibly self-destructive. The person who overcomes sex instead of being overcome by it—who is aware of spiritual as well as physical sexuality, and thus knows that there is a right way to channel sexual desires—can really achieve sexual satisfaction. But the person who mistakes all sexual desires for unchangeable physical appetites that cannot be channeled but must simply be gratified, and who therefore rearranges all of life in obedience to them exactly as they are, is headed for disaster. Nothing remains to hinder the gravitational forces pulling downward toward degradation. Materialism not only creates the force that pulls us down, it removes all obstacles that might stop or slow our descent. And one by one, all the other good things in a person's life will be brutally sacrificed on the altar of sex.

People who are enslaved by sex deny their responsibility for what they do. They blame their behavior on their unchangeable, uncontrollable, irresistible appetites. This is why, in order to get sex—and, even more, to get the kind of "great sex" they feel like they need to have—so many people are willing to lie, degrade themselves, squander huge amounts of money, betray their spouses, and expose themselves to all kinds of irresponsible risk and destruction. It's not their fault. They *have* to do these things.

Even ordinary people who don't lie, cheat, or do other obviously immoral things in the service of their sexual desires will still deny responsibility for the desires themselves. All of the degrading objectification we discussed in the previous section feels normal, natural, and good to people. The woman feels normal and natural when she offers herself as an object of male amusement, and the man feels normal and natural when responding, because this is just the way sex is. They feel a desire to do these things, and since the desire is merely physical, it can't possibly be wrong or disordered any more than the physical desire to eat. Only a prude or a weirdo would call you a pervert for eating. And such a person would obviously be a hypocrite, too, since you know he himself has to be eating. People who worry about sexual degradation must obviously be weirdos and hypocrites in the same way.

When society at large comes under the influence of enslavement to sex, the downward spiral of cultural degradation is also externalized. It's nobody's fault that Marilyn Monroe and Elizabeth Taylor made Mae West look like an uptight wallflower, and then Donna Summer and Madonna made Marilyn Monroe look like a choir girl, and then Britney Spears made Madonna look like a prude, and now Lady Gaga and Katy Perry are making Britney Spears look like a nun. This kind of sexual desire is just what everyone has really always wanted, deep down. The only reason we didn't get to this point a long time ago is because the prigs and hypocrites were in charge. As sensible and normal people have taken over the culture, the puritanical constraints of the past are fading away. We're finally free to live normal and healthy lives with normal and healthy sexuality—like sexualized pain and rape fantasies. Welcome to the land of freedom!

Worldly Sexuality Destroys the Family

Materialistic attitudes about sex also undermine our ability to think clearly about social structures like marriage and family. A lot of the leaders in our society have finally come to realize that it was a terrible mistake to legitimize divorce and illegitimacy. Yet they remain powerless to do anything about the problem, because they view sex as a physical act and miss its metaphysical implications.

Sex is not just an act. It is also a formative element of each person's identity. To be a human being is to be made to join in this comprehensive, transcendent, and permanent bond as either the male or female half. This defines who we are on a fundamental level. It shapes each person's overall personality, and extends to every individual part of it. Maleness and femaleness are stressed in the text describing the creative act: "In the image of God he created him; male and female he created them" (Gen. 1:27).

By definition, I couldn't enter into a total union with another person unless I were constructed to be able to do so. A receptivity to the union is part of my nature. And since the union is total, every part of me must be designed to enter the union. If there were some part of me that were not designed for sexual union with another human being, that part of me would not enter the union, and the union would not be total.

Thus, in one limited and particular sense, every aspect of a person is sexual. The maleness of a man and the femaleness of a woman isn't limited to their specifically sexual behaviors. It's expressed in everything they do.

That's not to say all men or women are the same. Any given man will embody a unique expression of maleness, and any given woman will embody a unique expression of femaleness. My eight-year-old daughter loves sports, and is looking forward to playing regularly as she grows up. This is a wonderful blessing from God—that I should have the privilege of raising a human being who glorifies God in this way. What would happen to this gift if I stifled it by telling her sports are for boys? (And what kind of hypocrite would I be, given that in spite of my maleness, I have loathed athletics my whole life?)

Or consider the vast difference in personalities and life choices between Deborah, Ruth, Esther, and Mary. Try to imagine the withdrawn, domestic Ruth (Ruth 2) singing Deborah's bloodthirsty battle anthem (Judges 5) or the forthright, no-nonsese Mary (Luke 1:46–55) navigating the delicate etiquette and secrecy of Esther's court intrigues (Esther 5–7). If you think they all represent a single expression of womanhood, you're seeing something I don't see. Yet they are all held up as godly women.

However, while every person's maleness or femaleness is unique, it's pretty easy to observe some generalities about the way men and women behave. Some common patterns are visible even across all times and places in history. For example, men are much, much more likely to be violent, both in good ways (soldiers) and bad ways (criminals). Yes, there are female soldiers and murderers, and there are male pacifists. But the plain fact is that they are exceptions, and if you want to think clearly about how culture works, you have to be aware that they are exceptions.

You can't manage a civilization very well without taking account of these patterns. Otherwise you're working in the dark. Many of our worst problems can be traced to the fact that the people running our civilization actually are working in the dark.

Consider, for example, the problems associated with the breakdown of marriage and family structures. Social scientists are finding that broken homes are a consistent indicator of everything from poor mother-infant relationships to early sex and low educational attainment to delinquency and criminality to poor health and early death. As one of them remarks, "I know of no other set of important findings that are as broadly accepted by social scientists who follow the technical literature, liberal as well as conservative, and yet are so resolutely ignored by network news programs, editorial writers for the major newspapers, and politicians of both major political parties."[15]

These patterns are not arbitrary. Human nature is a real thing. God made us as physical creatures with bodies and souls, so we have a biological and spiritual nature that works in certain ways. This nature shapes our behavior. If you don't take account of that, you're going to manage civilization poorly.

This leads us to some uncomfortable truths. Every civilization develops sex roles that train us to expect different behavior from men and women. These sex roles help society and its institutions manage the influence of sexual identity on human behavior. If we know, broadly speaking, what to expect from men and women, we can craft relationships and institutions better in response.

While sex roles are often dysfunctional, the disastrous harm being done by the breakdown of family structure illustrates the need for at least some sex roles. The leading institutions of American society destigmatized divorce and illegitimacy in the 1970s because they were unwilling to assert anything about sex roles. Once sex roles were off limits, they couldn't find plausible ways to insist that childbearing was legitimate only within marriage. By now, most of the people at the top of American society have realized what a disaster this was.[16] Yet they can't do anything about it because they are still, even now, unwilling to affirm even the most obvious difference between men and women: the different ways they respond to babies.

And, of course, there is the issue of gay marriage. So much is already being said about it that I need add little here. If government redefines marriage, this establishes that marriage is just an arbitrary piece of paper. Therefore marriage has no important meaning. It is whatever our passing whims make it, so it is really nothing at all. You can have gay marriage or you can have meaningful marriage—not both.

But gay marriage is not the real problem. It's only a symptom. Government redefining marriage is nothing new at this point. Government has been redefining marriage for two generations now, through liberalized divorce laws and other policies that destigmatized the broken home. Almost half the American population has never even known, as adults, a society in which marriage was *not* an arbitrary piece of paper with no important meaning. They have never lived in a society where marriage really meant something. Such a society can hardly avoid reaching the obvious logical conclusions: first gay marriage, and soon polygamy.

Before long, if there is no change of direction, I wouldn't be surprised to see some form of sexual indentured servitude reintroduced. Such arrangements have been perfectly normal throughout human history. We have been living through a very exceptional period when they have not existed, but we have no right to expect that unusual exception will go on forever. We are now raising generation after generation of young people in an environment where it is taken for granted that normal, healthy, and happy human sexuality consists of women degrading themselves for male amusement. How long can we normalize dehumanization before the law formally recognizes it?

Believe it or not, despite all this, I'm optimistic (within reason). I said I expected things to go down this nasty road *if there is no change of direction*. But I actually expect a change of direction.

Public disgust with the state of sexuality in America is palpable. People in high places are increasingly coming around to the idea that we need to reinstate marriage as the norm. If nothing else, the denormalization of marriage in the lower socioeconomic half of the population is creating extreme social disruptions that the top half can't ignore. Our leading cultural institutions have committed themselves to prioritize helping the poor, racial equality, women's dignity, children's well being, economic mobility and widespread opportunity, mitigation of class distinctions, and so forth. They're starting to notice that the breakdown of marriage is a dagger pointed right at the heart of all those goals. Nothing's guaranteed, of course, but I can see a near future in which gay marriage is legalized at the same time America's leading institutions start seriously restigmatizing divorce. And in the train of social change, government is always the caboose—the last to catch up with where we're really going.

Sex Is Not a Medical Condition

Many ideologies and thought patterns in our civilization reinforce the materialistic view of sex, legitimizing our movement away from the marital family. One of the most important of these is actually a strategy for resisting sexual degradation. Unfortunately, I think this strategy is ultimately just as materialistic as the materialism it tries to combat. This makes it even more dangerous; people who are worried about immorality (including most Christians) embrace this strategy because they don't recognize how materialistic it is.

I'm talking about the medicalization of sex. Americans extensively borrow the terms and thought categories of medicine when they think and talk about sex; the view that sex is a health issue is deeply ingrained. We see it in the way sex tips are classified as "health information" in magazines and bookstores. We see it in the way sexual behavior and teen pregnancy rates are tracked as "health statistics"—as if fornication and pregnancy were diseases.

We see it in the way the government's "health care reform" requires every American institution other than churches to subsidize contraception and abortion drugs. And we see it in the way critics of pornography constantly describe it as an "addiction." They seem to have no other frame of reference for thinking about porn besides it being a medical disorder.

Medicalizing sex is less materialistic than treating sex as a source of pleasure. It frames sex in terms of caring for people and healing them. This implies that we approach sex with a moral purpose, namely to help people. And it implies that there is a naturally existing, relatively stable boundary between sexuality that is good (healthy) and sexuality that is bad (unhealthy). Because it incorporates both a proper purpose of action and a proper model of development for human nature, medicalization does not reduce the human being to merely a physical body.

However, the medicalization of sex cannot avoid the strong undercurrent of materialism that dominates within medicine itself. In contemporary America, medical science is about the body. The limitation of medicine to matters of the body is stronger now than it has ever been. In the twentieth century, there were attempts to develop "medical" and "scientific" practices to address nonbodily causes of illness, especially mental illness. Freud thought of himself as a scientist, on the cutting edge of medical research. That is mostly gone now. Today, we draw a sharp dichotomy between medical science, which deals with bodily problems, and other forms of care such as counseling, therapy, and religious services. These other forms of care are often welcomed by medical professionals, but almost universally they are welcomed as something other than medicine. They are not medical or scientific *precisely because they do not deal with the body*.

The combination is toxic. If sex is medical and the medical is purely physical, then sex is purely physical. To the extent that we medicalize sex, we invite people to treat it materialistically. If sex is medical, all sexual desires and behaviors are healthy (good) unless you can show they create a specifically medical (bodily) harm. This undermines sexual morality right at its heart, teaching us that sex has no purpose other than the gratification of our immediate desires. The only moral rule is to make yourself healthy and happy without hurting anyone else. This removes all obstacles to the downward slide into degradation. It also confirms the transfer of sex out of the exclusive domain of the marital family, legitimizing whatever alternative sexual arrangements feel right to people.

We train ourselves to think about sex medically without even realizing what we're doing. This mode of thinking is just in the air around us. We breathe it in everywhere. That's why Christians have become so extensively captive to it.

I've already mentioned that Christians have felt a great deal of urgency to impact society's view and practice of sex. This is natural. Unfortunately, one side effect of this urgency has been an uncritical assimilation of these medical categories into most Christian leaders' thinking about sex.

Christian sex education programs generally stress the negative medical effects of premarital sex. Sometimes (but not often enough) they work in a discussion of theological perspectives somewhere. The headline message, though, is generally that people who have sex before marriage get diseases and have unhappy sex lives. Saving sex for marriage is the way to stay healthy and happy.[17]

Obviously, I think that headline is true. Saving sex for marriage actually is the way to stay healthy and happy. And it's not hard to see why we focus on that headline: our audience, the American public, wants to be healthy and happy. If we talk about sex in terms of the goals they already care about, they're more likely to listen.

The problem is, this relentless focus on staying healthy and happy implies that the purpose of sex is to make yourself healthy and happy. That's just not true. And it's basically a selfish message. We're training people to live for themselves.

Perhaps the most striking example of the medicalization of sex among Christians is how efforts to fight pornography have invested heavily in the concept of addiction. Almost every discussion of this issue seems to come back to this. And no wonder: addictive substances are just about the only things Americans still agree we should ban by law.

One of America's most prominent Christian writers on the subject of pornography has carried medicalization even further, campaigning for an effort to stigmatize porn as "sexual obesity." In one article, she defends the view that porn is addictive by pointing to the outpouring of vicious hate mail she and other authors receive every time they write on the subject. She remarks:

> Although academic experts may continue to battle over exactly what is meant by "addiction," surely the tremendously defensive response in the public square *by itself* settles the question to any reasonable person's satisfaction. What does it tell us that, when faced with any attempt to make the case that this substance should be harder to get than it is, some reliable subset of defenders can be counted on to respond more like animals than like people? If such is not the very definition of addiction, what is?[18]

So, any behavior that makes people behave in these vicious ways must be an addiction. Where does this leave the concept of sin? It would seem there is no room left in this line of thinking for wickedness.

This is not a trivial point about word choices. If we adopt "porn as obesity" or "porn as addiction," we send a strong message that *any and all sexual behavior is okay as long as it doesn't lead to negative health outcomes.* Far from slowing our decline into degradation, this will only facilitate it.

In our urgency to impact the culture, we have bent over backwards to speak the culture's language. We want to make sure that we will be heard, that we will be relevant. So we speak in a language that we know will be recognized as legitimate and important: medical language.

I believe this is the most important reason we haven't had more of an impact on the direction of sexuality in America. Because we have acquiesced in the medicalization of sex, we have disarmed ourselves against the real enemy. We have fought desperately to reduce the symptoms: smut, fornication, divorce, illegitimacy. But we have inadvertently reinforced the disease that causes them: materialistic assumptions about the nature and purpose of sex.

Redeemed Sexuality in the Church and the World

This survey of the social impact of materialistic attitudes about sex puts a new light on Scripture's claim that our sexual desires are our most badly disordered desires. Love of money or power is a heinous wickedness, but accumulating money or power in large amounts is very difficult and the amount that any one person can actually accumulate is limited. However, the cultivation of sexual indulgence can go on all day long, day after day. Even for a person who never goes beyond fantasies, porn, and masturbation, sexual gratification quickly becomes a routine part of the background of life, with little effort and few limitations. Our natural inclinations lead us more and more horribly awry, while rightly ordered sexuality comes to seem excessively severe (at best) or even weird and wrong (at worst).

Among Christians, this downward spiral is halted and reversed by the miraculous work of the Holy Spirit in revelation, regeneration, and sanctification—in our private hearts and in the faith community of the church. The Spirit shows us through Scripture and through biblical preaching and teaching what sex and family are really for—mostly by reminding us of the moral truths that we knew already but preferred to forget, but also by enlarging our perspective with additional "inside information." He works miracles in our hearts that transform us into people who are morally capable, however imperfectly, of struggling against our disordered sexual desires and reorienting ourselves toward a flourishing sexuality that manifests God's intentions. He sustains the shared life of the church where we support each other and build each other up in holiness, through everything from one-on-one counseling and discipling to accountability groups to appropriate church discipline. As much as the church may not live up to all God wants for it, it is the ark within which the Spirit is preserving something that resembles godly sexuality against the deluge of sexual immorality.

He also calls us out into the world to make use of all he has given us to be a blessing to our neighbors. He didn't light the lamp of godly sexuality in the church in order to hide it under a basket. The world needs our witness on sexuality like never before.

When civilizations are functioning normally, they create and enforce moral rules and social institutions that restrain people's sexual behavior. They do this because God is still at work throughout the whole creation, accomplishing his purposes by providential grace. These social systems don't create the same kind of flourishing sexuality that the Spirit creates in the church, but they do create the conditions for people to live normal, relatively humane lives.

Right now, our civilization is not "functioning normally" in that sense. What if the Lord is creating an opportunity for Christians? How can we be a blessing to our neighbors by helping them to remember the foundations in human nature upon which civilizations need to build their sexual morals and institutions?

Remember the formula for civilizational influence in chapter 2: first affirmation of the good, then within that framework, transformation of the bad through co-opted cultural entrepreneurship. We have to begin by affirming that marriage is good, then seek out opportunities to transform relationships in ways that demonstrate in practice how faithful marriage provides for human needs better than the alternatives.

Believe it or not, affirming that marriage is good is a major problem area for American Christians today! We usually do not affirm that marriage is good. We affirm that it is Christian and biblical. It *is* Christian and biblical, but that's not adequate as a basis for public advocacy. Saying we should support marriage because it's Christian and biblical implies that we want to pass laws that require people who are not Christian to live by Christian standards. That's wrong because it violates religious freedom and it expects people who don't have the Spirit to live up to standards only the Spirit can empower them to live up to. Our own dogmatic insistence that marriage is something *Christians* believe in may well be the main barrier to our non-Christian neighbors realizing that marriage aligns with their values, too.

Civil law should preserve the basic social conditions for humane sexuality. Lifetime monogamous marriage is not an exclusively Christian commitment. We can truthfully present it to our neighbors as the humane and decent development of natural civilization (in addition to being Christian and biblical, which of course it is also). As social breakdown in the lower half of society reaches greater and greater extremes, the humane and civilized basis of lifetime monogamous marriage is becoming more obvious. Actually enforcing the marriage contract instead of letting people just walk away from their marriages whenever they want is something Christians and non-Christians ought to be able to agree on.

But more important than the national debate on marriage and sex is the question of what Christians can do in our everyday lives. The key form of cultural entrepreneurship we need is not political advocacy (although I'm all for that). What we really need is for Christians coast to coast to become models of marital blessing, starting with their own homes but reaching out and blessing marriages around them as well. Our neighbors won't find the marriage message plausible until they see, in practice, how lifetime monogamous marriage is a blessing. Ordinary cultural contact with Christians is how that will happen, but only after Christians themselves change the way they live. How can we live out the joy of God in our own sexual and family lives, and what can we be doing in ordinary life that would make us a blessing to our neighbors?

As married couples, how can we stop approaching sex as a tool to extract pleasure, and free ourselves from selfish fantasy ("this girl will do whatever I want" or "men want me more than anyone else")? Can Christian husbands and wives just relax and enjoy doing whatever comes naturally, communicating to one another through words and sexual actions: "What I enjoy most about sex with you is just you—exactly the way you are, just doing whatever comes naturally, because what I care about sexually is *you*"?

As parents, how can we prioritize our children's nurture and growth as human beings, such that someday they will no longer need our tutelage? How can we build Christian families where the home is a place to live out our callings to bless one another? And how can we build homes where no one feels that the bonds between family members are potentially breakable, such that we have to constantly earn one another's loyalty?

What can you do in your community to honor and reinforce people's marital partnerships? Are there people you know with marriages and families in crisis? Can you support them—offer to cook a meal or babysit, be there to help them feel safe and supported?

What is your church doing to cultivate marriages and families in the congregation? Can your local church help people develop biblical knowledge about sex and family? Is your church using educational materials that inadvertently reinforce materialistic assumptions about sex, such as by medicalizing it or by overemphasizing that sexual morality will deliver more pleasure and keep you healthy and happy?

How can the church at large reintroduce the spiritual realities of sex to our nation? Are there ways of moving beyond just participating in the public policy disputes? Can we come alongside the national leaders of our culture, who are increasingly alarmed about the realities of family breakdown, and help them understand the deeper metaphysical causes? Can we resist the medicalization of sex as part of our public witness?

As the social disaster around us becomes harder and harder to ignore, the time is ripe for someone to prompt our non-Christian neighbors to rethink the sexual revolution. The leading cultural institutions have already realized there's a major problem. They're waiting for someone to help them understand why things aren't going the way they expected. We Christians have the inside information to explain the problem, and the Spirit's empowerment to show why marriage is a blessing. If we can overcome our need to insist that marriage is Christian and instead demonstrate that marriage is good, the opportunities before us are bountiful.

7

Work and the Economy

The LORD your God will bless you in all your
produce and in all the work of your hands,
so that you will be altogether joyful.

Deut. 16:15

We spend a lot of our lives working. In fact, when you add up
work on the job plus work in the home plus work in your neighborhood, church activities, civic life, and so forth, work takes up
the great majority of human life. God designed us that way for
important spiritual reasons. But too many people today have an
unspiritual view of work. And when we have a materialistic view
of work, we have a materialistic view of most of life.

Whether we understand work spiritually depends in large part
on whether we understand the economy spiritually. If we view the
economy materialistically, thinking that economics is just about
numbers on spreadsheets and arcane policy issues, we'll tend to
view work materialistically. On the other hand, if we have the vision to see that the economy is really a moral system, a vast web
of human relationships where people exchange their work with
one another, we'll tend to see the spiritual dignity and meaning
of our work.

That's why dramatic economic changes, like the ones we're all
going through right now, make people especially likely to despiri-

tualize their work. At such times, the older economic systems and institutions that had embodied the spirituality of work for earlier generations become obsolete. We lose the sense that our work is part of a greater social whole that has dignity and purpose. As a result, our own work loses its sense of dignity and purpose.

Here's an example from an earlier period of economic disruption that teaches a lesson for our own time. In the eighteenth century, at the dawn of the Industrial Revolution, the first factories would set up shop in a rural area and attract workers away from the local farms. Workers flocked to the factories because they paid better; the new economy was generating wealth. Agricultural life before the modern era consisted of endless backbreaking labor from early childhood to death, simply to scrape together enough food for everyone to barely survive. With everyone living right on the edge of subsistence, any natural disaster that seriously disrupted the food supply caused mass starvation. To help ensure the food supply, people were willing to live under rigid authoritarian power structures that dehumanized the individual. Now, at long last, the Industrial Revolution was beginning to bring people the more humane economic conditions of the modern world.

But the first factories were inefficient and inhumane. Because these workers had been suddenly separated from their families and communities, they lacked clear boundaries or moral structure. There was no preestablished sense of what ways of living were just or worthy in the context of the factory. So people lived in clusters of hastily constructed, filthy, squalid huts. These new pseudovillages had few religious, medical, or other normal community functions. Drunkenness reached extreme levels.

Under these conditions, people experienced their work as something burdensome and meaningless. When they showed up to work (which they didn't always do—absenteeism was rampant), they showed up as late as they felt like, in whatever state of drunkenness or hangover they happened to be in. They did whatever tasks happened to be lying around waiting to be done, and they did them halfheartedly and not very well. Then, when they felt like it, they knocked off from work to go drinking again. All these inefficient and inhumane conditions prevailed in the early years of industry because nobody (neither the owners nor the workers) had a social structure to signal to them that this state of affairs was unacceptable.

Thankfully, because God is always at work in the fallen world, times of change don't only bring decay. People are always inventing new economic structures to embody the spiritual significance of work for new economic conditions. And because Christians are specially transformed by the Holy Spirit, they have often taken the lead in this regard.

One eighteenth-century Christian in particular helped to revolutionize the early modern factory in an extraordinary way. His model was simple: I will give you a clean, well-built place to live, in a real human community; I will help you see your work as something meaningful because it produces good things that make the world a better place; and I will run my factory in a way that treats you with the dignity appropriate to you as a being who does work that makes the world a better place. In return, you will show up to work every working day; you will show up on time; you will show up sober; you will work hard all day; you will be assigned specific tasks for which you are responsible; and you will master those tasks and do them exceptionally. And if you produce shoddy work, I will drop your shoddy work product on the floor and smash it with my walking stick, since I don't tolerate shoddy work in my factory because *you are better than that*.[1]

It worked. The factory produced at an extraordinary level of both quality and quantity. The owner became world famous, and his products were highly sought after due to their superior craftsmanship. Other manufacturers copied the model, and workers gravitated toward factories run this way. The hard work and high expectations weren't a downside for the workers, they were part of what made the job attractive. They were an essential part of what gave the work dignity. The squalid pseudovillages and rampant drunkenness of the early Industrial Revolution gave way to the far more humane and spiritual environment of the late modern factory.

And here's the big twist: the Christian factory owner I'm describing was Josiah Wedgwood, the maker of Wedgwood china. Maybe you've heard of him due to his role in the antislavery movement; he leveraged his money and social prestige to promote abolition. But the only reason he had any money or prestige to lend to that noble and humane cause was because he played a much larger role in another noble and humane cause—the reinvention of the factory.

In fact, in some ways they were really the same cause. Slavery is an economic evil; its main function is to steal people's labor. Wedgwood was an economic reformer in both his invention of the modern factory and his antislavery work. He knew that slavery was wrong the same way he knew how to design a better factory: he had a spiritual view of economics.

Timothy Keller notes just a few of the many ways in which Christianity contributed to the emergence of the modern economy, such as the dignity of the human being as the basis of economic freedom, and generous service to others as the basis of an economy that serves customers with excellence:

> The Christian worldview has made foundational contributions to our own culture that may not be readily apparent. The deep background for our work, especially in the West—the rise of modern technology, the democratic ethos that makes modern capitalism thrive, the idea of inherent human freedom as the basis for economic freedom and the development of markets—is due largely to the cultural changes that Christianity has brought. Historian Jack Sommerville argues that Western society's most pervasive ideas, such as the idea that forgiveness and service are more important than saving face and revenge, have deeply biblical roots. Many have argued, and I would agree, that the very rise of modern science could have occurred only in a society in which the biblical view of a sole, all-powerful, and personal Creator was prevalent.[2]

Christianity was not the only factor that helped the modern economy emerge, but it was a very important one.

What's the lesson for our time? First, it says something about us that we remember Wedgwood as a champion of abolition and not as an economic reformer. He probably did much more good for many more people, both materially and spiritually, in his role as a factory owner than in his role as a sociopolitical agitator. We don't remember that because we don't think of work and the economy as moral, spiritual, and cultural phenomena. We think of them materialistically, even mechanically, as though the economy were a machine with buttons and levers. That's just not right—as Wedgwood and countless other economic heroes have proved. As I said in chapter 2, there are no morally neutral social systems, because social systems are just human relationships.

Wedgwood shows us something else as well. Because we spend most of our time working, the economy is a critical connection point between Christianity and society. Understanding the economy and participating in it in ways distinctively shaped by the Holy Spirit's work within us is one of the most important ways in which we manifest our discipleship within civilization and influence its direction. We can't all have the same huge societal impact Wedgwood had, but we all have some sphere of influence within which we can act. In your own work, whatever it is, you can be a Wedgwood in the way you do your work and interact with your coworkers. And those who have the opportunity can offer a bigger vision, reminding our civilization that the economy is not a machine but a moral system of human relationships—and proving it by using Christianity as a lens that reveals new and better ways of doing business in the new economy.

Work Is Most of Life—for a Good Reason

What is work? You might be surprised to hear that theologians have struggled and argued for years without settling on a definition. (On the other hand, if you know much about theologians, you might not be surprised.) The concept of work is central to Scripture. As we'll see, moral and spiritual teaching about work pervades the Old Testament, and the New Testament relies on this emphasis on work as a background assumption that shapes much of its instructions to the church. Yet drawing a line between "work" and other types of activities (rest, play, worship, etc.) often turns out to be very tricky in practice.

For our purposes, it will be good enough to say that work is everything we do to serve people and make the world a better place. Rest and play are things we do simply for their own sakes. Worship services, Bible study, prayer, and other religious works are things we do to cultivate our direct relationship with God. Just about everything else we do, we do to accomplish some good purpose beyond the activity itself (so it isn't rest or play) and with our eyes on the world and our neighbors as well as God (so they're not "religious works" in the narrow sense). That's the world of work.

This explains why work takes up most of life. God made us that way. It's simple, really. God wants human beings to serve and bless one another, so he designed us such that serving others and making the world a better place—working—is what we do most of the time.

This is why work is an essential element of human dignity. Part of being made in the image of God is being gifted with capacities to make the world a better place, and being called to use those capacities to bless people. This is why we admire people who work hard.

It's also why human beings have a natural desire to work. If you doubt that a desire to work is part of our nature, think about the indignity and frustration people suffer when they're unemployed. The loss of the paycheck isn't nearly as painful as the loss of the sense of worth and meaning that can only come from working.

The spiritual poison of sloth demonstrates the same point in reverse. People who can work but choose not to—whether they're rich people living off their fortunes, or poor people living off welfare, or middle-class people living off relatives or entitlement programs—are doing essentially the same thing drug dealers and pornographers do. They're violating their own most basic human dignity, living like animals and wallowing in uselessness, for the sake of what they materialistically believe will give them a comfortable life.

Of course, work is not the source of our dignity. That's the error of the workaholic. The image of God is the source of our dignity. But the ability and the calling to work are part of that divine image. So because we do in fact have the image and the dignity, work ought to follow. We don't have dignity as creatures because we work; we work because we are creatures with dignity, made in God's image.

Work Makes Us Fruitful

What does God want from our work? How does God want our work to be? The subject of work has been getting more attention from theologians lately than it has in more than a century. But we're still only just starting to get beyond the basics.

The obvious starting points are ethics and evangelism. God wants us to work ethically; he wants us to obey the moral law. Don't steal, don't lie, don't break the law or the rules of your workplace, don't cut corners. Work hard and do your work well, because you owe it to your employer to deliver value for the paycheck you're getting. That's just a basic rule of justice and fair play—you take someone's money, you owe him what he paid for. And in appropriate ways, you should manifest your faith to the unbelieving world in the workplace, both implicitly through the way you conduct yourself and explicitly as the occasion arises. Remember my relative from chapter 4, who became convinced Christ was alive because she saw Christ's power through the way her Christian coworkers did their work.

As I said, ethics and evangelism are the obvious places to start. They're obvious because any problems that arise in those areas are immediately urgent problems. If you're stealing from your employer or bullying coworkers, that's obviously wrong. If you don't view the workplace as a place of potential witness, that's obviously wrong.

But by themselves, with no deeper view of why God cares about work, an exclusive focus on ethics and evangelism in the workplace is legalistic. It's law without gospel. If we teach people to work ethically and to witness at work, and that's it, we're just cleaning the cup on the outside. The inside of the cup may still be full of worldly and materialistic assumptions about what work is for.

The next step in understanding work is to affirm that work is central to God's design for humanity, and that it is one of the most important ways in which we are called to glorify him. This is the level that more and more theologians are starting to rediscover in our time.[3] From the garden of Eden (before the fall), through the Mosaic Law and the Old Testament Wisdom Literature, to Jesus's own example and all New Testament teaching, work is consistently upheld as essential to God's design of human life.[4] This perspective is important because it connects work to our overall understanding of human life. Work becomes a central element of the story we tell ourselves about the meaning of our lives.

Yet even that is not quite enough. Understanding God's design is important, but if that's all we have, we risk overspiritualizing. Such understanding may change our mindset, but it's not likely to change our to-do list for Monday morning. "God designed you to work, so do your work for God's glory" doesn't give us enough practical guidance. What kind of work, and what manner of working, glorifies God most?

I have found it most helpful to think in terms of a calling to be fruitful. Our work ought to be authentically productive. We are called to serve people and make the world a better place. That means creating—producing—a better state of affairs. So work that is truly "productive" is work that does those things. It bears fruit in the form of a better world, whether that means goods and services delivered to customers in the marketplace, or children well taught in school, or a house where people and things are well cared for.

We can be fruitful because we are made in the image of a Father who creates. God created whole universes from nothing just by the word of his power. We're not that powerful! But we do work within the universe he produced to produce blessings within it. We receive the raw materials from him, and through our work we use those raw materials to create (produce) a better state of affairs than what we found.

We can also be fruitful because we are joined to a Son who united eternal divinity with the world of time and space in his own personhood. Jesus is simultaneously a human being within space and time, like us, and also the God who stands outside all space and time. We're not that cosmic! But in Christ we have become "partakers of the divine nature" (2 Pet. 1:4), so through the work of our hands, the divine nature is reorganizing that portion of the world that is within our stewardship. We incarnate the power of Christ when we work Christianly.

And we can be fruitful because we have the Spirit dwelling within us. The Spirit miraculously transforms our hearts. We're not that miraculous! But the change the Spirit makes in us affects everything we do, equipping us with strength, diligence, and joy for fruitful work. When we do our work spiritually, the Spirit is at work in us and through us.

Look again at Wedgwood's model. The key thing to grasp about it, the reason his factory quickly became world famous and was widely imitated, was that it was both more productive and more humane. It was more productive *because* it was more humane—and yet, it was also more humane *because* it was more productive. Treating people with dignity causes them to do better work and produce more value. But at the same time, setting high expectations for productivity is essential to treating people with dignity. It's the only way to treat people as though you really believe they are made in God's image and capable of making the world a better place.

I've described the fruitfulness of our work in terms of being productive. I know that for some people, the word "productivity" carries materialistic overtones. They think it refers only to a business context, and that it means whatever makes the most profit for the company. But I don't think the concept of productivity is limited in either of those ways. My wife is a full-time mother. If she tells me she had a productive day, that doesn't sound strange to me. I don't ask her, "What, you went out and got a job somewhere and you made money for your employer?" No, I know exactly what she means. She got her work done and it *produced* an improved world.

What Is Fruitful?

I said above that fruitful work should be "authentically productive." I use the word "authentically" because there's a lot of work out there that pretends to be productive, but really isn't. It doesn't actually bless people and make the world a better place.

My great-aunt used to work for the phone company. When my family was putting her affairs in order after her death (at a ripe old age), we discovered that she didn't own her phone. Right up until her last day, she was still renting her phone from the phone company. This practice was common in the early days of telephones, but it had died out more than half a century ago—or so we had thought. For the privilege of having a phone in her home, she was paying the phone company *every month* more than enough money to actually buy a phone—a better phone than the one she had—because she didn't know any better. Now, did no one at the phone company think to question this practice? Bilking little old ladies out of monthly phone rent may make money for the company but it is not productive work.

That's an obvious case, but there are many less obvious cases out there. We should be ready to think critically about work that's normally treated as legitimate. For example, if you buy an appliance or an electronic gadget, most stores will try to sell you an insurance policy on it. If you actually run the calculations for what the policy costs versus the chances you'll ever need it, the policies are usually a bad deal.

I once heard an ethics professor challenge the little vending machines that stores and restaurants keep in front, selling worthless trinkets for fifty cents or a dollar apiece. The trinkets won't entertain the kids who buy them for long; the machines are really just there to prompt kids to demand their parents buy them something. In effect, the machines are there to create discord in families so the owners of the vending machines can blackmail parents.

However, ethical questions are not just for those who work in gray areas. Every worker needs to understand what it is about his work that truly serves others and creates a better world. Even when we look at legitimate work, how we measure productivity needs to take into account all its authentically productive aspects. For example, an employer who rewards workers for making a lot of units without regard to the quality of their work is financially shortsighted, because if his products are no good, people will stop buying them. But that is not all; he is also cultivating an empty, materialistic view of work in his company. Workers in such environments need to have the independence of mind to see what is truly productive even if their employers do not.

This question of "quality" leads us to another issue. When we talk about what is or is not fruitful or authentically productive, we need to avoid making judgments based on our own personal preferences or what values happen to be fashionable. There is a widespread tendency to pass judgment on goods and services based on whether they please the person making the judgment, not whether they serve the needs of others who may have different circumstances and priorities.

One person may look at, say, a cheap table sold at a discount store and call it "shoddy" because it's not aesthetically impressive and it's not made to last a hundred years. To what extent is that judgment informed by the perspective of a comfortable, upper-middle-class suburban household that can easily afford to buy a more impressive table? For people of more limited economic means, inexpensive goods are a godsend. For them, the alternative to the cheap table is not a better table. It's either no table, or giving up something else they need to get a table. And the cheaper table may make more sense even for some people who could afford the superficially better table. They may have other, better uses for the money. An inexpensive and aesthetically unimpressive table can be "high quality" if it does the job it's supposed to do.

I'm not saying it's wrong to buy beautiful and long-lasting things! Beauty and durability make the world better. But another thing that makes the world better is efficiency, which allows us to offer goods and services at lower prices, so people (especially people struggling to make ends meet) can live better lives.

This principle was first disseminated by two great medieval theologians: Albertus Magnus and his student, Thomas Aquinas.[5] Different people have different needs and circumstances, so it is legitimate for them to value things differently. Each customer ought to seek the tradeoff between what they get and how much they pay that is right for him. Paying more to get more is not, by itself, morally superior to paying less for less (and vice versa). The very definition of what counts as "more" or "less" quality varies widely depending on the person and the situation. Today, economists refer to this principle as "the subjectivity of value"; it is one of the bedrock principles of modern economics.

Similarly, we need to be careful how we think and speak about special categories of work. Many people have a sense of romantic mystique about certain professions such as artists, scientists, doctors, teachers—and, for that matter, pastors and missionaries. Others have a special reverence for work that targets poverty relief, environmental improvement, or other causes. And still others pay special attention to those whose jobs give them leadership and power.

All these special focuses can be justified to some extent. There really is something mysterious and magical about making art.

There really is something different about a business that hires only ex-convicts looking for a new start. There really are unique issues and questions that people in elite positions urgently need to think about but others just don't.

Yet none of this makes it okay to create an implicit spiritual caste system where these kinds of work are better, more spiritual, or more Christian than other kinds of work. A relentless focus on "special" work can be discouraging and oppressive to the people who do "ordinary" work. For example, it's not uncommon for more educated and privileged people to describe repetitive physical labor on factory lines and farms as dehumanizing. That kind of snobbery is what's really dehumanizing; it dehumanizes the millions of people who cultivate creation and serve their neighbors by performing these vitally important tasks. As the "knowledge economy" creates greater and greater economic separation between white-collar and blue-collar workers, it's going to be increasingly important to remember the dignity of ordinary line work.[6]

If you really look for it, you can find something mysterious and magical in any kind of legitimate and fruitful work. Martin Luther once gave an enthusiastic sermon on the incredibly transcendent spiritual experience of changing dirty diapers.[7]

Productivity itself is mysterious and magical. It's the byproduct of our being made in the image of a God who (in the person of the Father) created everything from nothing just by speaking, who (in the person of the Son) united eternal divinity and material humanity in a single person in whom all things hold together, and who (in the person of the Spirit) dwells within us to empower and sustain us. Any time we're productive, we're living into the three-personal life of the Triune God who creates, integrates, and empowers.

If Work Matters, the Economy Matters

Because work is central to God's plan for human life, the economy is central to it as well. The economy is the social system through which people organize their work and dispose of its fruits. Its main characteristics include employment and pay, property ownership, exchange, profit-making business, and investment. But the basic fact of all economies is that human work creates economic value. The economy is critical to everything that happens in human civilization. You can't reduce civilization to merely the economy; Marx was wrong to think that everything in human life is just a mask for economic forces. Yet nothing happens in civilization without some kind of economic work being involved. Suppose a group of friends gets together on a Saturday for a baseball game. This activity presupposes that someone has earned enough money to buy the bat and balls, and that a company exists somewhere making them. Someone had to build and maintain the playing field, usually a municipal government spending tax revenue— revenue that could only be raised thanks to a productive economy. Marx's economic reductionism is wrong, but there's a reason it's so plausible to some people. Wherever you look in civilization, you do find economic things happening everywhere.

Much of what we said about family in chapter 6 is true of the economy as well. Social systems have to reconcile two things: natural human proclivities that are basically the same everywhere, and the particular conditions that are different in every society. Thus, there are some universal characteristics common to all economic systems, and there are some ethical and spiritual imperatives that are obligatory in every society. But economic systems do vary to a large extent, and it's legitimate that they do so, because they must respond to the needs and conditions of their time and place.

Employment and pay—exchanging money or other valuable goods for work—is one of the universal features. Wages are a huge issue in the Bible. In the Old Testament, in both the Law and the Prophets, God is constantly admonishing employees to earn their wages, and employers to pay people the wages they're owed and not cheat them. And in the New Testament, parables and teachings repeatedly describe God's kingdom and other spiritual realities by using employment and wages as illustrations.[8] That's because the moral and spiritual significance of wages is intimately familiar to us. Jesus realized that if you talk to people about wages, they'll know you're talking about something with deep importance.

The idea that there is a natural hostility between labor and management, or labor and investors, is antibiblical. The idea that the relationship between employer and employee is by nature competitive rests on the assumption that all human beings are always greedy and should never be expected to rise above greed. The most basic economic reality, in this view, is that everyone is out to seize as much as possible for himself; evil is more powerful than good, and who gets how much is more important than human relationships. I can see why a militant materialist like Marx (whose theory this is) could find all this plausible. Why anyone else would accept it is beyond me.[9]

Yet this theory is the primary basis of all American labor law. As a result, we have policies that force companies and unions into a constant state of conflict with one another. In much of Europe, by contrast, labor law encourages companies and unions to cooperate. This is one reason Germany was able to weather the recent economic storms so much better than we did; unions and managers trusted each other enough to work together flexibly to adjust to new realities. American labor law, with its Marxist assumption that whatever benefits the employer must be hurting the employees, doesn't even permit some of the solutions that helped the Germans save jobs.[10]

Another universal economic reality is markets and prices. Every economy is a "market economy," because people in every society meet their economic needs by exchanging goods and services. Markets and prices are one of the most important tools God built into human nature for helping us serve one another and create a better world. Albertus and Aquinas were among the first to describe how the price system serves human needs. Wherever prices aren't fixed in some way, the price level fluctuates to indicate what is in high demand or low demand, relative to what is easily available or in short supply. When buyers and sellers respond to this information, goods and services find their way most quickly to those who value them most, relative to their availability. The exchanges that take place through the market as people buy and sell don't just move stuff around. Human work is productive, but the ability to exchange our work with others makes it a thousand times more productive. The modern economy is so fantastically productive, partly because the workers themselves are more productive now, but mostly because the modern system liberates the great exchange of human labor far more effectively than the ancient economy did.

Just think about what it would take to make even one ordinary item—say, a shirt or a pen or a chair—if you had to make the whole thing from scratch yourself, using nothing produced by anyone else's work. You couldn't start by making the item, you'd have to start by making the tools you would need. Actually, you'd have to make some other tools just to make those tools, and so forth back through generations of tools! You might spend a lifetime making one shirt. But since you live in a world with other people in it, you don't have to. You can take the money you earned just from one hour of labor and buy a shirt—and a much, much better shirt than the one you would have made from scratch.

Obviously markets are not some automatic machine that will ensure the best result regardless of our character. On the contrary, what kind of market we have depends on what kind of people we are. Virtuous people who freely choose to serve one another with their work will create a flourishing market economy. In a selfish society, markets break down from lack of trust.[11] Markets also must be supervised to ensure fair play and opportunity for all, and some goods and services need to be banned outright or strictly controlled. On the other hand, the authority to enforce justice can itself become a cover for exploitation and injustice. For example, today some people think nostalgically about the medieval "guilds." At the time, however, some theologians denounced guilds as price-fixing monopolies that fattened the rich and well connected at the expense of the poor and less powerful.[12]

Like wages, markets and prices are of central concern in the Bible. Market exchange is frequently blessed as a system through which people serve one another and satisfy one another's needs. And the danger of cheating is ever-present. The Prophets and Wisdom Literature constantly admonish us to use fair weights and measures, to deliver to others the goods and the price that we promised them, not to exploit social status or political power to squeeze a better deal out of weaker parties, and so forth.

For one striking example, read through the famous description of the godly woman in Proverbs 31 and see how many times market exchange is affirmed as an important element of her godliness. She works very hard and is generous to those in need, but she is also blessing people through economic transactions:

- Her household grows wealthy from her fruitful labor (v. 11).
- She acquires the raw materials she needs for her work (v. 13).
- She acquires other things her household needs (vv. 14–15).
- After careful deliberation, she purchases land (v. 16).
- She produces goods that she can sell for more than they cost to make (v. 18).
- She goes to the market and sells those goods (v. 24).
- Her household is not dependent upon others for economic support (v. 27).
- Through the sale of her goods in the marketplace ("in the gates"), her productivity has a ripple effect on the whole community that manifests God's glory to all (v. 31).

This godly woman brings to all these exchanges a keen intelligence and a careful determination to manage them with good stewardship, because she knows that the marketplace is a place where God's purposes are accomplished. Why is she praised as godly and virtuous for buying wool and flax (v. 13)? Presumably because she does it with excellence, always getting the best price but doing so with integrity.

Perhaps the most basic universal economic institution is wealth and property ownership. It's important to note that wealth means a lot more than just money. Anything that has economic value is a form of wealth. In recent years, academic economists have been paying a lot more attention to intangible forms of wealth, such as your education, skills, and personal qualities (which economists call "personal capital") as well as your relationships with others and knowledge of social systems (your "social capital"). Money is just a means of exchange that allows us to move wealth from one person to another more efficiently—it's very important, but it's not the most basic reality. Wealth comes first; money is a tool we use to transfer it.

Like wages and markets, wealth is a topic of great importance in the Bible. On the one hand, wealth is consistently described as a blessing in Scripture. In both the Old and New Testaments, wealth is one of the many ways in which God showers down blessings on humanity, and God wants us to work so that we and our neighbors will flourish economically.[13] The "prosperity gospel," which promises that wealth will magically follow from faith, is false. But the calling to work hard for economic productivity that produces the blessing of wealth (among many other blessings) is real.

On the other hand, Scripture consistently warns us of the dangers of wealth. Do a text search for "greed" if you doubt it! We saw in chapter 6 how common it is for people to idolize sex; money is just about the only thing that competes with sex as the most tempting target for idolatry. Beyond the issue of greed, Scripture warns against the equal and opposite sins of squandering wealth (Luke 15:11–32) and hoarding wealth, removing it from use entirely (Luke 12:13–21). By contrast, Scripture commends caring for the needs of our own households and other close relations (1 Tim. 5:8), and after that, giving generously for relief of others' needs (James 2:15–17). Scripture also praises investment that makes wealth available to others who can use it productively, so the community can flourish (Ps. 112:3–5).

The imperative to show generosity is especially stressed. In the Old Testament, when God tells his people he's going to bless them abundantly, he remarks: "There will be no poor among you; for the LORD will bless you in the land that the LORD your God is giving you for an inheritance to possess—if only you will strictly obey the voice of the LORD your God" (Deut. 15:4–5). In the New Testament, James warns: "What good is it, my brothers, if someone says he has faith but does not have works? Can that faith save him? If a brother or sister is poorly clothed and lacking in daily food, and one of you says to them, 'Go in peace, be warmed and filled,' without giving them the things needed for the body, what good is that?" (James 2:14–16).

There is no contradiction between God's calling to productivity and his warnings against greed. Their harmony is well expressed in Proverbs 28:20: "A faithful man will abound with blessings, but whoever hastens to be rich will not go unpunished." In other words, good behavior (the behavior of a "faithful man") has a tendency to make you rich, but wanting to get rich is a sin. It is the love of money, not money itself, that is a root of all kinds of evils (1 Tim. 6:10). God warns against abusing wealth not because wealth is bad, but because he knows that we are bad.

A good case in point is God's warning to the Israelites in Deuteronomy 8:11–20. God warns the Israelites not to forget about him after they get rich in the Promised Land. So getting rich does create a temptation to forget about God. But throughout the warning, God assumes that the Israelites will in fact get rich in the Promised Land. Why? Because they're *supposed* to get rich in the Promised Land! That's God's plan to bless them (Deut. 15:4). It's precisely because God intends to bless them with wealth that he knows they need a warning not to abuse his blessing.

Growth Creates Threats, but Also Opportunities

The simultaneous goodness and danger of wealth presents us with a problem, especially in the modern economy, because the modern economy grows. In the ancient economy, the amount of wealth stayed more or less the same, or grew so slowly that nobody noticed. But in the modern economy, we aren't just moving stuff around; our work and exchange are productive, so we have more wealth and the economy grows.

Economic growth provides indispensable spiritual blessings. It expands our opportunities both for human dignity through work and for human dignity through the enjoyment of God's wonderful creation order. Growth also creates a much greater variety of ways to glorify God. Instead of being forced to spend your life doing whatever job your father did, you can actually go find your calling from God among countless potential opportunities. Instead of having stewardship over no more wealth than only what your bare subsistence requires, you can glorify God by enjoying and generously sharing what he has richly provided.[14]

Growth also creates material blessings that are beyond measure. Rock star Bono, who is nobody's idea of a corporate shill, sums it up: "Entrepreneurial capitalism takes more people out of poverty than aid. We need Africa to become an economic powerhouse."[15]

Globally, the number of people living on one dollar per day dropped an astonishing 80 percent just from 1970 to 2006, and living-standards measurements have more than doubled. Antipoverty programs didn't cause this improvement. Rather, many undeveloped nations embraced the modern economy and began growing. Global inequality is plummeting as millions of people who used to be poor in places like China and India are rapidly rising toward the rest of us. After the economic transformations in Asia and South America in the past generation, sub-Saharan Africa is now the only major global region where growth remains the exception rather than the rule.[16]

Yet economic growth also creates threats to spiritual life. Economic growth disrupts social structures. Existing institutions were designed to handle things a certain way, but economic growth introduces new ways of doing things. The old structures struggle to keep up; they're always disrupted, and sometimes they're destroyed.

We rely on social structures to restrain evil and help people find meaning in their work. So when they're disrupted, evil can slip loose and work can seem to lose its meaning. Consider the first half of Wedgwood's story. Agricultural society had developed a whole constellation of institutions and customs to organize and moralize agricultural life. But when the Industrial Revolution began to take workers out of the countryside and gather them in factories, all those humanizing structures became irrelevant. Wedgwood arrived on the scene of a moral disaster. That's the kind of threat economic growth creates.

As a result, there are always some Christians who are afraid of economic growth. John Wesley pronounced that "wherever riches have increased, the essence of religion has decreased in the same proportion."[17] How he squared that with the Old Testament depiction of the Promised Land as a place of fantastic riches, I don't know. But this strain of thought continues to crop up pretty regularly in our own day.[18]

I understand why some people fear growth. As I've already noted, Deuteronomy 8:11–20 gives us much to ponder. Yet wherever there are threats, there are also opportunities.

Don't forget the second half of Wedgwood's story! In the end, workers and customers flocked to support the humane factory model Wedgwood invented because it filled the moral gap. And it did so while also delivering the blessings of economic growth—the early factories were tough work, but premodern agricultural labor conditions were a lot worse. Give me Wedgwood's factory any day over breaking my back my whole life in order to generate just enough food to live on.

Disruption of institutions also produces critical benefits. Jesus himself disrupted a lot of institutions! He didn't attack them with violence or try to tear them down directly. But he did declare and demonstrate a superior path that the existing institutions weren't following. He stole people's hearts to his new and better way. As a result, even as Jesus explicitly taught people not to violently rebel against either religious or political institutions, both those institutions saw him as a direct threat to their existence and their power. They were right!

When institutions are guaranteed a permanent existence, they tend to become self-serving and oppressive. This happened to the church itself during the late Middle Ages. The church got away with a lot of exploitation and corruption because, "We're the Holy Catholic Church—no one's allowed to disagree with anything we do!" But institutions that get disrupted will be forced to remember why they exist. Rome cleaned up its act only after it became clear the Reformation couldn't be stamped out, and that it was even threatening to displace the Roman Church unless Rome got its house in order. It was when Rome had to make a choice between reform and extinction that the abuses finally stopped. One of the greatest blessings of economic growth is to force institutions to serve people in order to survive.

This is why the famous idea of the "cultural contradictions of capitalism" is false. Sociologist Max Weber feared that the desire to maximize profit would inevitably drive us to rationalize all of life economically, trapping us in a dehumanizing "iron cage" that would leave no room for the soul. Weber wrote in 1905 at a time when the latest business fad was to scientifically identify the one best way to do every task, down to the tiniest details.[19] But that whole idea failed and vanished, just like the early factories that had run on alcoholism were swept away by Wedgwood's superior model. In the long run, dehumanizing practices fall apart because people don't respond well to dehumanization. Cultural entrepreneurs keep us both more humane and more productive by sweeping such practices away.[20]

To me, the debate about economic growth seems very similar to the debate about church growth. Forgive me, but I'm going to draw some unfair, oversimplified caricatures of that debate for just a moment. On one side you have people who sound like they believe church growth is an end in itself: the mission of the church is to grow, so do whatever brings people through the doors. On the other side you have people who seem to be afraid of church growth: by gum, in our ministry we do things God's way, and if people aren't coming into our church, it must be because they don't like how we do things God's way!

Both of these approaches, in their pure forms, are inadequate. You can't make growth an end in itself because the life of the church will become spiritually empty. If the content of church life is guided and determined solely by the imperative to grow, there's nothing left about the church that makes it a church. In that case, why would people keep coming? The church needs to be dedicated to a mission that has integrity apart from growth—manifesting God's kingdom.

And yet, if you're afraid of church growth, you'll stifle the life of the church. A church that's doing its job extending the kingdom will normally be growing. If you create fear about growth, you'll teach people not to take initiative and create flourishing ministries. When leaders discourage growth, stagnation and cynicism set in. Show me a church that's afraid to grow and I'll show you a church that's in the process of dying.

Of course, in real life neither side of the church-growth debate takes the extreme, absolute positions I've depicted here. There's a lot of gray area in the middle. But the extreme positions that I've described illuminate a basic tension that really does exist between the two sides. And if you look around, it's not hard to find people who go too far in one direction or the other.

We have the same basic tension in the debate about economic growth. On one side you have people who sound like growth is an end in itself: the mission of a business is to grow, so do whatever maximizes profit. The people on the other side sound like they're afraid of economic growth: by gum, our traditional social structures do things God's way, and if people don't like being forced to live within the constraints of traditional social structures, it must be because they don't like doing things God's way!

Both of these approaches, in their pure forms, are inadequate. You can't make growth an end in itself because the life of the business becomes spiritually empty. If the content of working life is guided and determined solely by the imperative to grow, there's nothing left about the business that's authentically productive. In that case, what will you have to sell that's worth buying? A business needs to be dedicated to a mission that has integrity apart from growth—serving customers. And yet, if you're afraid of economic growth, you'll stifle the life of the business. A business that's doing its job serving customers will normally be growing. If you create fear about growth, you'll teach people not to take initiative and work diligently at making the world a better place. When leaders discourage growth, stagnation and cynicism set in. Show me a business that's afraid to grow and I'll show you a business that's in the process of dying.

And what I've just said about individual businesses can also be said about the economy at large. If society's cultural leaders teach people that growth is an end in itself, the economy becomes spiritually empty and (therefore) unproductive. But if they teach people to be afraid of growth, they kill the drive to work productively by serving customers and making the world a better place. Both these approaches equally reinforce the materialistic assumption that work is unspiritual. This is why they both end up doing the same thing in practice: cultivating greed and materialism.

As with church growth, in real life neither side of the economic growth debate takes the extreme, absolute positions I've depicted here. There's a lot of gray area in the middle. But the extreme positions I've described illuminate the basic tension that really does exist between the two sides. And if you look around, it's not hard to find people who go too far in one direction or the other.

Integrating Growth and Generosity

The way forward on economic growth seems clear to me. We are called to do authentically productive work. This will normally lead to economic growth, because productive work creates value, and it therefore increases the total amount of value in the economy. So we should welcome growth. But we have to be careful not to make growth an end in itself; our motivation is to make the world a better place, not get rich. And we have to teach people how to use their wealth as stewards of God to benefit their neighbors, not squander it or let it go to waste.

What does that look like in practice? We have to integrate, into our lives and our message to the world, two equally important imperatives: the imperative to authentic productivity and the imperative to generosity. In John Wesley's famous adage about what to do with money: "Make all you can, save all you can, give all you can."

In fact, the imperatives to productivity and generosity are mutually reinforcing. It's difficult to have one without the other. That's because they both come from the same source: God's intention that we should live lives that serve others and make the world a better place.

I have a personal stake in both growth and generosity. If I come across like I'm personally biased toward advocating generosity, that's because I am. I'm employed full time at a grant-making foundation, so I'm part of what might be called the generosity industry. My salary is paid because my benefactors want to give money away.

But if you think I'm personally biased toward advocating economic growth, that's also true. My wife has a serious chronic illness, and her life is sustained by medicines that would never have existed without the explosive growth of the US economy in the past half-century. As I write this, it has only been about a week since my wife's doctor commented that as recently as thirty years ago, a woman with her condition would have been dead by now. So yes, if you accuse me of being in the tank for a strong economy, I'll wear that badge without apology.

Each of these imperatives has a tendency to degenerate into an excuse for greed and materialism in the absence of the other. Without the call to generosity, the call to productivity makes people feel entitled to live materialistic lives—as long as they accumulate their wealth by working productively. But without the call to productivity, the call to generosity makes people feel entitled to live materialistic lives—as long as they pay off God by tithing their 10 percent.

The only way to root out materialism is to reorient people's attitudes about their entire economic lives. If you only lead people to do good work (productivity), they'll use their wealth selfishly. If you only lead them to get their use of wealth right (generosity), they won't orient their lives to good work. The whole life of a person has to turn away from selfishness and serve God and neighbor. As someone once said, the only effective place to intervene in a vicious circle is everywhere at once.

As I've described this integrated call to productivity and generosity, many of you will have identified, in your minds, the type of economic system it represents. The trouble is, some of you will have identified it as "capitalism," others will have identified it as "socialism," and still others will have identified it as "a third way."

I once heard a panel discussion in which two of America's most distinguished evangelical Bible scholars fell into exactly this trap. They quickly and easily agreed, in general terms, that fruitful work plus generosity is what we want. Then they spent most of their time arguing over whether such a system would be "capitalism, just capitalism with generosity" (as one of them insisted) or "neither capitalism nor socialism" (as the other insisted).[21] I wish I could say this was an isolated incident, but in my experience it is far more common than not for people to agree on the substance and then fight about terms.

The root of this problem is that the terms mean radically different things to different people. To one person, capitalism means any system based on greed while socialism means any system based on generosity. To another person, capitalism means any system based on productivity while socialism means any system based on envy and sloth. Behind this linguistic dispute lies a whole host of complex historical, economic, and sociological disagreements going back more than a century.[22]

I would like to propose a way out of this impasse. Let's temporarily set aside the whole host of complex historical, economic, and sociological disagreements over the origin and nature of "capitalism" and "socialism." Let's even set aside those terms, since we can't seem to use them without reopening all the old arguments. These debates matter; I have some pretty strongly held views about them myself. But right now these debates are paralyzing us. Since we agree (broadly) that we need both fruitful work and generosity, let's focus on accomplishing that goal. If we do that, we can return to the complex arguments later, probably with new illumination. At the very least we'll have learned how to talk to one another.

Two Lies for Two Kinds of Workers

How does work go wrong? Just as we saw with sex in chapter 6, work goes wrong when we take a materialistic attitude about it. And just as with sex, there are two mutually reinforcing lies that both lead to the materialistic conclusion.

However, while the two sexual lies are naturally complementary—one appeals to the male and other appeals to the female, but they both lead to the same behavior, so the two sexes cooperate in debasing themselves—the economic lies are not. They lead to opposing behaviors more often than they cooperate. While some people believe both lies, for the most part one lie appeals to one kind of person and the other lie appeals to a different kind of person. The two personality types despise one another, and each group is reinforced in its debased approach to life by its revulsion and disgust at the other, opposite group.

As we've seen, the working life that we're called to live is fruitful and productive. In economic terms, that means we *create value* for others. Yet we don't rest on value creation as a source of dignity or security. We work fruitfully not because we want to gain dignity and security, but because we already have it, in God.

One of the materialistic lies about work is that the good life, the life worth having, is getting as much economic value as you can from others while doing as little work as possible. In other words, live by *extracting* value rather than *creating* value. This is the lie behind sloth, dependency, and the entitlement mentality that expects others to provide for you. We find this at every level of society, from ethically empty Wall Street financiers to crony capitalists in both political parties to able-bodied people who live on welfare generation after generation just because they can.

It's also the lie behind all forms of theft, fraud, and exploitation. This includes everything from illicit drugs and pornography to employers and employees who cut corners in the workplace to the catalog companies that make money by charging little old ladies $50.00 for "collectable" dolls that they could buy in the local big box store for $15.99. Think about the phone company that rented a phone to my great-aunt for decades.

The opposite lie is that productive work is the fundamental source of human dignity and security. This is the lie that lies behind workaholism, the mentality that drives people to prove their self-worth by producing success. Once again, we find this lie at every level of society. People desperately cling to their work for dignity and security in both the boardroom and on the shop floor. I've known people who were eaten up by anxiety and fear of failure, and I've known people smugly complacent that they must be good people because their work is successful. It's not a pretty picture either way.

This is also the lie that lies behind all types of elitist attitudes and social structures that allocate different levels of human dignity to people who do different work. The banker or professor or artist (or missionary) who looks down on the plumber or line worker or beautician (or pastor) is violating the image of God in his neighbor. The policymaker or employer who arbitrarily allocates special privileges to certain workers, companies, or sectors of the economy is doing the same.

Two Kinds of Economic Oppression

The economy goes wrong when social structures incorporate the two lies about work. Because the two lies are perennial, you can find both of them embodied in economic arrangements pretty much everywhere. But because they are not naturally compatible, you will usually find one lie predominant in one part of society while the other lie predominates somewhere else.

Historically, ancient economic arrangements were very fallen. To take the gravest example, slavery was universally accepted around the world as normal and natural before the rise of Christianity. Even since then, it has proven stubbornly difficult to keep down. Although slavery has political and familial aspects, it is most immediately an economic arrangement. Its essence is a certain definition of property ownership (defining some people as property), and its purpose is to organize work and dispose of its fruits in a certain way.

Slavery is the natural endpoint of the lie that the good life is to be had by extracting value from others. Slavery grows from this mindset, and also cultivates it—not only in the slave owners but also the slaves. Those who have been enslaved are constantly tempted to internalize the horribly dehumanizing message implicit in their social status. It's little wonder the gospel did so well among enslaved people in America; the structure of meaning for human life that the gospel provided stood in stark and very favorable contrast to the structure of meaning implicit in slavery.

This lie also lies behind all forms of economic patron/client relationships. Throughout history, the rich and the poor have used patron/client relationships to get along with each other without requiring either side to acknowledge the human dignity of the other. While these relationships have taken on a bewildering variety of forms, from feudal lords and their serfs to western governments propping up third-world dictators with "aid" payments, the basic arrangement is always the same. The rich pay the poor to stay quiet and obey. Think of the patron/client relationship as a kind of "slavery for hire"—if the rich can't keep the poor down with chains, they'll do it with money. Each side views the other as illegitimate and less than fully human. The rich think of the poor as lazy blackmailers (because they extract other people's wealth by threatening to riot) and prostitutes (because they do what they're told once they're paid off). The poor think of the rich as bullies (because they're willing to pay for the privilege of being the boss) and misers (because it takes the threat of a riot to get them to share their wealth). In fact, each side is focused entirely on extracting what it wants from the other while giving as little as possible. They may hate each other, but they understand one another very well.

Finally, this lie is behind economic ideologies based on "enlightened self-interest." The idea here is that it's sufficient for society to forbid the use of force or fraud, and otherwise set few or no ethical expectations for economic behavior. In this view, people are invincibly selfish, but if you keep them from lying or stealing and otherwise leave them to their own devices, they will discover that it's in their self-interest to practice the classical virtues—hard work, honesty, self-control, etc. Some Christians find this view appealing because it seems to provide for public order without requiring a high level of virtue from fallen people who don't have the Spirit. It has never lacked for proponents, but it got a big boost from the revolutionary work of Adam Smith in the late eighteenth century. This tendency was carried all the way to its natural conclusion in the philosophy of self-worship formulated by Ayn Rand, whose views are conveyed by the title of one of her books: *The Virtue of Selfishness*.

Set aside for a moment whether a society driven by enlightened self-interest would be worth the effort to sustain. In fact, the economics of enlightened self-interest don't work. The reason is so simple, I marvel that so many smart people can't see it: if there is no shared public morality other than enlightened self-interest, what justifies forbidding force and fraud? Why isn't it in my self-interest to lie, cheat, and steal whenever I can get away with it? The apostles of enlightened self-interest, from Thrascymachus to Hobbes to Rand, have spent more than two thousand years struggling desperately to articulate an answer to this question. They have produced reams and reams of arguments, all of them chock full of gaping logical holes and glaring contradictions. There is really no solution to the problem, and the whole exercise is a colossal waste of time.

There's an even deeper problem with enlightened self-interest. What actions should count as force or fraud? We all agree murder is wrong, but what counts as murder? Our debates over abortion and bioethics are just the tip of the iceberg for that problem. We all agree theft is wrong, but what counts as theft? In 2009, a judge retroactively changed the bankruptcy laws, with no clear legal authority to do so, in order to strip some GM bondholders of rights they would otherwise have been entitled to during the company's bankruptcy. Was that theft? A lot of people think so, but a lot of people think not. Laws have to be grounded in a social consensus on public morals that goes deeper than just bare labels like "force" and "fraud." Enlightened self-interest can't provide such a consensus.

The opposite lie, that work is the basis of our dignity and security, lies behind economic arrangements based on vocational hierarchies that allocate different levels of dignity to people in different professions. These were less frequent in the ancient world, simply because in a primitive economy there are few people who do the kind of special work that lets them claim to be superior. But priests, rulers, artists, and a few others did benefit from exploitative social arrangements based on the theory that their work made them better people who deserved to control the lives of others. In modernity, this has become more of a problem, as improved education and living conditions allow larger numbers of people to do work that can stake a claim to be special.

This lie is also behind arrangements that use control over other people's work as a false source of security. This is the main reason societies with primitive economies almost always have authoritarian political regimes. In an agricultural economy, food security is always fragile. Even a small decrease in food production could take a whole society to the brink of starvation. A drought or some other natural event could do it at any moment. Social unrest could do the same. People want to know that a firm authority figure is ready to step in and make sure everyone's back is to the wheel, and no one gets out of line. Relatively free and democratic political regimes have no space to develop until economic growth secures the food supply.[23]

The modern economy has produced its own version of this evil. Throughout the twentieth century, a series of economic ideologies sought to maximize economic growth by forcing people to do whatever jobs were assigned to them by a technocratic elite of economic planners. This never succeeded in producing growth, but it did succeed in brutally enslaving people to the technocrats. The technocrats appear to have found this a satisfactory outcome.

The materialistic obsession with growth for its own sake, at all costs, has taken a terrible toll in death, slavery, and misery. The most extreme form was of course Communism, which killed over 100 million people and reduced many more to slavery under totalitarian control.[24] Yet this kind of thinking has been a constant presence in Western democracies as well; from the beginnings of the modern economy to the present day, every democratic country has had a substantial socialist movement.[25] Even after the track record of the last century, which shows where socialism must always lead, some people are still so obsessed with economic growth that they think they can get it by controlling other people's work.

As with sex, so with work—we have been in a unique moment in history. We have enjoyed a society that has been simultaneously one of the most productive, freest, and most generous in history. Yet the old ways are returning. Both of the two lies are gaining ground. They feed off one another—the growth of one drives people to champion the other against it. Value extraction is becoming a way of life at the top (as headlines from Wall Street and Washington show), at the bottom (as levels of nonwork among the able-bodied continue their unprecedented rise among the noncollege-educated), and in the broad middle class (almost 70 percent of Americans take more from government than they give it).[26] The economy sputters as people cease to value fruitful work that produces value. And what solutions are offered? On one side, we hear promises to restore growth through ever-increasing government control of the economy, while on the other side we get promises to restore growth by cultivating enlightened self-interest.

I don't want to paint the picture too bleak. As with sex, so with work—within reason, I'm optimistic. There are some promising signs of renewal. I don't think the majority of the American people believe in the typical economic solutions being offered by either party. That's a hopeful sign, because politicians are good at reading public sentiment and then slavishly following it.

Redeemed Work in the Church and the World

Christians are specially enabled to navigate between these equal and opposite errors by the miraculous work of the Holy Spirit in revelation, regeneration, and sanctification—in our private hearts and in the faith community of the church. He shows us through Scripture and through biblical preaching and teaching what work and the economy are really for—mostly by reminding us of the moral truths that we knew already but preferred to forget, but also by enlarging our perspective with additional "inside information." He works miracles in our hearts that transform us into people who are morally capable, however imperfectly, of building a working life that focuses on cultivating blessings for others through our work, and participating in the economy as value creators rather than value extractors. And he sustains the shared life of the church, where we can support each other and build each other up to be fruitful workers and generous givers.

He also calls us out into the world to be a blessing to our neighbors, and I believe economic work provides the most powerful opportunity to do so in our time. At the beginning of this chapter, I pointed out that Christians spend most of their lives working in the economy. Later, I observed that the economy is critical to human civilization; nothing in society happens without economic work. If you put those two observations together, you get a powerful conclusion: when Christians integrate their faith with their work, performing their work as a manifestation of discipleship and prioritizing fruitful service to their neighbors, they spend most of their lives infusing the impact of the Spirit's work in their hearts directly into the very bloodstream of human civilization.

I don't have words to express how critical I think this insight is to rebuilding a Christian influence on American civilization. We are passing through a transitional period much like Josiah Wedgwood's: old economic structures are being disrupted. The future will belong to the people who create new economic structures that function better in these changed circumstances. Here we must ask, just as we asked in the last chapter regarding sex, what if the Lord is creating an opportunity for Christians? Believers like Wedgwood have taken the lead in creating new and better economic structures before. Why not now? How can we be a blessing to our neighbors by helping them to remember the foundations in human nature that shape how civilizations do their work and build their economic institutions?

Remember the formula for civilizational influence in chapter 2: first, affirmation of the good, then, within that framework, transformation of the bad through co-opted cultural entrepreneurship. We have to begin by affirming that work and the modern economy are good, then seek out opportunities to transform relationships in ways that demonstrate in practice how fruitful work and virtuous exchange provide for human needs better than the alternatives.

If affirming marriage is a major problem area for American Christians today, affirming work and economics is an area where we need even more growth. In chapter 5 I wrote at some length about the church/work dualism that has grown extensively in American churches. Having an impact on our civilization through the economy starts with breaking that dualism. The task of building godly lives, of being Spirit-transformed disciples instead of superficial converts, takes place outside the walls of the church, in daily life where we participate in human civilization. Most of that time is spent working. When our churches identify our daily work as a central place where we learn how to live godly lives, we'll have reached the starting line.

But work is not enough. Human beings aren't just individual creatures, we're also social creatures. The cultural structures of the economy shape the meaning of our work; if we're not talking about the economy, we're not really talking about work. In fact, if we don't teach people to see how their work interacts with other people's work through economic exchange, we're in grave danger of setting them up for exploitation. The last thing we want to do is teach people God wants them to do their jobs without teaching them to see how their jobs impact other people!

We don't have to get involved in partisan disputes to speak about what kind of economy we should have. Because the economy is human action, it's a moral system. A well functioning economy can only come from a commitment to moral principles and practices that are shared across partisan boundaries. The church can affirm those trans-partisan moral commitments: that economic productivity and growth are good, and that they come from old-fashioned hard work and entrepreneurial innovation, not from gimmicks and technocratic tricks hatched by elites in New York and Washington; that companies should strive to turn an honest profit by serving customers with excellence; that the market economy needs to be grounded in ethical integrity, the rule of law, and expansion of economic opportunity to everyone; and so on.

But more important than the national debate is the question of what we all can do in our everyday lives. The key form of cultural entrepreneurship we need is not political advocacy (although I'm all for that). What we really need is for Christians coast to coast to become models of economic blessing, starting with their own work and their own companies, but reaching out and blessing those around them as well. Our neighbors won't find our message plausible until they see, in practice, how hard work and humanely productive companies are a blessing. Ordinary cultural contact with Christians is how that will happen, but only after Christians themselves change the way they live. How can we live out the joy of God in our own working and economic lives, and what can we be doing in ordinary life that would make us a blessing to our neighbors?

As stewards of our work, how can we support ourselves by creating value for others instead of extracting value from others? How can we prepare Christians to find ways to use their work to make our faith meaningful, and to produce more than they consume? As stewards of wealth, how can we encourage saving, investing, and giving?

In your workplace, how can you help to keep serving the customer and getting the job done right front and center? How can you make your workplace more productive and humane? If you have management responsibilities, even in only a small part of the company, how do these questions apply to you especially as a manager—how can you lead and set an example and expectations for those under your stewardship?

Because businesses determine the shape of our work so extensively, we especially need Christian business leaders who can act as modern Wedgwoods. Today, most Christians in business leadership (like most non-Christians in business leadership) care about more than profits; they care about serving the customer and taking good care of their people. However, if the economy is going to be a place where we rebuild Christianity's impact on civilization, that has to be taken to the next level. We need innovative entrepreneurs who use Christianity as a lens to examine how we do business and to invent new and better systems, ways of doing business that are both more productive and more humane.

In your community, are there ways to accentuate the goodness and beauty of fruitful work and generosity? Where do you see people diligently cultivating blessings for their neighbors and giving generously? Where do you see people extracting value without contributing, consuming more than they produce, or squandering wealth instead of saving and giving? What can you contribute to address needs in your community through the economic skills, abilities, resources, and relationships you've been blessed with?

In your local church, what teaching and preaching opportunities are there to help develop biblical knowledge about work and the economy? Are you ceding all that territory, which takes up most of human life, to the world? Can small groups study the topic? Does your church inadvertently teach a narrow view of "stewardship" by focusing only on how people can give to and serve the church, rather than helping people see themselves as God's stewards in all of life?

How can the church at large reintroduce the spiritual realities of work and the economy to our nation? Are there ways of helping America navigate between the two great errors—a dehumanizing collectivism on one side, and mere "enlightened self-interest" on the other? Can we come alongside the national leaders of our culture, who are increasingly alarmed about the realities of economic breakdown, and help them understand the deeper moral causes? Can we make good stewardship of our work and our national economy a bigger issue in our public witness?

America is suffering from a widespread moral anxiety about its economy. The Tea Party movement and Occupy Wall Street may be on opposite ends of the political spectrum, but they really have the same source. We are worried about what kind of people we are becoming. Does it still pay to work hard and play by the rules in America, or is this a country where scoundrels succeed and slackers get a free ride? These debilitating moral doubts are only going to become more severe in the years ahead, because our economic challenges aren't going to get much easier. If Christians become cultural entrepreneurs who manifest a better way for work and the economy, we can show our neighbors the answer to their economic anxieties.

8

Citizenship and Community

I caused the widow's heart to sing for joy.

Job 29:13

We come at last to that bugbear, politics. Many of you have been waiting to see what I will say about this since you first opened the book. Some may worry that I'm going to recommend charging into political combat to enact a Christian policy agenda. Others may worry that I'm going to denounce politics and recommend we withdraw from it completely. And still others may worry that I'm going to offer a hopelessly vague "third way" with nebulous generalities about "steering a reasonable middle course" that don't say anything useful or interesting about the political problem. I will do my best to do none of those things.

Democratic Restrooms

Part of the reason politics has become such a problem for us is because there are actually two different things that are both called "politics," and we don't always distinguish which one we mean. One is the contest for power between parties and factions, especially during elections; we're all familiar with that. The other is something more basic, something that's actually shared by all parties and factions because it's embedded in the social order itself.

This "deeper politics" is the shared set of beliefs about justice that define the nature and boundaries of all political action in a given society. It's the set of background assumptions that stand behind the electoral contests, the partisan disputes, and the whole apparatus of law, policy, regulation, and adjudication. It's a set of shared beliefs we all have in common about what kind of behavior should be expected of everyone who wants to live in our society, versus what kinds of behavior people are free to disagree about. The editors of the journal *First Things* once described politics in this deeper sense as "free persons deliberating the question, How ought we to order our life together?"[1]

Here's the best illustration I've ever come across of that deeper politics. Back in college I started reading comic books. (Laugh all you like.) One story in a favorite title of mine took place in 1979, in London, on the day Margaret Thatcher was elected. Our hero is a dyed-in-the-wool Labor voter, and so are all his friends and everyone in his neighborhood and everyone else he knows. Anything else is unthinkable. Thatcher's victory is heartbreaking, a travesty, and it shakes his faith in his country.

He's sitting at the bar, spouting off at length about the evils of the Tories. He finishes up with, "Who would vote for them?" The barkeeper, one of his oldest and most trusted friends, puts down a glass. "Actually, I voted for them."

Shock, betrayal, amazement—the floor is opening under our hero's feet. The world is upside down. They argue. Our hero pleads with his friend to see reason. But the man remains mild and unflappable. Labor had been in power a long time, they were doing a poor job, things were really starting to go badly, and it was time to let the other side have a turn.

Our hero stands up and declares that he needs to use the facilities. Bitterly, he asks: "Is it still all right with you if a *Labor man* uses your WC?"

Still mild, the barkeeper shrugs and replies: "I'm a democrat. Anyone can use my WC."[2]

That was a powerful scene for me. It's not just the personal drama of two longtime friends struggling with a sudden estrangement. And it's not just the striking example of virtue in this bartender who remains so decent and restrained in the face of persistent abuse from a longtime friend.

Notice what the barkeeper could have said at the end, but didn't. He could have said, "I'm still your mate." He could have said, "I'm hospitable." He could have said, "I'm a barkeeper, not a polltaker." He could have said, "My bar's still on this street, not Downing." He could have said, "I'm an Englishman." Any one of those—friendship, general hospitality, profession, neighborliness, or national solidarity—could have been his reason for reassuring our hero that the WC was still open to him.

Instead, his reason for providing his WC to voters of all parties is itself political: democracy. He knows that when bars start refusing their restrooms to people based on party affiliation, democracy will be over. He refuses to discriminate in the use of his facilities because he believes in a broader "democratic" way of life that defines the nature of his civic community and shapes its political constitution. That's the deeper layer of politics that stands behind the partisan contest.

Equally important, notice that the barkeeper doesn't feel he has to deny or conceal his partisan position in order to sustain this civic solidarity. He voted Tory and he doesn't care who knows it. But that doesn't mean he's compromised his deeper "democratic" identity as a barkeeper whose WC anyone can use. He's comfortable with both. They don't have to be in competition.

A Shared Sense of Justice

The survival of the political system—any political system—depends on people behaving like that barkeeper. We can't have a humane civic life if you risk losing your bathroom privileges at the local bar based on how you vote. If partisan conflict becomes absolutized in that way, that deeper sense of civic duty that makes us treat people right across partisan boundaries withers away. Only the partisan contest remains, released from any sense of moral boundaries. Cynicism and brutality quickly follow.

Members of a given society have a sense of shared identity and way of life. Not everything is shared, of course, but society would not exist if we had no sense of sharing anything in common. If you gathered a bunch of randomly selected people from around the world and locked them in a hotel together, they would have to find a way to get along with each other, but that wouldn't make them a "society." They would have no sense of shared identity and way of life. But over time, if they were locked in long enough, they would eventually develop that shared sense, and become a society.

Many people think we don't really share a common way of life in modern America anymore, but we do. We all agree about representative democracy, the rule of law, personal liberties, and government that exists to serve the governed. We all agree that able-bodied people should work and others should be generously cared for, and that the economy should be driven by business and entrepreneurship but tempered by reasonable regulation and a safety net. We all agree that women should be treated with equal dignity, that young people should choose their own marriage partners instead of parents choosing for them, and that when you get married it's always wrong to cheat. And we all agree the social order should aspire toward religious freedom. If you think all of this is obvious or trivial, you should get to know how people live in the rest of the world.

One of the most important aspects of the shared identity and way of life that makes us a society is a shared sense of justice. That's not the only part of our shared identity, but it is one of the most important. A society isn't a society unless it shares at least some agreement about what kind of behavior is fair and what actions can and can't be tolerated. Again, there are limits—no society has total agreement about justice in all respects. But there is also no society that has no agreement about justice at all.

Some people think we don't have a shared sense of justice in modern America. Admittedly, sometimes our political disputes are so rancorous that they seem to "go all the way down." But that's really just a surface impression. In fact, there's a lot we agree about.

In a recent book, psychologist Jonathan Haidt documents his research on areas of moral agreement between the political left and right in America. Haidt summarizes the areas of agreement within two broad categories: you shouldn't cause harm or suffering without a really good reason, and you should bend over backwards to make sure those who are at a disadvantage aren't mistreated. As simple as that sounds, in practice it covers a lot of ground. In many places in the world, these simple moral ideas are highly controversial! Haidt also illustrates how America struggles for moral clarity in some other areas, which he describes as "liberty, loyalty, authority, and sanctity." But even these are topics of ongoing debates rather than lost causes. Haidt interprets his data through the lens of an evolutionary psychology I don't share, but I think his data show that moral consensus isn't as far gone as some believe.[3]

Politics Is about Justice

Our shared sense of justice is critical to our social identity. Without it, we aren't a society. We're just a random jumble of people who happen to live in the same space.

That's why politics is so important. Politics is the main institutional embodiment of our shared sense of justice. Of course, this doesn't mean we can just forget about justice and leave it to the state to worry about, as if we don't all have an individual responsibility to behave justly! It's exactly the other way around. The state exists because of our individual responsibility to justice—because our shared sense of justice guides all of us in everyday life.

In the history of political philosophy, one of the most important questions is the relationship between power and justice. There has always been a cynical minority, people like Thrascymachus, Machiavelli, and Hobbes, who argue that politics is fundamentally about power. As a result, their theories have no place for any concept of intrinsic human dignity or the public good. Politics is simply a means by which individuals impose their will upon others. In this view, the highest political good is order—not peace in the biblical sense of *shalom*, blessedness, or flourishing, but order in the narrow sense of restraining violence. It doesn't matter how much people hate each other, it only matters that they keep quiet.

Over against this view, the great majority of political philosophers, as well as humanity at large, agree that politics is fundamentally about justice. The purpose of the state is not to impose the will of the rulers upon the ruled, but to see to it that the community's shared sense of justice prevails. The state is an agent of the community and works for its good. The good toward which it works is not an absence of violence but a positive, constructive good—the doing of justice, so people can love and flourish.[4]

The basis of politics is the community's moral consensus about justice. It is not necessary for the community to agree about everything—no community does—but it is necessary for the community to agree about some things. People have to be able to take for granted, without having to stop and argue it out in every single case, at least some broad outlines of what it means to play fair and treat people (and things) the way they ought to be treated. Otherwise society couldn't function; we'd spend all day arguing about justice every time we engaged in even the simplest transactions. You couldn't buy your groceries or drive down the street or take your kids to school without getting into all kinds of disputes with your neighbors. Worse, whenever we'd come into conflict about fair play, we'd have no common ground on which to adjudicate our disputes.

So the most important task in political life is to build moral consensus. In that phrase "build moral consensus," all three words are important. If politics is not guided by the *consensus* of society, government is just a tool of brute force that factions fight each other to control. But if the consensus is not *moral*, government is just a cynical machine people use to gratify selfish desires. Either way, there is no space for justice, freedom, or the intrinsic dignity of the human person.

But the most important word is *build*. Because we live in a fallen world, moral consensus does not come easily. It deteriorates whenever it is not being intentionally built up. Yet because God's grace remains active throughout creation and his law is written on all human hearts, moral consensus does emerge when we work to build it. God's providential grace empowers the natural human processes of reason, history, culture, and socialization to be vehicles for producing moral consensus.

Partisan disputes are not bad in themselves. They don't have to undermine moral consensus; that's the lesson of the barkeeper with his democratic restroom. In fact, there are important virtues to party politics, and especially the two-party system. It may feel like the party system forces us into conflict, but that's an illusion. Conflict, including political conflict, is inherent in fallen human nature. Approaches to politics that seek to eliminate conflict have historically ended in disaster. The approaches that succeed are the ones that assume conflict will always occur and seek to manage it. Channeling politics through parties helps us manage conflict by forcing people to build coalitions and compromise. Restricting the system to only two parties ensures that the parties have an incentive to stay flexible and avoid developing permanent ideological, geographical, or (worst of all) ethnic identities. But as valuable as the party system is, it needs to rest on a deeper stratum of moral consensus about justice.

Two Levels of Justice: Theological and Natural

When we say societies must have at least some moral consensus about justice, we have to be careful about the word *justice*. Like *politics*, *justice* has two layers of meaning, and it has become a bugbear for us because we don't always distinguish what sense of *justice* we mean when we talk about it. If we don't keep the difference clear, we run the risk of promoting either theocracy or a cultural captivity of the church.

On the one hand, there is *theological justice*. This is the complete, ultimate righteousness that we need to stand before God without fear of condemnation. It includes the track record of our actions as well as the content of our personal character.

That kind of justice is not humanly enforced. God reserves exclusively to himself all authority to enforce theological justice (Rom. 12:14–21). Human beings can't see into one another's souls, so we can't reliably judge how other people are or aren't conforming to ultimate theological justice. Moreover, as fallen and sinful creatures we can't live up to that ultimate standard in our own strength, so enforcing it on earth is impossible anyway.

That's not to say we can't encourage and admonish one another to live up to this standard. We can and must. The state of our neighbors' progress in holiness should be of the deepest concern to us. God has even given the church the authority to conduct church discipline as one important form of teaching and admonishment.

What we can't do is enforce this standard as if we were judges. At the bar of theological justice, we're all in the dock as fellow criminals. One criminal can encourage and admonish another criminal to mend his ways. But God is on the bench, and only he can dispense the punishments—or forgiveness.

On the other hand, there is another type of justice, which is humanly enforced. For lack of a better term, let's call it *natural justice*. In a famous passage (Rom. 2:12–16), Paul says that the behavior of human civilizations proves that the law of God is written on the human heart. He describes how God uses the natural human processes of reason, history, culture, and socialization as vehicles of his grace, moralizing the human community.

Government requires our outward actions to conform to a more simple standard of justice. By his grace, God has sustained the ability of fallen and sinful human beings to know this simpler standard of lawfulness, to judge whether the actions of others conform to it, and to administer justice in the world according to this standard. As Paul makes very clear in Romans 13:1–7, God delegates to human communities the power of judgment and enforcement in this kind of justice.

But what does natural justice require? Mostly, it requires us to treat people with basic respect and play fair. We have to be good citizens, respecting the rights of others and participating constructively in society. We might think of it as "peace-oriented lawfulness." The classical philosophical language for it is "giving to each what is due to him."[5]

Natural justice applies at both the individual and social levels. Each of us individually needs to live up to this standard. We also need to maintain a naturally just society, such that our society is *the kind of place* where people treat each other with basic respect, playing fair and giving to each his due. The individual level is where government spends most of its time; rectifying individual acts of injustice is its main function. But the social level of concern, maintaining the kind of society where natural justice can prevail, means the state can't just give us a set of rules to follow and then enforce them. It is also responsible to see to it that the rules don't become a gameable system that people can exploit for their own advantage. Moreover, it means politics has to be concerned with some issues that reach beyond merely enforcing the rules.

Two Places of Justice: Church and State

Just like family and the economy, the embodiment of natural justice in the social order is universal to some extent, and to some extent it's adapted to particular circumstances. We find some rules that are the same basically everywhere—don't kill, don't steal, keep your promises, help your neighbor. Famously, in one of his books C. S. Lewis collected citations from a wide variety of civilizations throughout history, showing these areas of common morality.[6] Barbaric societies don't extend these rules to the treatment of outsiders, but civilized societies recognize them as moral rules applicable to all human beings simply because they're human. That's almost the definition of what makes a society barbaric or civilized.[7] At the same time, there is a great deal of variation in defining the terms of the rules (e.g., what counts as murder?) and applying them.

An interesting problem for politics is that almost no one is loyal to natural justice simply as such. People will live and die for God, or for gods, or historical forces, or their nations or ethnic groups or families, but very few will do much for the sake of "ethics" as a concept. Throughout history there have been people who have wanted to take the set of rules that we find universally enforced in human civilization, and set that up as an ethical code on its own. All such efforts have failed; few have ever gotten beyond the faculty lounge.

That is to say, natural justice presupposes theological justice. This brings us back to something we saw in chapter 1. You can't keep people moral, even in just their public behavior, unless they cultivate a comprehensive view of the universe. This makes sense; there is only one God, and he doesn't have one morality for some people and another morality for others.

At the same time, the difference between the two types of justice is important, and the two have to be distinguished. There is only one morality, but it contains within it multiple levels. There is one level (natural justice) that God calls human beings to enforce, and another (theological justice) that he forbids us to enforce.

The purpose of the distinction between these levels of justice is clear. We need to have a sense of justice that we share with our neighbors; otherwise we couldn't experience human community with them. But we can't expect to share theological justice with our neighbors, because they don't have the redeeming power of the Spirit at work in their lives. The civil community is a place of compromise and consensus among people of different spiritual orientations, so any sense of justice that's genuinely shared will fall short of the fullness of theological justice. Therefore, God provides for one level of justice that's shared (creating civil community) and another level of justice that isn't (preserving the integrity of the church). He has provided for both at an institutional level as well. We have the state to cultivate natural justice in a shared way for the whole community, and the church to cultivate theological justice among believers. The contrast between church discipline and political rule is instructive. Church discipline, which concerns theological justice, is declarative and spiritual. It does not involve the use of force to either punish past behavior or restrain future behavior. By contrast, political rule concerns natural justice and is explicitly connected to the use of force in Romans 13. The difference between the status of human authority over one type of justice and the other is clear.

The delicate task of Christian citizenship is to distinguish and carefully navigate between the two levels of justice, while never leaving either of them behind. If we charge into the political realm and try to enforce theological justice, we'll be overstepping our boundaries. Yet if we allow the church's social witness to be limited merely to natural justice, we will fail to witness ultimate theological justice to the world. We have to find ways to participate in the social order that *witness* theological justice without *enforcing* it, while also building moral consensus to support the enforcement of natural justice.

No Escape from Politics

These days, some people have started to resist the idea of calling this moral consensus about natural justice "political."[8] I can understand the reasons for that tendency. We want to protect natural justice from degenerating into a tool of partisan conflict.

However, natural justice can't be separated from politics. We see that in the way the barkeeper used political language: "I'm a democrat." There are three reasons for this.

One reason is that virtually all the great figures in Western history, regardless of where they stood on anything else, have always used political language to describe natural justice. Inventing a new language from scratch that breaks away from how all the most influential people in your civilization have always spoken and acted is a very dangerous thing to do. It pulls up people's cultural roots and leaves them feeling like there are no limits and everything is up for grabs. And it separates people from a lot of the inherited cultural wisdom they need.

The second reason is that there's a deep intersection between a society's moral consensus about natural justice and the design of its political constitution. While there are a lot of common moral threads across societies, there are also a lot of differences. And, uncomfortable as it can be to acknowledge this, these differences tend to align closely with different kinds of political constitutions. Describe what assumptions about natural justice are shared among the citizenry in a given country, and I'll tell you whether that country is a democracy, an aristocracy, an oligarchy, or whatever else. We're kidding ourselves if we think it's just a coincidence that the United States is structured as a democratic republic and the shared assumptions about natural justice that underlie social life in America emphasize equality of human dignity ("all men are created equal") and personal liberties ("endowed by their Creator with certain inalienable rights").

The third reason why natural justice can't be separated from politics is that, if you rule out political terminology like "democracy," you have to describe the moral consensus with other terminology—and the alternatives are even more dangerous. Abstractions like "the culture" or "natural law" or "social solidarity" are insufficient. No one is going to make sacrifices or change his way of life out of devotion to an abstract intellectual generality. We need something that has the same specificity and tangibility as "our democratic way of life." But all the other tangible terms we could use are jingoistic and tribal: our country, our people, our traditions, our preferences. Describing the moral consensus in these terms alone would reduce the moral consensus to merely the assertion of some group's will.

Only politics can sustain ideas of natural justice that aren't defined by membership in a certain social group. Political language and concepts (in the American context: democracy, the rule of law, equal dignity, personal liberties, etc.) are unique in their ability to help people develop a sense of natural justice that is more than merely the expression of one group's preferences. That is the special calling and glory of politics in God's design of the social order.

Good Citizenship in Everyday Life

So how do we relate politics to the rest of social life? Let's return to the idea that, at least to a certain extent, the members of a society need to have a sense of shared identity and way of life. Politics, both in the form of partisan competition and at the deeper level of moral consensus about natural justice, is one important element of this. But it is not the only one.

To help describe this further, I will use the term *citizenship* to talk about how we participate in all the shared aspects of our society's identity and way of life. This includes political activity in both senses (partisan competition and moral consensus) as well as all the nonpolitical ways we participate as members of society. I know that this way of using the term may make some uncomfortable. I don't think this word choice is essential. Yet we have to talk about this somehow, and *citizenship* seems to me to be the best word available.

Unfortunately, these days we Americans have a tendency to think about citizenship only in terms of the partisan contest for power. Good citizenship means showing up to vote once every four years. (*Really* good citizens vote every two years!) The only other context we seem to have for talking about *citizenship* anymore is immigration policy. But I'm talking about much more than those things.

In a deeper sense, good citizenship is something we do every day. It means keeping an eye out for each other in our communities, not because some government program makes us do so, but because we want to. It means working together to solve problems and in general "owning" our special responsibilities to one another as members of the same society. That barkeeper feels both a sense of civic duty and a sense of civic pride in making his facilities available to everyone regardless of how they vote. The act itself may seem trivial, but the meaning it has for him is vital to how he behaves in daily life. People feel the same way about pitching in to a community cleanup project or volunteering as a tutor—or, trite as it may sound, helping a little old lady across the street. That's what I mean by good citizenship.

The social sphere of citizenship is more difficult to define than the social sphere of family or the economy. Citizenship is a bond that connects you to a much broader set of people. In your family, you are intimately related to a relatively small number of people. Even if you have a big family, with lots of cousins and uncles and whatnot, it's still a pretty small group compared to the whole population. Economic relationships are not usually as intimate as familial ones (although they sometimes are). Still, there is a relatively small set of people you are economically related to on a daily basis—the people in your workplace being the most obvious example. Citizenship isn't like that; you are bonded by citizenship to every other member of your society. That barkeeper could have had exactly the same "I'm a democrat" conversation with a complete stranger who walked through his door for the first time that day.

Yet citizenship doesn't simply mean your general duty to be a good neighbor to everyone you come into contact with. If I meet a foreigner, whether I travel to his country or he travels to mine or we sail out and meet in international waters, I have a moral duty to treat him rightly simply because he's a person. That's not a citizenship thing, it's a humanity thing. So citizenship doesn't cover all human interaction.

Citizenship is specific to a community. Just as sexuality defines family as a social structure and work defines the economy as a social structure, citizenship defines communities. Good citizenship means being a good member of a community and participating in the life of the community in a virtuous way.

We usually think of citizenship only in terms of the national community, but that's not adequate. Community is not the same thing as nation. The national community is important, but we are members of multiple communities—nation, state, region, county, city, neighborhood. Citizenship involves participation at all these levels. How could I call myself a good American citizen if I didn't lift a finger to make my neighborhood a better place?

Good Citizens Are Generous Neighbors

So what does good citizenship—being a good member of a community—look like, and what role is played by the two forms of politics (partisan competition and moral consensus about natural justice) as opposed to other aspects of shared community life? As with so many other things, to some extent the answer to that question is universal, because human beings have some universal natural proclivities. And to some extent it's adapted to the particular needs of each society's time and place.

We already know what politics supplies: natural justice. This is something communities need. So participating in politics to promote natural justice within the moral consensus of society is one aspect of good citizenship.

Moreover, we've already talked about something we shouldn't do. We shouldn't try to use politics to enforce theological justice. When we engage in politics, whether it's voting or through our everyday behavior (like the barkeeper), we need to orient ourselves toward natural justice. Otherwise we risk undermining religious freedom and inviting theocracy. Whenever we find ourselves in situations where a witness for theological justice is called for, we should be proactive in "taking off our political hats" and speaking in nonpolitical modes.

Admittedly, sometimes the boundaries between natural justice and theological justice are tricky to navigate in practice. There are many occasions where it isn't clear which one we're dealing with, and reasonable people will disagree. The important thing is not to lose sight of the distinction and run headlong in one direction or the other.

So the next question is: what else do communities need besides natural justice? That will tell us what else good citizenship requires besides politics.

In one sense, the answer to that question is so large that it's hard to put it into words. Go looking for needs in your community that won't be met by people simply treating others with respect and playing fair and you'll find no end of them. Respect and fair play don't require me to offer babysitting to a single mom, or help someone find a job, or volunteer to clean up a park, or do any of the thousands of things ordinary people do for each other every day.

A broad generalization that more or less covers all of this might be generous neighborliness. We need to interact with our neighbors in generous ways, working with others to solve problems and making the community a better place. And it's not enough just to be generous when we happen to interact with our neighbors; we have to go out and do this proactively. Defending his works, Job declares: "I was a father to the needy, and I searched out the cause of him whom I did not know" (Job 29:16). That's a deeply convicting verse!

This generous neighborliness is a difficult calling. One reason people are tempted to seek a political solution to every problem is because it's easy. Anyone can vote. People will also seek financial solutions to problems because it's easy to write a check. But generous neighborliness means going out in daily life to sacrificially improve life in your neighborhood.

Generous neighborliness is the key thing that makes a community more than just a political unit. This is what gives us a sense of social solidarity with other people even if we come into economic competition or partisan conflict. Generous neighborliness is the social basis for sustaining that substratum of moral consensus running underneath the surface of civilization. It's how we remind ourselves that we really aren't so different, because we're all human.

We can destroy space for real community and invite politics to take over everything in two ways. One is when we cease to strive to be generous neighbors. People fall back into a contented state of "enlightened self-interest" where they take no delight in their neighbors, and think their *only* duty is to obey the laws of natural justice. That social substratum where moral consensus is maintained disappears.

The other is when we try to enforce neighborliness by law. If everything's forced, there's no space for generosity—because it's not generous if it's forced. There's no space for community here, either; the tasks of neighborliness are taken away from people in daily life and transferred to institutionalized bureaucracies. That's why generous neighborliness is what we came up with when we asked what communities need *other than* the natural justice that's enforced by politics.

Natural justice and generous neighborliness are different things that supplement one another; each goes bad without the other. Yet they have one important thing in common. Both require the individual to subordinate himself voluntarily to the interests of his neighbors. Community life can only remain humane and healthy if people spontaneously recognize it as right and desirable to subordinate their own desires to their neighbors' needs.

The key difference is that natural justice can be enforced where people fail to do it spontaneously, while generous neighborliness can't. Enforceability is why we call natural justice both natural and just; it's fair to enforce it because everyone knows it by nature and is accountable to it. Unenforceability is what makes generous neighborliness both generous and neighborly; it only happens when people really want to do it, which means it's an expression of genuine love.

Why Politics Takes Over Everything

How does citizenship go wrong? A growing number of people sense that in America today, partisan conflict—the contest for power—is taking over everything. People are no longer confident that we share a citizenship that is more than merely political, nor are they confident that our politics can be based on a moral consensus about justice. Politics is coming more and more to mean soley partisan conflict, and more and more areas of human life are becoming subordinated to that conflict.

This is not a new phenomenon. In fact, it's the way citizenship typically has gone wrong throughout human history. Aristotle wrote about it at some length almost 2,500 years ago, and with some exceptions, his observations have been vindicated by subsequent history. (There's a reason people still read him.[9]) James Madison described the same dynamic in his famous paper on the United States constitution, Federalist No. 10. (There's a reason people still read him, too.[10])

The problem starts within the political sphere. People start using politics mainly as a way to look out for their own interests, or those of their cultural subgroups. Natural justice gives way to the specific interests of various individuals, factions, and subcultures as the main motivator of political activity.

The critical turning point comes when people begin to identify the desires and interests of their own social faction or subgroup with the general interest of society and natural justice. I convince myself that what I want, or what my group wants, is really what "the community" wants, what the community needs, and what justice demands. Meanwhile, you convince yourself that what you want or what your group wants is really what "the community" wants and needs, and what justice demands.

This is the critical turning point because it causes us to lose any sense that the community exists and has integrity outside the sphere of political conflict. The community's wants and needs are simply identified with a given political agenda. Justice itself comes to mean the implementation of my agenda. The stage is set for political conflict to slowly begin taking over all of life.

The big lie that makes citizenship go wrong is right at the heart of human sin. What leads people to identify their own desires with justice and the general good? Most basically, it is the sinful desire of the fallen human being to live in an egocentric universe where his wishes define reality. Sin begins with a willful self-deception—the illusion that "you will be like God" if you just *act* like you're God (Gen. 3:5).

As the reach of politics extends, it degenerates morally. When justice becomes defined simply as one side's agenda, the moral consensus aspect of politics withers away. Politics becomes reduced to a competition for power. In the absence of moral consensus, the competition for power is not restrained by any sense of boundaries. This gives it an internal drive to expand and conquer new territory. Meanwhile, the decay of moral consensus increases the level of conflict in society at large, and thus creates incentives to use power in spheres where it wasn't previously used. So for both internal and external reasons, partisan conflict expands to encompass more and more of social life.

While this is not a new phenomenon, it has specific causes in our time. It goes back to the history we looked at in chapter 1. In the early twentieth century, America lost what was historically its moral center. Societal agreement on natural justice is deteriorating. We have less and less of a shared sense of what's right or fair in our public conduct. As a result, we have more social conflicts, and the social conflicts we have are harder to resolve peacefully. So we increasingly turn to the use of state force as a way of settling disputes. Hence, the partisan contest for control of the state takes over more and more of life.[11]

This is why we now think of "good citizenship" solely in terms of voting. We know that good citizenship means upholding the moral center of the community. But the moral center of the community is increasingly moving out of the substratum of generous neighborliness and into the surface world of partisan conflict.

A friend of mine once said that people turn to extreme ideologies when they lose confidence that their culture has answers to the moral crises it faces.[12] Today, extreme ideologies that leave no room for real community outside the political sphere have a greater presence than they used to. On one side is an extreme ideology that advocates an ethics of pure self-interest. If you tell adherents of this ideology that they have a responsibility to generous neighborliness, that smells to them like the thin end of the wedge for socialism and political collectivism. So they actually mobilize to fight against anyone calling for generosity. On the other side is an extreme ideology that views politics and government programs as the source of generous neighborliness. If you tell these adherents that when neighborliness is mandated by law and administered through the state, it becomes politicized, cynical, and ungenerous, that smells to them like an excuse for selfishness. So they actually mobilize to defend government bureaucratization of neighborliness. Neither group wants to politicize everything, but both are effectively taking us in that direction.

An additional challenge is the increasing separation of Americans into like-minded neighborhoods.[13] Direct interaction between different kinds of Americans is becoming less common. That means neighborliness among people of different beliefs and ideologies is all the harder to cultivate.

Our increasing physical isolation from one another is affecting our political system. As the polls opened on Election Day, 2012, Michael Barone—for many years one of the most prominent and well-informed political commentators in America—drew on research by Bill Bishop to make this observation: "In 1976, only 27 percent of voters lived in counties carried by one presidential candidate by 20 percent or more. In 2004, nearly twice as many, 48 percent, lived in these landslide counties. That percentage may be even higher this year." When the votes were counted, Barone discovered that he had called the election wrong where he wanted to be right (he's a conservative and had predicted a Romney win) but he was, alas, right on the money where he wanted to be wrong, in terms of our increasing political isolation. The headline of his column: "America Is Two Countries, Not on Speaking Terms."[14]

As in chapters 6 and 7, it's important not to overstate the case here. As before, I'm optimistic, within reason. Ideologies that exclude the possibility of moral consensus do not yet have active support from a majority of Americans. They do have substantially more influence than they used to. More and more people are talking about this problem and looking for a solution. A renewal of commitment to building moral consensus and real community through generous neighborliness is needed if the unlimited expansion of political conflict is to be stopped. People seem to realize that this is needed, and I suspect those who go out on a limb in this direction will be rewarded.

Redeemed Citizenship in the Church and the World

Christians are specially enabled to overcome the selfish desire to identify their own desires as the public good by the miraculous work of the Holy Spirit in revelation, regeneration, and sanctification—in our private hearts and in the faith community of the church. He shows us through Scripture and through biblical preaching and teaching what citizenship and the community are really for—mostly by reminding us of the moral truths that we knew already but preferred to forget, but also by enlarging our perspective with additional "inside information." He works miracles in our hearts that transform us into people who are morally capable, however imperfectly, of generously blessing all our neighbors regardless of where they stand with the Lord, and participating in the community (including the political system) in ways that cultivate justice and flourishing for all citizens. And he sustains the shared life of the church, where we can support each other and build each other up as a people who value natural justice and generous neighborliness, without losing sight of the higher theological justice that we know is really at the heart of the universe.

Here we see how cultivating discipleship within the church is not a separate, isolated activity from going out into the world to be a blessing to our neighbors. Good citizenship has been right at the heart of Christian discipleship as far back as history records. In the middle of the second century, Justin Martyr argued that the Roman emperor should tolerate Christianity because *Christians are such good citizens that when Christianity flourishes, non-Christians are better off.*[15]

Some in our own time want to suppress Christianity by force. We ought to be able to say the same thing to them that Justin said to the Romans. Can we?

In addition to being good citizens in the community every day, we can bless our neighbors by building a moral consensus with our non-Christian neighbors based on natural justice. Remember the formula for civilizational influence in chapter 2: first affirmation of the good, then within that framework, transformation of the bad through co-opted cultural entrepreneurship. We have to begin by affirming that the natural justice we share with our neighbors is good, even if it doesn't rise to the level of God's ultimate theological justice. Then we seek out opportunities to transform relationships in ways that demonstrate in practice how generous neighborliness provides for human needs better than the alternatives.

We don't need to fear that our neighbors won't welcome the effort. The desire for natural justice is not confined to the church. That's exactly what makes it "natural" justice instead of theological. God is still at work throughout the entire creation, accomplishing his purposes by providential grace even where this does not lead all the way to redemption. One of the things God does is equip all people with a desire for natural justice, as Paul's comments in Romans 2 make clear. That's part of what it means to be made in God's image. The natural processes of reason, history, culture, and socialization help people develop a sense of natural justice and teach them that they ought to live by it. The fact that they do not, in fact, live by it does not mean that they don't know they should. In fact, if they didn't know they should, they wouldn't be culpable for the fact that they don't!

And yet, at the same time, we Christians are equipped to build moral consensus in a way that most of our neighbors are not. Remember that natural justice presupposes theological justice, and moral consensus relies on generous neighborliness. Right now, these moral foundations of the social order are withering away. As moral consensus becomes weak and generous neighborliness is stretched thinner and thinner, politics becomes little more than a contest for power between parties. However, as believers we have a higher loyalty to a higher standard of justice, and an imperative to put our neighbors' needs ahead of our own desires. That gives us standing to renew the practice of "politics" at the deeper level, "politics" as a moral imperative to good citizenship and natural justice.

Unfortunately, for reasons discussed in chapter 1, in the twentieth century evangelical leaders often fell into the same trap as the rest of America. They knew they were the *theological* heirs of the old Protestant consensus that had exercised central moral authority in American life; usually they didn't realize they were not the *sociological* heirs of that consensus. So they frequently identified the moral consensus of the community and the cause of natural justice with the agenda of their cultural subgroup. As it became increasingly clear that America no longer had a moral center and non-Christians were changing institutional arrangements in alignment with their beliefs, they felt like they were under attack. So as they strove to place themselves at the top of American civilization, a position that "evangelicals" as such had never before occupied, they believed that they were only defending themselves against vicious assaults by those who hated them.

These problems are increasingly recognized among American Christians. In fact, I'd go so far as to say that the old model of evangelical politics is now effectively dead, and has been for some time.[16] Consider how George W. Bush worked hard to avoid triumphalist rhetoric and the defensive narrative. He stressed that he wanted to represent not only "people of faith" but also "people of no faith" and their concerns. Throughout his presidency, one of his most important premises was that all human beings (Christian, atheist, Muslim, whatever) share a basic set of universal values. I don't think that approach is adequate; it assumes moral consensus always exists everywhere, neglecting the need to *build* consensus. But at least it shows what a stark difference there is between Bush and Pat Robertson.

With the old model dead and nothing else clearly taking its place yet, the time is ripe for a new model of Christian citizenship to emerge. To my mind, citizenship should mean generous neighborliness in everyday life, not just voting. We have to build moral consensus with the whole American community, both in our formal political involvement and in our everyday citizenship.

Rethinking the American founding in the way I described back in chapter 1 will be an important part of this. Religious liberty for all is at the heart of our national identity. America has always been a truly shared possession; that's what's so special about it. Partisan conflict is fine, and we should be comfortable with it both in society at large and among Christians themselves. But that conflict needs a substratum of moral consensus underneath it. Christians can be a force for rehumanizing the political sphere by prioritizing the religious freedom of those who aren't Christians.

The first step to making that happen will be learning to practice good citizenship. We must continue to stand up for natural justice in the public square, but we must learn not to identify victory for natural justice with victory for our social group. We have to detach moral victory (that is, victory for marriage, for human life, etc.) from religious victory. The way the issues have been framed in the last generation, a vote for moral public policy was the same thing as a vote for Christians to impose Christianity on the public. We can reframe the needs of natural justice as the basic preconditions of decent human civilization (which they are) rather than as exclusively Christian teachings (which they are not). We also need to make extra efforts to fight back against the absolutization of politics. We must challenge the widespread assumption that our moral disagreements about public issues make us into mortal enemies. The decay of our politics has reached a point where it is simply taken for granted that there is no moral common ground or shared citizenship. Enmity has become institutionalized. We have to work to deinstitutionalize it by bending over backwards to demonstrate that we, at least, do not see those who disagree with us as enemies. They are fellow citizens with whom we disagree.

Above all, we must invest in generous neighborliness so the ties of citizenship are rebuilt across lines of conflict. How can Christians use their membership in communities (neighborhood, city or town, nation, etc.) as occasions for being a good neighbor? How can we be the kind of neighbors who make others say, "I can't imagine this place without you?" When issues of justice are at stake in our immediate lives, such as in a workplace conflict or an issue in the neighborhood, how can we reach out to unbelieving neighbors and build moral consensus with them? How can we show that we *want* to live in a society where non-Christians are equally valued as citizens and members of the community?

In your local community, how can you practice generous neighborliness through institutions like schools, businesses, sports, and activity groups? In what ways do you see people and institutions building moral consensus among people who disagree? What opportunities do you have to cultivate the expectation that people in your community look out for each other?

In our national community, are there national causes we can support that contribute to our sense of civic solidarity as a nation instead of just moving money and stuff around? Are there opportunities in your local community to connect these virtues to our national identity, such as when celebrating national holidays? Are you overly invested in national causes at the expense of involvement in your local community?

In your local church, what is your church doing to cultivate discipleship through good citizenship? Is it a topic that comes up once every four years? Does your church inadvertently teach a dualistic approach to life that separates discipleship from good citizenship? Or does it inadvertently undermine moral consensus by identifying justice and the public good with an agenda limited to political issues?

How can the church at large reintroduce the spiritual realities of citizenship to our nation? Are there ways of distinguishing justice and the public good more clearly from the agenda of our cultural group? Life in civilization requires compromise and coalition building, particularly in the area of politics. Can we do more to build moral consensus in the American community around natural justice?

I like to remember that on 9/11, Flight 93 was prevented from crashing into the White House by a gay man and an evangelical. When America's survival was at stake, they had no difficulty linking arms and fighting together to save it, even unto death. In the coming decades, Americans are going to be discovering that the absolutization of our social conflicts is likewise threatening to destroy the country. Like the heroes of Flight 93, we will have to make the choice to come together despite our differences. If they could find a way to die together, we can find a way to live together.

Conclusion

He Rules the World
with Truth and Grace

The joy of the LORD is your strength.

Neh. 8:10

Infusing the joy of God into our daily participation in human civilization involves countless little things. There's no formal program or "eight easy steps." And yet, while from one point of view it involves countless little things, from another point of view, it's really just one very big thing.

You have to develop the wisdom to build a single, integrated, whole life that honors and follows Jesus in your home, workplace, and community. You have to wrestle with what's called for in each area of your life, without losing sight of how all the areas fit together. That means not only figuring out a lot of questions that are unique to you, but also keeping your wits about you—because your situation will change over time and you'll often be confronted with unexpected dilemmas.

To look at your whole life in a new way requires intentional and sustained effort. You may have heard of the story "Acres of Diamonds," which was written in the 1860s by Baptist pastor Russell Conwell. Conwell founded Temple University with the revenue he made on the lecture circuit giving his "Acres of Diamonds" speech thousands of times. (His name is also preserved in American evangelicalism in Gordon-Conwell Theological Seminary.) The story tells of a rich man in ancient Persia who becomes obsessed with diamonds after first hearing about them from a traveler; he sells his estate and spends his life looking for them. He lives a frustrated life and dies unhappy, having never seen a diamond. But the people to whom he sold his estate discover a diamond mine right underneath the man's house.

The wonders we seek are right in front of us, if we have the wisdom to dig in our backyards and find them. The point is not geographic localism; it's developing the insight to see what really matters. Conwell closes the speech: "Bailey says: 'He most lives who thinks most.' If you forget everything I have said to you, do not forget this, because it contains more in two lines than all I have said. Bailey says: 'He most lives who thinks most, who feels the noblest, and who acts the best.'"[1]

To train and prepare yourself to infuse the joy of God into your daily participation in human civilization, I would stress four things. You will need to develop sensitivity to the "unwritten rules" of social life in our civilization, and learn how to practice your faith not only explicitly but also in the way you respond implicitly to these unspoken patterns of life. You will need realism about what you can accomplish; each of us needs to engage in careful strategic thinking to identify goals that are reachable. You will need perseverance; most of the fruit you should hope to see from your efforts will take time to grow. But perhaps most of all you will need encouragement. We should all remind ourselves, every day, that God is constantly at work in our lives, and not only in our lives but in everything that happens in the world. He has promised us that however bad things may seem, our efforts to embody his joy in our lives will not be in vain.

Civilization and the Gospel: Both Explicit and Implicit

American evangelicals have received two wonderful, incredible gifts from God that are in tension with one another. We have, on the one hand, our passionate desire to show God to our neighbors, and, on the other hand, our passionate desire to show our neighbors that we love them and want their good. We want everyone to see, feel, and experience the joy of God, but we're worried about coming across like we're picking fights or presenting God as an enemy. We want people to know just how amazingly the joy of God transforms every aspect of human life for those who receive it. We're worried about how to tell them about this without creating hostility.

Thank God for both of these gifts, because we need both. God bless evangelicals for wanting to show God and the joy of God to people, and also for wanting to show people that we are (and God is) for them and not against them. Both are basic to who we are in Christ.

Unfortunately, too often we cultivate only one or the other of these gifts. Some of us have developed a tendency to try to make everything in human life explicit. We can see how the joy of God impacts every area of human life and we (rightly) want to make that explicit so others can see it, so some of us (not so rightly) try to shoehorn an explicit discussion of God, his law and his gospel, and their applications into every social situation. Others shy away from *ever* making the gospel explicit, for fear of creating discomfort or confrontation. We always leave the gospel implicit, assuming that people will recognize it or have a chance to hear it from someone else.[2]

There is a time and a place for everything. Unto everything there is a season, and a time for every purpose under heaven. The explicit gospel and all its applications need to be actively circulated so they're available to everyone, but they don't need to be crowbarred into every social situation. All believers ought to participate in the process of evangelization, but that does not mean all of social life must be subordinated to this imperative.

We see this exemplified in the New Testament. Jesus, the apostles, and believers at large share the gospel explicitly in situations where it is appropriate. They share it in private spiritual conversations. They share it in the temple and other teaching places. They share it in the marketplace, which was used as a place for the exchange of ideas in Greco-Roman tradition. But there's no indication they subordinated all their human relationships to this imperative. I have a hard time believing that Jesus talked to everyone he met at every well he ever drank from in the same way he talked to the Samaritan woman.

When we drag things back to an explicit connection to God in an unnatural way, our neighbors feel like we view them only as potential converts, not as people. They feel dehumanized by this, and they're right to feel that way. Our relationships with them become hollowed out, because all the implicit human interactions are suddenly overridden. Peter helping Mrs. Jennings fix a porch rail, sending the implicit message "I enjoy blessing you," suddenly becomes CHRISTIAN EVANGELIZING A HEATHEN. Lisa ordering her regular lunch from the server she sees every week, sending the implicit message "I trust you so much that I'm willing to eat what you put in front of me" suddenly becomes CHRISTIAN EVANGELIZING A HEATHEN. Bob chatting with Frank about a ball game, sending the implicit message "I'm like you and I enjoy the things you enjoy," suddenly becomes CHRISTIAN EVANGELIZING A HEATHEN. A movie telling a morally edifying story shoehorns in an artistically awkward gospel presentation scene, and all the implicit edification is suddenly replaced by CHRISTIANS EVANGELIZING HEATHENS. The fixing of the rail, the buying of a cup of coffee, the conversation about a game, the uplifting story—and the deeply humanizing messages they implicitly send—all disappear, replaced by two-dimensional artificialities.

There's a good reason not to try to shoehorn the explicit gospel into every social interaction. It's not because the spread of the gospel should be limited. It's precisely because the spread of the gospel should be unlimited!

Civilization exists on two levels—let's call them explicit civilization and implicit civilization. Any time you interact with other people, you are following two sets of rules: the written rules and the unwritten rules. Explicit civilization is the written rules: laws and regulations, workplace rules and policies, house rules. Even the rules that aren't formally written down but are explicitly expected ("that's not the way we do things around here") are part of explicit civilization. Implicit civilization is the rules that are never named, rules that are "enforced" through facial expressions, tones of voice, using one word rather than another. Usually we don't even think about these expectations as we're setting them. It's the difference between saying "That's great!" or "That's nice," or "That? Really?"

Implicit civilization needs to be evangelized. But only an implicit gospel can be infused into implicit civilization. Whenever you take things to the explicit level, you leave the implicit level behind; that's what it means to call it "implicit." So by the very nature of things, the explicit evangelism only evangelizes explicit civilization. Crowbarring the explicit gospel into every situation prevents us from ever applying the gospel to the implicit level of civilization.

You may think "implicit gospel" is a contradiction in terms. Consider 1 Peter 3:1–2: "Wives, be subject to your own husbands, so that even if some do not obey the word, they may be won *without a word* by the conduct of their wives, when they see your respectful and pure conduct." Of course, a few lines later Peter brings the explicit gospel back in: "In your hearts honor Christ the Lord as holy, always being prepared to make a defense to anyone who asks you for a reason for the hope that is in you" (v. 15). But he immediately adds the implicit gospel again: "Yet do it with gentleness and respect, having a good conscience, so that, when you are slandered, those who revile your good behavior in Christ may be put to shame" (vv. 15–16). We need both; one without the other will not do.

As 1 Peter 3 suggests, we actually undermine evangelism when we only use the explicit gospel. Our way of life, our implicit commitment to the gospel in how we conduct ourselves and treat people, is what makes the explicit evangelism seem plausible and legitimate. This is the same principle that we saw at work in chapter 8, where the substratum of generous neighborliness sustains the moral consensus upon which explicit politics is based. So shoehorning the gospel into every situation is not only bad on its own terms (because treating people in dehumanizing ways is a bad thing), it's self-defeating.

The implicit gospel is like the heavens "declaring" the glory of God (Psalm 19). The heavens don't talk; they declare God's glory simply by being what they are. So do we, if we are truly being transformed by the Spirit. Timothy Keller argues that just as God reveals himself to all humanity through the "wordless speech" of the heavens and the mountains and the flowers, he also reveals himself through the "wordless speech" of human culture.[3] Isaiah 28:23–29, for example, tells us it is God who instructs farmers how to farm. Romans 2:12–16 tells us it is God who instructs lawmakers in justice. If Christians don't manifest a Spirit-transformed participation in these activities, we aren't declaring God's glory.

I think this idea of evangelizing implicit civilization with an implicit gospel *in addition to, not instead of,* the explicit gospel is part of what Keller is talking about when he talks about building a "gospel ecosystem."[4] Keller describes how most American evangelicals are unprepared to deliver the gospel in ways that will make sense to people who are formed by contemporary American civilization. He recommends intentionally building networks of Christians who figure out what the gospel looks like when it's lived out in a variety of cultural settings—different professional fields, different ministry objectives, different people groups, and so forth. He offers this not as an alternative to explicit evangelization but precisely as a necessary background or foundation for conducting explicit evangelization. Why is it necessary? His point seems to be that American evangelicals need to train themselves more diligently in the implicit gospel before they can present the explicit gospel credibly.

Of course, this is not to say you can never present the explicit gospel except within ongoing relationships where the other person has seen you living out the implicit gospel. I've done sidewalk evangelism, and I've seen God convert people through that. But rest assured, when that happens it's almost always because those people have seen the implicit gospel lived out in other contexts. Remember my relative from chapter 4? My wife and I shared the explicit gospel, but she only found it plausible because for years and years she saw the implicit gospel in her Christian coworkers.

The implicit level also acts as a "carrier" that helps transmit cultural influence across barriers of hostility. When people develop a dislike for a cultural group—say, evangelical Christians—all the explicit messages from that group are filtered out. C. S. Lewis writes in his autobiography that for a long time, he paid no attention to Christian claims because he had Christians mentally "placed" in a certain way. One of the most important things that changed his mental state was the behavior he encountered among Christians he knew.[5] I went through exactly the same thing myself, and so have other converts I know.

Even where the explicit Christian message is never accepted, the implicit carrier can transmit the gospel into implicit civilization with dramatic impact. That was the theme with which I opened this book—"Joy to the World!" The joy of God can have influence in civilization far beyond the sphere of actual conversion, if we give it space.

That's why, over the long term, this implicit carrier is indispensable to Christianity's impact on civilization. Only implicit evangelism can take Christians' distinctly Spirit-shaped ways of participating in civilization and spread them out into the world beyond the scope of the Spirit's supernatural saving work. As long as we stay at the explicit level, Christianity can never influence people who aren't converted, so by definition the church can't influence civilization beyond its own walls.

And, of course, we need to keep the explicit gospel front and center in church life. It's necessary not only for its own sake, but also to sustain the implicit element. Remember, implicit evangelization doesn't just mean "be a nice person." It means infusing the radical, life-changing gospel into everything we do. You can't do that if you don't constantly remind yourself and others about the gospel you're infusing. That's the Spirit's work we looked at in chapters 3–5.

Prudence: Neither Naive nor Cynical

Human civilization is extremely complex and changes only very slowly. The ways in which it changes are subject to countless millions of factors that interact in unpredictable ways. Even a small slice of civilization—say, a home or a factory floor—will contain within it a bewildering variety of cultural factors interlocking in ever-changing nexuses and ganglions. Modern civilization in particular is vast, complex, and highly differentiated.

So if we want to influence people, we have to be realistic. Our reach should not exceed our grasp. For centuries, the church used to teach that there were four "cardinal virtues" that were central to living a good human life, and one of them was prudence.[6] Prudence might be summarized as the moral virtue of being realistic.

Today we tend to think of prudence or realism more as a manifestation of intelligence or savvy. But there were good reasons the church historically classified this as a moral virtue, an integral part of being a good person. Realism is essential to responsible behavior. It means you care whether your actions are actually improving the world and blessing others rather than destroying and burdening. Naiveté is not quaint, innocent, and morally purifying. It's horribly destructive. Maybe some people can't help being naive in some respects, but for the most part, naiveté is a serious sin. It's lazy and irresponsible.

Realism does not mean despair or cynicism. Those are also serious sins. They deny that God is still at work in the world through providential grace. Despair denies that God is in control of the world, while cynicism denies that human beings still possess the conscience and moral agency they were made with in God's image. In fact, despair and cynicism are actually forms of naiveté. No one could be more naive than the man who believes, in the teeth of all the evidence showing otherwise, that the bad guys always win and good things always fall apart and come to nothing. No one could be more naive than the cynic who believes, in the teeth of all evidence showing otherwise, that all human behavior is motivated exclusively by selfishness. These, too, are lazy and irresponsible people—they want excuses to avoid working and sacrificing to achieve good things.

Being realistic—neither naive nor cynical—means thinking carefully about what is under your control and what is under other people's control, and how other people are likely to respond if you act this way or that way. You can use that insight to figure out the best, most effective course of action to accomplish good results. Just as important, it means always paying attention to the results of your actions and continually feeding those results back into your thinking, so you can stop doing anything that turns out not to work, and get better and better over time at identifying what gets good results and what doesn't.

Notice that the starting point of realism is to be aware of spheres of control: what is your sphere of control, what is each other person's sphere of control, how do others respond within their spheres to your actions, and how can you act within your sphere to get the best reactions and results. There is a theological reason why spheres of control are so critical. Human beings were made to be stewards of creation. That means we have control over it—each of us has control over some portion of it—and we are called to use that control to cultivate blessings for God's glory. We are all kings of creation under God, our great high King.

Your sphere of control is limited. It may be large if you are a wealthy, powerful, or influential person. Or it may be small. (The Bible is clear that God intends people to have different sized spheres, but he also intends that all people have equal dignity regardless of how big their spheres are. This is one point of the parable of the talents.) But whatever size your sphere is, it's limited. God made things that way so others could have spheres of control, too. If you controlled everything, others would have no kingship, no opportunity to be stewards.

For this reason, we need to distinguish two things: the sphere of things you are able to control, and the sphere of things you ought to actually control. If you set down your wallet near me and then turn your back, I have the ability to take control of it by picking it up and putting it in my pocket. But I ought not to do that. So within the larger sphere of things that you can control if you chose to, there is a smaller sphere of what you *ought* to control. This smaller sphere is your true sphere of kingship, the proper sphere for exercising your stewardship. Dallas Willard describes this as "what you have say over."[7]

This point is critical to engaging civilization with realism. When we work to influence things going on in the world, whether in our own homes or in the country at large, we have to remember two limitations on our spheres of control. First, we have to be aware of what is really within our control and what is not. Cultural change is hard to produce; we need to figure out which goals we can really accomplish and which ones are desirable but not realistically attainable. Second, even where we can do something, we shouldn't do it by taking control of things that rightfully belong to other people's spheres of control. Otherwise we're taking away our neighbors' stewardship. Those who don't live up to godly standards of behavior do not thereby forfeit their right to control their own lives.

The good news is, our membership in civilization and all its structures (home, workplace, community, etc.) is part of our sphere of control. That's because people are social creatures, as we saw in chapter 2. Our stewardship includes our relationships with others. We are responsible to be stewards of the way we treat other people and interact with them. We're responsible to be good sons, daughters, brothers, sisters, husbands, wives, fathers, and mothers; employees, employers, managers, coworkers, students, teachers, clients, customers, and vendors; friends, neighbors, members, and participants. Through our stewardship of relationships, a sphere of social influence opens up. Our daily participation in civilization gives us opportunities, over time, to change social dynamics in a godly direction.

By changing the way I treat others and steward my relationships with them, I can—within limits—affect the way they behave within their spheres of control. I don't take their control away. I change my relationship with them, which (because they are social creatures) impacts them as people. The better a husband I am to my wife, the better a mother she will be to my daughter. The better a boss I am to my subordinate, the better a coworker he will be to everyone else in our workplace. If I become a better neighbor, my neighbors will also become better neighbors.

Realism means neither overestimating nor underestimating my ability to change social dynamics and get positive results. I need to set goals that are neither too ambitious nor too timid. If my goals are too ambitious, I'll only waste my effort—and possibly create a bad witness that drives my neighbors away from Christ. But if my goals are too timid, I won't live out the joy of God; and when I stand before my Master in the end, I won't have much of a good report to make about my stewardship.

That means I have to think carefully about my sphere of control. The goal "everyone in my workplace will feel fairly treated" might be ridiculously overambitious if I'm just a line worker, or if my workplace is riven with longstanding conflicts. But it would be setting the bar too low, making things too easy on myself, if I'm the manager of a small workplace that already has a strong organizational culture. The line worker might select a small working group and make it a goal to gently encourage better teamwork there. In a workplace riven with conflicts, it might make sense to pick just one conflict and focus on ameliorating it. Meanwhile, the manager whose workplace has a strong *esprit de corps* might think about more boundary-pushing ideas. Could that workplace do more to be a blessing to the community at large?

Setting the right goals also means I need to think about my strategy for achieving them.[8] If I don't have a strategy, that means I haven't thought my goals through and don't really know if they're achievable. And my goals should be more or less ambitious depending on how much control I have over the means of achieving them. Within my own home I should challenge myself to create a lot of Christlikeness; otherwise I'm not really living out the calling of discipleship. In my country at large or when reaching around the world, I should be more careful in thinking through what is really possible.

Perseverance: Getting Everyone from A to B

We have to give up our dreams of immediate victory. They tend to distract us from our real divine calling, which is the real source of a satisfactory life: to do the right thing in the right way for the right reason, in childlike reliance on God. What I have described in this book is obviously not a quick and easy path to dramatic results. It's a call to perseverance in doing things the hard way. But although this path is longer and harder, it's also more fulfilling and satisfying, because it maintains both integrity and effectiveness.

We are sometimes fooled by what appear to be rapid victories for this or that issue in the struggle for cultural change. A cause—stigmatizing tobacco use, for example, or promoting gay marriage—seems to make the leap from marginal to mandatory overnight. That's an illusion. These sudden victories are always the result of slow social change over long periods of time. The anti-smoking cause (which I support) leapt to sudden victory because for a century, American culture had been gradually medicalized; health has now become the supreme public good. The gay marriage cause (which I oppose) leapt to sudden victory because for a century, American culture had been gradually refusing to think of sex as a metaphysical reality and sex roles as legitimate and necessary. In both cases, the defenders of the old ways had been slowly losing their place at the center of civilization for a long time. The "sudden" victories occurred when the reformers—having patiently waited through a generation or more of diligent work building up their cultural position—saw that their time had finally arrived.

In the past generation, American evangelicals have heard more than their share of empty promises—claims that big cultural changes were just around the corner, or were already underway. At this point, I think we're finally through with empty promises of cultural miracles. At least, by now I sure hope we are. (Please, Lord, let my statement that "we're finally through with empty promises of cultural miracles" not turn out to be just another empty promise of a cultural miracle!)

That doesn't mean we give up. It means we remember that God made us as historical creatures who change and accomplish things over time. Look back at the first point in chapter 1: Christianity is uniquely a religion of history. God likes history. He works within it and through it. He works through social processes that unfold over time.

You can see how God likes to work through history in how he's built the church. It took about three centuries for the gospel to spread just to the whole Roman Empire. It took six centuries for the church to settle its basic doctrinal questions concerning the Trinity and the incarnation. It took ten centuries—a thousand years—for the church to repudiate "ransom" theories of the atonement and formulate the language that justification occurs through forensic imputation. It took another five centuries after that before we even started having the fight over whether justification *only* occurs through forensic imputation! Today we are witnessing the breathtaking spread of the gospel in the Global South. God's bringing in so many millions of people from so many people groups in so many places all at once is going to change the church in ways we can't possibly predict. For all we know, as little as a century from now people may look back on our time as the most important turning point in the two-thousand-year history of the church. Who's to say? But if you ask why it took God two thousand years to get to this point, I think the answer's pretty obvious. He has always preferred to accomplish things in his own good time, through the unfolding processes of human history.

The same principle is visible in the history of Christianity's impact on human civilization. It took three centuries just for the church to persuade the Roman state to tolerate its existence. It took more than a full millennium before Christianity's influence succeeded in eliminating slavery, prompting greater dignity for women, and cultivating the emergence of early modern democracy within Europe. And it took centuries more for these changes to reach their full fruition: When the age of exploration brought slavery roaring back through the international slave trade, it took three centuries to tamp it back down. Democracy and the rule of law didn't come into their own until the eighteenth century. Letting young women choose their marriage partners instead of having their fathers choose for them emerged at about the same time.

Historical processes are messy and unpredictable. The apostles clearly saw that doctrinal controversies were going to be an ongoing problem in the church, but I suspect that if you'd asked them how many centuries they thought it would take before the church developed a clear and systematic witness on all the key issues, they couldn't have predicted it. Some might have predicted it would happen quickly, others might have predicted it would never happen at all. "It'll happen in six centuries" is something I think they wouldn't have been equipped to foresee. And if they couldn't foresee that, we're certainly not equipped to foresee where American civilization is going or what our own impact is going to be.

One thing we can easily predict is that anything worth accomplishing will take time, and the bigger our goals are, the more time they will take. I once saw an organizational leadership textbook that showed two diagrams. One showed Point A and Point B with a short, straight line connecting them. It was labeled something like, "This is what it looks like when a leader goes from Point A to Point B." The other diagram showed Point A and Point B connected by a long, winding line that snaked all the way around the picture before it finally found its way over to where it was going. It was labeled, "This is what it looks like when a leader goes from Point A to Point B *and brings everyone else in the organization there, too.*" Cultural impact never happens except through this messy process of bringing "everyone else" along with us to the point where we're going. We should expect a long, winding path.

Here's another point. I think this is extremely important, but not enough people learn it. Let's imagine we have to get people from Point A to Point Z. Sometimes, you'll be able to say to people who are at A, "I know it's a long way from here, but you really need to get to Z, and here's why." However, most of the time people who are at A just won't buy the idea that they need to get to Z. After all, if they were going to find Z plausible, they would have probably realized they needed to get there a long time ago and already started going in that direction. So when you call them to Z, they don't budge. But suppose you say to them instead, "You'd be much better off at G, and here's why." It's a true statement. G really is better than A; it's closer to Z! And unlike Z, G is something they'll buy—it's much more plausible. Then, as you work to help them get to G, somewhere around D or E they'll start to get a better view of the landscape, and they may realize that G isn't sufficient. That's when you start talking up how L is even better than G. Maybe they'll refuse to listen; if so, you'll still have done them a lot of good by getting them to G. But you'd be surprised how often people will agree to move the goalposts from G to L. And then, as they're passing through J or K, you can drop a hint that T is an even better destination than L, and see how that flies. You can actually get a lot more people to Z by *not* telling them Z is where they need to be until they're practically there.

Let's say a pastor returns from a conference on worship and

announces to his church that because of what he learned, he's making changes—even relatively small ones—to the order of worship. Any pastor can tell you what happens next: conflict and resistance. People don't understand what lies behind the change, what motivates it and shows that it's necessary. It's scary to them. But suppose the pastor instead just does one small thing differently, once, without announcing it ahead of time or making a big deal out of it. People get to see what it looks like, and he can gauge their reactions. If they like it, he keeps the change; if not, he thinks of something else to try after a suitable period of time goes by. Do this over a few years and you can get the changes you want without conflict. Over a decade, you can really turn people's perspectives around on what the church does.

This point is closely related to "implicit civilization" and "implicit evangelism." As you *explicitly* bring people to G, by the very act of doing so you're also *implicitly* preparing them for the message that they'd be even better off at L, and so forth. If you do the implicit stuff right, the explicit stuff goes a lot easier.

We do need to make sure that this call to realism and perseverance doesn't become an excuse for inaction. We are called to action. "Stay dressed for action and keep your lamps burning" (Luke 12:35). This is especially true when a change of direction is called for. As the saying goes, you can't steer the car while it's parked. If we want to change the way Christianity engages American civilization, we will have to focus more on starting new efforts than on stopping old ones.

This is why perseverance is so important. The only way to avoid both recklessness and inaction is to select realistic goals and a realistic timetable for accomplishing them—which means persevering through the long and messy process that realistic approaches require. We need to set both short-term goals (to keep us moving) and long-term goals (to keep us from falling into an unproductive rut). The goals and timetables need to be realistic, but not complacently so.

Another aspect of perseverance is persevering through failure, so we can learn from it. We are called not only to action, but to pay attention to the results of our actions so we can fix what's not working and redouble our efforts on what is. Virtually everyone who has accomplished anything worthwhile agrees that the ability to persevere in the face of failure and learn lessons from it is essential to success. A marketing campaign once used billboards with images of famous people like Abraham Lincoln and Thomas Edison. The tagline on each billboard ran: "Failed, failed, failed, failed, failed. And then . . ." The lesson applies not only for the famous, but for all of us. We're not all in a position to change history, but if you want to change your home, workplace, or neighborhood, you have to be ready for failure, failure, failure, failure, failure. And then . . .

A final point: perseverance is not all teeth-gritting and will-power. The Lord's mercies are new every morning, and the spiritual rewards of obedience in the arenas of civilization life begin immediately. They don't wait until the goals are accomplished. Set your mind on persevering in doing the Lord's work, and the Spirit will flood you with the grace to sustain you.

Encouragement: Joy for the World

The challenges of our time can seem daunting. I've already emphasized that we need to be realistic and recognize the limits of what can be accomplished. However, it's equally important that we take courage. Despair is a sin; it denies God's providential grace. I've already said several times that I'm optimistic within reason. I chose the words "within reason" because I believe it's *rational* to be moderately optimistic.

Evil is not stronger than good, not even in this fallen world. God is still at work in the world, accomplishing all his purposes. By his creative power, he uses the natural human processes of reason, history, culture, and socialization to infuse moral awareness into fallen humanity, even where the saving power of the gospel hasn't taken root. And by his redeeming power, he transforms our minds, hearts, and lives to bring the joy of God out into the world, manifesting the Spirit's work in a way that is intricately, extensively, unavoidably, and permanently embedded within human civilization.

I believe American evangelicals are well equipped to face the challenges of the coming century, and even to take the lead in doing so. We believe in the freedom-of-religion society that the American founders wanted to build—perhaps more strongly than any other Americans do. We're highly adaptive; we don't know for sure what a successful new model of social engagement would look like, but we don't need to. We'll keep trying things out until we find what works. The reason we'll keep trying is yet another asset: evangelical theology emphasizes getting out of the church building to make our faith active in the world. We also have a robust appreciation of the fall, so we know better than to think we can change the world just by having the best arguments.

Oh, and one more thing. We know our Bibles. When operating a complex system, it never hurts to study the instruction manual.

God doesn't owe us success. If we fail, his Word will go forward in other places. If nothing else, he will use our failure as a teaching example to the church throughout the rest of the world. Contemplating the destruction of the Roman Empire, a theological genius in Africa rose up to write *City of God*, describing how God's glory had gone forth in the world with Rome and would go forth in the world without it, too. It became the most important book about the church and society since the Bible itself and a key inspiration for Western Christianity's integration of discipleship with life in civilization for 1,600 years and counting. Likewise, if we fail, perhaps some new theological genius will rise up to contemplate our failure, and from it write a new masterpiece to guide the church in places like Africa, Asia, and Latin America for the next two millennia.

However, I believe better things can and should be hoped for. May the Lord's will be done, not mine. But as I look around the American landscape, I expect the Lord isn't done with his church in this country yet. Not by a long shot.

Recommended Reading

The Church and Society

Berger, Peter. *The Sacred Canopy*. New York: Anchor, 1967.

Crouch, Andy. *Culture Making*. Downers Grove, IL: InterVarsity Press, 2008.

de Tocqueville, Alexis. *Democracy in America*. McLean, VA: Trinity Forum, 2010. This is an excerpt of de Tocqueville's original two-volume work.

DeYoung, Kevin, and Greg Gilbert. *What Is the Mission of the Church?* Wheaton, IL: Crossway, 2011.

Hunter, James Davison. *To Change the World*. New York: Oxford University Press, 2010.

Kuyper, Abraham. "Rooted and Grounded: The Church as Organism and Institution." Grand Rapids, MI: Christian's Library Press, 2013.

Sherman, Amy. *Kingdom Calling*. Downers Grove, IL: InterVarsity Press, 2012.

Thompson, Greg. "The Church in Our Time." New City Commons Foundation, 2012. http://newcitycommonsfoundation.com/perspective/church-our-time.

Wittmer, Michael. *Heaven Is a Place on Earth*. Grand Rapids, MI: Zondervan, 2004.

Sex and Family

Bavinck, Herman. *The Christian Family*. Grand Rapids, MI: Christian's Library Press, 2012.

Burk, Denny. *What Is the Meaning of Sex?* Wheaton, IL: Crossway, 2013.

Girgis, Sherif, Ryan Anderson, and Robert George. *What Is Marriage? Man and Woman: A Defense*. San Francisco: Encounter Books, 2012.

Keller, Timothy, with Kathy Keller. *The Meaning of Marriage*. New York: Dutton, 2011.

Lewis, C. S. *The Four Loves*. Orlando, FL: Houghton Mifflin Harcourt, 1991.

Veith, Gene, and Mary Moerbe. *Family Vocation*. Wheaton, IL: Crossway, 2012.

Winner, Lauren. *Real Sex*. Grand Rapids, MI: Brazos, 2006.

Work and the Economy

Bolt, John. *Economic Shalom*. Grand Rapids, MI: Christian's Liberty Press, 2013.

Claar, Victor, and Robin Klay. *Economics in Christian Perspective*. Downers Grove, IL: InterVarsity Press, 2007.

Corbett, Steve, and Brian Fikkert. *When Helping Hurts*. Chicago, IL: Moody Publishers, 2009.

Recommended Reading

DeKoster, Lester. *Work: The Meaning of Your Life*. 2nd ed. Grand Rapids, MI: Christian's Library Press, 2010.

Grudem, Wayne. *Business for the Glory of God*. Wheaton, IL: Crossway, 2003.

Guinness, Os. *The Call*. Nashville, TN: Thomas Nelson, 2003.

Keller, Timothy, with Katherine Leary Alsdorf. *Every Good Endeavor*. New York: Dutton, 2012.

Nelson, Tom. *Work Matters*. Wheaton, IL: Crossway, 2011.

Schneider, John. *The Good of Affluence*. Grand Rapids, MI: Eerdmans, 2002.

Stevens, R. Paul. *Work Matters*. Grand Rapids, MI: Eerdmans, 2012.

Van Duzer, Jeff. *Why Business Matters to God (And What Still Needs to Be Fixed)*. Downers Grove, IL: InterVarsity Press, 2010.

Veith, Gene Edward. *God at Work*. Wheaton, IL: Crossway, 2011.

Wong, Kenman, and Scott Rae. *Business for the Common Good*. Downers Grove, IL: InterVarsity Press, 2011.

Citizenship and Community

Douthat, Ross. *Bad Religion*. New York: Free Press, 2012.

Forster, Greg. *The Contested Public Square*. Downers Grove, IL: InterVarsity Press, 2008.

Gregg, Samuel. *The Commercial Society*. Lanham, MD: Lexington Books, 2007.

Haidt, Jonathan. *The Righteous Mind*. New York: Pantheon, 2012.

Hunter, James Davison. *The Death of Character*. New York: Basic Books, 2000.

Murray, Charles. *Coming Apart*. New York: Crown Forum, 2012.

Novak, Michael. *On Two Wings*. San Francisco: Encounter Books, 2002.

Willard, Dallas. *Knowing Christ Today*. New York: Harper, 2009.

Williams, Daniel. *God's Own Party*. New York: Oxford University Press, 2010.

Notes

Acknowledgments

1. C. S. Lewis, interview by Sherwood Wirt, "The Final Interview of C. S. Lewis," *Decision* (September 1963); also available at The Christian Broadcasting Network, http://www.cbn.com/special/narnia/articles/ans_lewislastinterviewa.aspx.
2. William Shakespeare, *A Midsummer Night's Dream*, act 2, scene 2.

Introduction: Let Every Heart Prepare Him Room

1. Pew Forum on Religion and Public Life, "Global Survey of Evangelical Protestant Leaders," June 22, 2011, 11.
2. Peter Berger, "A Global Evangelical Elite," *Religion and Other Curiosities* (blog), *The American Interest*, February 29, 2012, http://blogs.the-american-interest.com/berger/2012/02/29/a-global-evangelical-elite.
3. See D. Michael Lindsay, *Faith in the Halls of Power* (New York: Oxford University Press, 2007).
4. C. S. Lewis, "What Christmas Means to Me," in *God in the Dock*, in *The Collected Works of C. S. Lewis* (New York: Inspirational Press, 1996), 507. See also "Xmas and Christmas: A Lost Chapter from Herodotus," 505–6.

Part 1: Let Men Their Songs Employ

1. See Abraham Kuyper, "Rooted and Grounded: The Church as Organism and Institution" (Grand Rapids, MI: Christian Library Press, 2013). The text was originally the inaugural address Kuyper delivered in the Nieuwe Kerk in Amsterdam on August 10, 1870.

Chapter 1: Christianity and the Great American Experiment

1. Billy Graham, quoted in Daniel Williams, *God's Own Party* (New York: Oxford University Press, 2010), 25.
2. On the importance of getting the story right in addition to getting the facts right, see Timothy Keller with Katherine Leary Alsdorf, *Every Good Endeavor* (New York: Dutton, 2012), 155–60.
3. Among many books looking at the evidence for this view, see Marvin Olasky, *Fighting for Liberty and Virtue* (Washington, DC: Regnery, 1995); Michael Novak, *On Two Wings* (San Francisco: Encounter Books, 2002); Samuel Gregg, *The Commercial Society* (Lanham, MD: Lexington Books, 2007); Greg Forster, *The Contested Public Square* (Downers Grove, IL: InterVarsity Press, 2008); and Peter Wehner and Arthur Brooks, *Wealth and Justice* (Washington, DC: AEI Press, 2010).

4. Ross Douthat, *Bad Religion* (New York: Free Press, 2012), 6–8.
5. On this topic, see Forster, *Contested Public Square.*
6. Martin Luther, *On Secular Authority,* in *Martin Luther: Selections from His Writings,* ed. John Dillenberger (New York: Anchor, 1961), 385.
7. See Williams, *God's Own Party,* 11–48.
8. William Ward Ayer, quoted in Williams, *God's Own Party,* 12.
9. Harold Ockenga, "The Challenge to the Christian Culture of the West" (address at the inauguration of Fuller Theological Seminary, October 1, 1947). Available in the archives of Fuller Seminary.
10. See Patrick Henry, "'And I Don't Care What It Is': The Tradition-History of a Civil Religion Proof-Text," *Journal of the American Academy of Religion* (March 1981): 35–47.
11. D. R. Myddleton, *They Meant Well* (London: Institute of Economic Affairs, 2007), 18.

Chapter 2: The Church and the World

1. The story of Adam and Eve's creation shows us that the individual person is precious in God's sight by the very fact that God intervened to provide Adam with the companion he needed. If Adam was of no value without Eve, why was it not good that Adam should be alone?
2. While there is only one God, in terms of personal identity the one God is Father, Son, and Spirit. These personalities are defined by their relationships to one another: to be the Father is to be the one who eternally begets the Son, while to be the Son is to be the one eternally begotten by the Father, and to be the Spirit is to be the one who proceeds from both. Obviously, our knowledge of these matters is limited to what is revealed to us in the Bible; we have no direct knowledge of the internal life of the Trinity. But insofar as the Bible reveals these things to us, it appears that the personal identity of the three persons arises from their relationships to one another.
3. The Gospel Coalition, "Theological Vision for Ministry," 3.3.1, http://thegospelcoalition.org/about/foundation-documents/vision/.
4. For example, the social institutions of family, economy, and civil community are all affirmed in 1 Peter 2:13–3:7. On family, see also Ephesians 3:14–15. On the economy, see also Colossians 3:23–24. On civil community, see also Romans 13:1–7.
5. Planned Parenthood of Southern Pennsylvania v. Casey, 505 U.S. 833 (1992).
6. The word translated here as "welfare" is *shalom,* which is used with multiple layers of meaning in the Old Testament. *Shalom* in its strictest meaning represents the full flourishing of human life in all aspects, as God intended it to be. Obviously the fallen world cannot achieve *shalom* in this sense apart from redemptive grace. But although the fall redirected the world against *shalom,* God's redeeming work transforms Christians in a way that reorients them toward *shalom.* This redirection will be fully realized only at the end of history, but in the present life we experience a foretaste of the perfect eschatological *shalom,* and this foretaste is also (by metonymy or association) called *shalom.* This transformation of the heart in believers always results in active service to others in civilizational activities (Matt. 25:14–46). As a result, wherever redeemed and redirected people are present, human civilization will be impacted by their redirection. In this way, even those who are not directly transformed by the Holy Spirit

benefit from, and are influenced by, the *shalom* of those who are. This indirect experience of *shalom* does not create a redeeming relationship with Jesus Christ, but its impact bears a likeness to the impact of that redeeming relationship, and is therefore (again by metonymy or association) also called *shalom*. For discussion of *shalom* in these three different but related senses, see Amy Sherman, *Kingdom Calling* (Downers Grove, IL: InterVarsity Press, 2012); and Kevin DeYoung and Greg Gilbert, *What Is the Mission of the Church?* (Wheaton, IL: Crossway, 2011). Sherman emphasizes the continuity of the three senses while DeYoung and Gilbert emphasize their discontinuity, but both books acknowledge both aspects, and the inevitable tension between them.

7. See James Davison Hunter, *To Change the World* (New York: Oxford University Press, 2010); and Greg Thompson, "The Church in Our Time: Nurturing Congregations of Faithful Presence," New City Commons Foundation, October 2011, http://newcitycommonsfoundation.com/sites/default/files /The%20Church%20In%20Our%20Time%2C%20A%20New%20City%20 Commons%20White%20Paper_4.pdf.

8. See Thompson, "Church in Our Time."

9. Timothy Keller with Katherine Leary Alsdorf, *Every Good Endeavor* (New York: Dutton, 2012), 69–70.

10. See, for example, the apologetic writings of Justin Martyr.

11. See Greg Forster, *The Contested Public Square* (Downers Grove, IL: InterVarsity Press, 2008), 62–141.

12. I first found this idea in Hunter, *To Change the World*, 231–36. I have since discovered it is a much older idea.

13. See note 4.

14. I owe this point to my friend Joe Loconte.

15. See Forster, *Contested Public Square*, 62–83.

16. See Hunter, *To Change the World*.

17. Michael Novak, "Two Battles That Saved the West: Lepanto 1571 and Vienna 1683" (Bradley Lecture, American Enterprise Institute, Washington, DC, December 8, 2008).

18. By necessity, I've greatly oversimplified the story. Two good histories of the emergence of the modern economy are Rodney Stark, *The Victory of Reason* (New York: Random House, 2006); and Joyce Appleby, *The Relentless Revolution* (New York: Norton, 2011).

Part 2: Let Earth Receive Her King

1. Timothy Keller, "What's So Great about the PCA?" (paper for the 38th PCA General Assembly, Nashville, TN, June 2010).

2. See C. S. Lewis, *Mere Christianity*, in *The Complete C.S. Lewis Signature Classics* (San Francisco: HarperCollins, 2002), 80–82.

3. C. S. Lewis, *The Pilgrim's Regress*, in *The Collected Works of C. S. Lewis* (New York: Inspirational Press, 1996), 150. *Resurgam* is Latin for "I shall rise again." *Io paean* was an ancient Greek cry of triumph, exaltation, praise, or thanksgiving. The "worm" referenced in the final line is the dragon Virtue killed.

Chapter 3: Doctrine: Teaching and Preaching

1. The line is from B. B. Warfield's sermon on Acts 22:10. See Fred Zaspel, *The Theology of B. B. Warfield* (Wheaton, IL: Crossway, 2010), 106.

2. Aida Edemariam, "Was Jesus a Woman?" *The Guardian*, June 22, 2006.

3. Augustine, *Confessions* (New York: Oxford University Press, 1991), 254.

4. Mark Chaves and Shawna Anderson, "Cumulative Data File and Codebook," National Congregations Study, Duke University, 2008, question 32. In this survey, 3.5 percent of congregations included were non-Christian (see question 9).

5. Jackson Carroll, et. al., "Codebook," Pulpit and Pew National Survey of Pastoral Leaders, National Opinion Research Center, 2001, question 258. Only Christian clergy were asked this question. The survey found results on pastors' educational attainment similar to those of the National Congregational Study (see question 256).

6. See Alister McGrath, *C. S. Lewis—A Life* (Carol Stream, IL: Tyndale, 2013), 209.

7. I first realized this critical point when I read Dallas Willard, *Knowing Christ Today* (New York: Harper, 2009).

8. D. Michael Lindsay, *Faith in the Halls of Power* (New York: Oxford University Press, 2007), 233–48.

Chapter 4: Devotion: Worship and Spiritual Formation

1. I heard Franklin Graham say this on a radio broadcast in approximately 2004.

2. I owe this point to John Piper.

3. C. S. Lewis, *Mere Christianity*, in *The Complete C. S. Lewis Signature Classics* (San Francisco: HarperCollins, 2002), 60.

4. See Aristotle, *Metaphysics*, book 7.

5. For an excellent treatment of the Lord's Supper, see Keith Mathison, *Given for You* (Phillipsburg, NJ: P&R, 2002).

6. "What I, like many other laymen, chiefly desire in church are fewer, better, and shorter hymns; especially fewer." C. S. Lewis, "On Church Music," in *Christian Reflections*, in *The Collected Works of C. S. Lewis* (New York: Inspirational Press, 1996), 240.

7. C. S. Lewis, "The Inner Ring," in *The Weight of Glory* (New York: HarperCollins, 2001), 156–57.

8. Ibid.

Chapter 5: Stewardship: Calling and Discipleship

1. A small sample of the many recent books on this topic: Os Guinness, *The Call* (Nashville, TN: Thomas Nelson, 2003); Michael Wittmer, *Heaven Is a Place on Earth* (Grand Rapids, MI: Zondervan, 2004); Darrell Cosden, *The Heavenly Good of Earthly Work* (Peabody, MA: Hendrickson, 2006); Lester DeKoster, *Work: The Meaning of Your Life*, 2nd ed. (Grand Rapids, MI: Christian's Library Press, 2010); Jeff Van Duzer, *Why Business Matters to God* (Downers Grove, IL: InterVarsity Press, 2010); Tom Nelson, *Work Matters* (Wheaton, IL: Crossway, 2011); Kenman Wong and Scott Rae, *Business for the Common Good* (Downers Grove, IL: InterVarsity Press, 2011); Amy Sherman, *Kingdom Calling* (Downers Grove, IL: InterVarsity Press, 2012); and Timothy Keller with Katherine Leary Alsdorf, *Every Good Endeavor* (New York: Dutton, 2012).

2. See also Luke 19:11–27; Ephesians 4:28; 1 Thessalonians 4:11; 2 Thessalonians 3:10–12; 1 Timothy 5:8; and 2 Timothy 2:6.

3. I was first impressed with the significance of this juxtaposition after reading DeKoster, *Work*.
4. Some read the parable of the talents as speaking exclusively about evangelism. For a detailed treatment of the parable that shows the weaknesses of this view, see Craig Blomberg, *Interpreting the Parables* (Downers Grove, IL: InterVarsity Press, 1990), 214–21: "God entrusts all people with a portion of his resources, expecting them to act as good stewards of it. . . . The money distributed among the servants must not be equated with any specific type of gift or ability" (214–16). Klyne Snodgrass, who puts more emphasis on the eschatological nature of the parable, still comments that "parables about the future are not intended to set a sequence of events. Rather, 'one speaks about the future for the sake of the present.' The concern is for right living." Klyne Snodgrass, *Stories with Intent* (Grand Rapids, MI: Eerdmans, 2008), 542.
5. Sherman, *Kingdom Calling*, 120–26.
6. Keller, *Every Good Endeavor*, 68.
7. I first encountered this connection between deep satisfaction and Christian liberty in William Messenger, "Calling in the Theology of Work" (paper presented at the Evangelical Theological Society annual meeting, November 17, 2010).
8. Timothy Keller, "Vocation: Discerning Your Calling," Redeemer City to City, 2011, 3.
9. Gene Edward Veith, "Vocation: The Doctrine of the Christian Life," *Journal of Markets and Morality* (Spring 2011): 119.
10. Ibid.
11. For a discussion of the issues, see Colin Gunton, *The Triune Creator* (Grand Rapids, MI: Eerdmans, 1998), 193–211.
12. See Marvin Olasky, *The Tragedy of American Compassion* (Wheaton, IL: Crossway, 2008); and Robert Lupton, *Toxic Charity* (New York: HarperCollins, 2012).
13. "The fact that you are giving money to a charity does not mean that you need not try to find out whether that charity is a fraud or not." C. S. Lewis, *Mere Christianity*, in *The Complete C. S. Lewis Signature Classics* (San Francisco: HarperCollins, 2002), 48.
14. See Peter Greer, *The Poor Will Be Glad* (Grand Rapids, MI: Zondervan, 2009); and Steve Corbett and Brian Fikkert, *When Helping Hurts* (Chicago: Moody, 2009).
15. See Amy Becker, "The New School Choice Agenda," *Christianity Today*, April 9, 2012.
16. See Sherman, *Kingdom Calling*, 199–222.

Part 3: He Comes to Make His Blessings Flow

1. I have drawn heavily on Peter Berger, *The Sacred Canopy* (New York: Anchor, 1967), for this section.

Chapter 6: Sex and Family

1. Augustine, *Confessions* (New York: Oxford University Press, 1991), 147.
2. G. K. Chesterton, *The Everlasting Man* (San Francisco: Ignatius Press, 1993), 116.
3. David Courtwright, *No Right Turn* (Cambridge, MA: Harvard University Press, 2010), 4.

4. C. S. Lewis, *Mere Christianity*, in *The Complete C. S. Lewis Signature Classics* (San Francisco: HarperCollins, 2002), 61.
5. I adapted these from statements in Dennis Prager, "What Do Men Want?" *National Review Online*, December 21, 2010; and Dennis Prager, "What Do Women Want?" *National Review Online*, December 28, 2010. Prager's formula: A man wants to be admired by the woman he loves, a woman wants to be loved by a man she admires.
6. C. S. Lewis, *The Screwtape Letters*, in *The Complete C. S. Lewis Signature Classics* (San Francisco: HarperCollins, 2002), 162. Lewis is writing here in the character of Screwtape, a demon, but is expressing Lewis's own view.
7. Lewis, *Mere Christianity*, 61.
8. I owe this point to my friend Kyle Ferguson.
9. One classical source on this is Bronislaw Malinowski, *Sex, Culture, and Myth* (Boston: Harcourt Trade, 1962; orig. 1930). Malinowski popularized the concept of "legitimacy" for understanding familial structures. See Charles Murray, *Coming Apart* (New York: Crown Forum, 2012), 160.
10. Some of the reasons for this tendency are discussed in Christopher Kaczor, "The Perils of Polygamy," *Public Discourse*, May 21, 2012, http://www.thepublicdiscourse.com/2012/05/5338.
11. In this book I am not addressing the question of the husband having "headship" in the home. That is not because I'm afraid to tackle controversial and uncomfortable issues, as I hope you've seen by now! It's also not because I don't know what I think—I believe husbands ought to serve their wives through the practice a self-sacrificing spiritual headship. C. S. Lewis remarks that the Bible crowns the husband, but only with a crown of thorns (*The Four Loves* [Orlando, FL: Houghton Mifflin Harcourt, 1991], 106). However, precisely because the husband's headship is spiritual—indeed, it is a great theological mystery—and also because the Christian community is divided over it, I don't think it will play a large role in Christian public witness.
12. Gene Veith and Mary Moerbe, *Family Vocation* (Wheaton, IL: Crossway, 2012), 76. See also Lauren Winner, *Real Sex* (Grand Rapids, MI: Brazos, 2006).
13. C. S. Lewis, "We Have No 'Right to Happiness,'" in *God in the Dock*, in *The Collected Works of C. S. Lewis* (New York: Inspirational Press, 1996), 519.
14. Augustine, *Confessions*, 151.
15. Murray, *Coming Apart*, 158.
16. Some of them realized it relatively early. See Barbara Dafoe Whitehead, "Dan Quayle Was Right," *The Atlantic*, April 1993. I don't know if anyone has done a formal survey of American elites to confirm my impression that most of them have come around on this topic, but for at least some recent evidence see Isabel Sawhill, "20 Years Later, It Turns Out Dan Quayle Was Right about Murphy Brown and Unmarried Moms," *Washington Post*, May 25, 2012.
17. For more on this subject, see James Davison Hunter, *The Death of Character* (New York: Basic Books, 2000), 129–45.
18. Mary Eberstadt, "The Weight of Smut," *First Things* (June/July 2010).

Chapter 7: Work and the Economy

1. See Joyce Appleby, *The Relentless Revolution* (New York: Norton, 2010), 148–51. See also Glenn Sunshine, "Josiah Wedgwood (1730–1795)," *Christian*

Worldview Journal, Chuck Colson Center for Christian Worldview, February 27, 2012, http://www.colsoncenter.org/the-center/columns/indepth/17482 -josiah-wedgwood-1730-1795. What I offer here is an exegesis of what I take to be the deeper cultural messages and significance at work in Josiah Wedgwood's actions. I don't know whether Wedgwood was the kind of man who would actually say "you are better than that" in explaining why he smashed shoddy work with his walking stick. What I do feel confident asserting is that his workers flourished because that message was implicit in his actions.

2. Timothy Keller with Katherine Leary Alsdorf, *Every Good Endeavor* (New York: Dutton, 2012), 180.

3. Just a few of the burgeoning list of books on this topic: Os Guinness, *The Call* (Nashville, TN: Thomas Nelson, 2003); Michael Wittmer, *Heaven Is a Place on Earth* (Grand Rapids, MI: Zondervan, 2004); Darrell Cosden, *The Heavenly Good of Earthly Work* (Peabody, MA: Hendrickson, 2006); Lester DeKoster, *Work: The Meaning of Your Life*, 2nd ed. (Grand Rapids, MI: Christian's Library Press, 2010); Jeff Van Duzer, *Why Business Matters to God* (Downers Grove, IL: InterVarsity Press, 2010); Tom Nelson, *Work Matters* (Wheaton, IL: Crossway, 2011); Kenman Wong and Scott Rae, *Business for the Common Good* (Downers Grove, IL: InterVarsity Press, 2011); Amy Sherman, *Kingdom Calling* (Downers Grove, IL: InterVarsity Press, 2012); and Keller, *Every Good Endeavor*.

4. For example, see Exodus 20:9 and 35:30–35; Psalms 90:17; 128:2; Proverbs 12:11–14; 16:3; 18:9; 22:29; 24:27; 31:13–31; Ecclesiastes 3:22; 5:6; 9:10; Matthew 25:14–30; Luke 19:11–27; John 5:17; Ephesians 4:28; Colossians 3:23–24; 1 Thessalonians 4:11; 2 Thessalonians 3:10–12; 1 Timothy 5:8; 2 Timothy 2:6.

5. See Rodney Stark, *The Victory of Reason* (New York: Random House, 2006), 65. See also Thomas Aquinas, *Summa Theologica*, 2b.77.1; and John Mueller, *Redeeming Economics* (Wilmington, DE: ISI Books, 2010).

6. Keller, *Every Good Endeavor*, 47, 49–50.

7. See Martin Luther, "The Estate of Marriage," 1522, http://pages.uoregon .edu/dluebke/Reformations441/LutherMarriage.htm.

8. See Matthew 6:24; 7:24–27/Luke 6:47–49; Matthew 13:52; 18:23–35; 20:1–16; Matthew 21:33–41/Mark 12:1–9/Luke 20:9–16; Matthew 24:45–51/Luke 12:42–46; Matthew 25:14–30/Luke 19:12–27; Mark 13:33–37/Luke 12:35–38; Luke 7:41–43; 16:1–12; 17:7–10.

9. Even the distinction between labor and capital doesn't hold up under scrutiny. Business owners are laborers whose work bears fruit. Active investment is also a form of labor—it uses talents (talents that not everyone has) in the service of the business. Inactive investors (such as owners of mutual funds) are not contributing their labor to the flourishing of the business, and this can create important challenges. Businesses lose their mission when they can't look beyond the quarterly earnings reports so cherished by absentee stockholders. But the important distinction is between those who do and don't contribute their labor to the business.

10. See Kevin Hassett and Dean Baker, "The Human Disaster of Unemployment," *New York Times*, May 12, 2012.

11. For an introduction to this large topic, with links to many helpful books, see Greg Forster, "Greed Is Not Good for Capitalism," The Gospel Coalition,

Notes

August 15, 2012, http://thegospelcoalition.org/blogs/tgc/2012/08/15/greed
-is-not-good-for-capitalism.

12. Raymond de Roover, "The Theory of the Just Price," *Journal of Economic History* (December 1958): 418–34.

13. See, for example, 1 Kings 3:10–13; Psalm 112:1–3; Proverbs 12:9–11; Matthew 25:14–30; and 1 Timothy 5:8; 6:17–19. See also John Schneider, *The Good of Affluence* (Grand Rapids, MI: Eerdmans, 2002).

14. For biblical reflections on how economic growth provides opportunities to glorify God, see Schneider, *The Good of Affluence.*

15. Bono (speech at Georgetown University, November 13, 2012); see http://www.georgetown.edu/news/bono-speaks-at-gu.html.

16. Maxim Pinkovskiy and Xavier Sala-i-Martin, "Parametric Estimations of the World Distribution of Income," National Bureau of Economic Research, October 2009. Other researchers' estimates yield different numbers, but all estimates agree that the drop in global poverty has been very large.

17. John Wesley, quoted in Ross Douthat, *Bad Religion* (New York: Free Press, 2012), 78.

18. In one of the most important books on American religion in recent years, Ross Douthat offers a hope that an "age of diminished expectations" in economic growth will be good for the church (*Bad Religion*, 283–84). Interestingly, Douthat also points to America's present sexual and political dysfunctions as opportunities for the church. I've done much the same in chapters 6–8 in this book, so clearly we're thinking along similar lines. What worries me is that Douthat and those discussing his book sometimes sound like they're suggesting economic dysfunction is something the church should welcome. A quick thought experiment about whether the church ought to similarly welcome sexual and political dysfunctions will show why I find this troubling. Economic dysfunction can only create opportunities for the church, as Douthat and I both hope, if the church is offering society something that will lead back to superior economic functioning—and that means growth. So a positive attitude about economic growth will be an important component of any attempt to pursue the opportunities we may have.

19. See Peter Baehr and Gordon Wells, "Introduction," in Max Weber, *The Protestant Ethic and the "Spirit" of Capitalism, and Other Writings* (New York: Penguin, 2002), ix–xxxii.

20. For more, with links to related books, see Forster, "Greed Is Not Good."

21. Wayne Grudem and Craig Blomberg made these remarks (respectively) during a session on "Theology of Work and Economics" at the 2011 annual meeting of the Evangelical Theological Society, San Francisco.

22. At the heart of these disputes is Weber's cultural contradictions thesis. Weber has erroneously taught people that capitalism thrives when a spirit of greed predominates. For more, see Forster, "Greed Is Not Good."

23. See Appleby, *The Relentless Revolution*, 56–86.

24. See Mark Kramer, *The Black Book of Communism* (Cambridge, MA: Harvard University Press, 1999).

25. For a good history, see Friedrich Hayek, *The Road to Serfdom* (Chicago: University of Chicago Press, 2007, orig. 1944). For an important contemporary example, see Robert Miller, "Waiting for St. Vladimir," *First Things* (February 2011).

26. On nonwork rates, see Charles Murray, *Coming Apart* (New York: Crown Forum, 2012), 168–88. On 70 percent of Americans taking more than they pay see Arthur Brooks, "America and the Value of 'Earned Success,'" *Wall Street Journal*, May 8, 2012.

Chapter 8: Citizenship and Community

1. "The End of Democracy? Introduction," *First Things* (November 1996).
2. I quote from memory, but the scene took place in *Hellblazer*, 1.3.
3. Jonathan Haidt, *The Righteous Mind* (New York: Pantheon, 2012).
4. For a history of political philosophy, especially as it bears on Christianity, see Greg Forster, *The Contested Public Square* (Downers Grove, IL: InterVarsity Press, 2008).
5. See Aristotle, *Politics* (New York: Oxford University Press, 1992), 100 (where Aristotle comes closest to the formula that would later be used to summarize his views, "giving to each his due") and 106–36 (his analysis of justice).
6. See C. S. Lewis, *The Abolition of Man*, in *The Complete C. S. Lewis Signature Classics* (San Francisco: HarperCollins, 2002), appendix.
7. Some readers will wonder how this applies to Islam. That is a complicated question we can't get into here. For a starting point toward addressing it, I recommend Bernard Lewis, *What Went Wrong?* (New York: Oxford University Press, 2001); and Bernard Lewis, *The Crisis of Islam* (New York: Random House, 2004).
8. See, for example, James Davison Hunter, *To Change the World* (New York: Oxford University Press, 2010), 80.
9. See Aristotle, *Politics*.
10. See Alexander Hamilton, James Madison, and John Jay, *The Federalist Papers* (New York: Mentor, 1961).
11. See Hunter, *To Change the World*, 101–10.
12. I owe this point to my friend Charlie Self.
13. See Charles Murray, *Coming Apart* (Crown Forum: New York, 2012), 16–115.
14. Michael Barone, "America Is Two Countries, Not on Speaking Terms," *Washington Examiner*, November 6, 2012.
15. See Justin Martyr, *First Apology*, http://earlychristianwritings.com/text /justinmartyr-firstapology.html.
16. See Daniel Williams, *God's Own Party* (New York: Oxford University Press, 2010); and Greg Forster, "Evangelicals and Politics," *Public Discourse*, May 1–3, 2012, http://www.thepublicdiscourse.com/2012/05/5213.

Conclusion: He Rules the World with Truth and Grace

1. Russell Conwell, "Acres of Diamonds," Temple University, n.d., http://www .temple.edu/about/history/acres-diamonds. "Bailey" is Philip James Bailey, an English poet.
2. This is the main topic of Matt Chandler's excellent book *The Explicit Gospel* (Wheaton, IL: Crossway, 2012).
3. Timothy Keller with Katherine Leary Alsdorf, *Every Good Endeavor* (New York: Dutton, 2012), 186–90.
4. Timothy Keller, "What Is God's Global Urban Mission?" (advance paper, Lausanne Conference, Cape Town, South Africa, May 18, 2010), http:// conversation.lausanne.org/en/conversations/detail/10282.

5. C. S. Lewis, *Surprised by Joy,* in *The Inspirational Writings of C. S. Lewis* (New York: Inspirational Press, 1994), 117–25.

6. The other three are justice, temperance, and fortitude.

7. I heard Dallas Willard say this at the Kern Pastors Character Conference, Green Lake Conference Center, Green Lake, Wisconsin, July 6–8, 2010.

8. I first encountered this point about the importance of strategy in Greg Thompson, "The Church in Our Time: Nurturing Congregations of Faithful Presence," New City Commons Foundation, October 2011, http:// newcitycommonsfoundation.com/sites/default/files/The%20Church%20 In%20Our%20Time%2C%20A%20New%20City%20Commons%20White %20Paper_4.pdf.

General Index

absolutism, 40
accommodationism, 60
American Protestantism, 49–51,
    115–16, 273–74
anti-Christian intellectual move-
    ments, 35
antinomianism, 22, 121–22
Aquinas, Thomas, 224, 227
aristocracy, 40, 262
Aristotle, 148, 268, 305
asceticism, 193
assurance, 143
atheists, 138
Athens, 13–16
Augustine, 22, 85, 99, 116, 182,
    196–97
Ayer, William Ward, 52–53

Babel, 81–82
Berger, Peter, 18
biblical knowledge, 130–33

calling, 161–62, 168–72, 220–21
capitalism, 234–35, 238–39
celibacy, 196
Chesterton, G. K., 182
childrearing, 189–90
Christian leadership, 99–102,
    248–49
Christian liberty, 171–72
Christian scholarship, 59
Christian sex education pro-
    grams, 205–6
Christianity

and American's founding,
    34–42, 59, 71
and good citizenship, 263–68
organizational vs. organic,
    30–32
and social influence, 60–64
church
authority of, 115–20
and balance of doctrine,
    devotion, and stewardship,
    104–9, 176
and balance of mission and
    exile, 69–71
and city building, 81–87
and cultural engagement,
    88–97
discipline, 261
growth of, 234–35
and influence of the world,
    72–76
and influence on the world,
    76–79
and redeeming sexuality,
    207–11
and redeeming work, 245–50
and state, 42–43, 259–61
civic duty, 254
civil government, 258–61
collectivism, 72–73
Communism, 35, 244
community, 121–22, 162, 174,
    256–58, 263–71, 275–76
confessionalism, 40
conversion, 144, 146–47, 186,
    197

Scripture Index

Real Calvinism Is About Joy

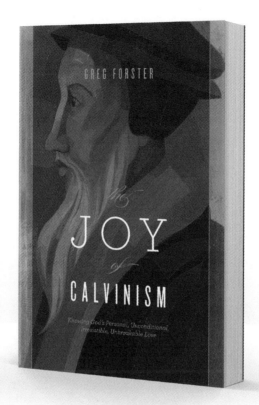

This positive guide to the principles of Calvinism shows how God's love and our joy lie at the heart of this often misunderstood theology.

"A refreshing, clearly written, thought-provoking, truly enjoyable book that will help overcome many misconceptions and deepen people's faith and joy in God each day."

WAYNE GRUDEM, Research Professor of Bible and Theology, Phoenix Seminary

"Calvinism gets a lot of bad press because of its joyless believers. Yet joyless Calvinism is an oxymoron. Forster has helped reframe this beautiful understanding of God in a way that is attractive and compelling."

DARRIN PATRICK, Lead Pastor, The Journey, St. Louis, Missouri

For more information, visit crossway.org.